FRANCE IN THE GISCARD PRESIDENCY

To
Naomi, Kate and Lucy

France in the Giscard Presidency

J. R. Frears

London
GEORGE ALLEN & UNWIN
Boston   Sydney

First published in 1981

GEORGE ALLEN & UNWIN LTD
40 Museum Street, London WC1A 1LU

British Library Cataloguing in Publication Data

Frears, J. R.
  France in the Giscard presidency.
  I. Title
  944.083'6   DC417   80–42288

  ISBN 0–04–354025–2
  ISBN 0–04–354026–0 Pbk

Set in 11/12 point Times by Computacomp (UK) Ltd, Fort William, Scotland
and printed in Great Britain by Billing and Sons Ltd, Guildford, London and Worcester

Contents

Preface

The electors of France have not, as I write, yet decided whether this book on the presidency of France shall be an epitaph or a mid-term balance sheet. At all events this is an account of a *septennat*, the hopes, ideas, policies, actions of a President richly endowed with both intellectual gifts and political power. His central aim has been a more cohesive national community united in the task of building French economic strength, reaffirming France's rank in the world and creating a more liberal democracy. However, it is precisely because France is not a particularly liberal democracy and there are very few checks and balances on executive power that Giscard d'Estaing, supported by a technocratic and administrative elite subject to few democratic controls, has been able to pursue the vigorous policies of his predecessors in the spheres of economic or foreign affairs. This is one of the many paradoxes of French democracy that this book tries to examine.

In writing this book I have been greatly helped by a Research Fellowship from the Nuffield Foundation, by an invitation from the Rockefeller Foundation to work at the legendary Villa Serbelloni in Italy, by Patricia King who typed the manuscript, and by many colleagues and officials in Great Britain and France. I would like to express my grateful thanks to all.

List of Abbreviations

1 Political Parties

Gaullism
RPF	Rassemblement du Peuple Français (1947–53)
UNR	Union pour la Nouvelle République (1958–67)
UDR	Union des Démocrates pour la République (1968–76)
RPR	Rassemblement du Peuple pour la République

Centre and 'Giscardiens'
MRP	Mouvement Républicain Populaire
CD	Centre Démocrate
CDS	Centre des Démocrates-Sociaux
CNIP	Centre Nationale des Indépendents et Paysans
RI	Républicains Indépendents
PR	Parti Républicain
UDF	Union pour la Démocratie Française

Socialists and allies
SFIO	Section Française de l'Internationale Ouvrière (Socialist Party 1905–69)
PS	Parti Socialiste
CERES	Centre d'Etude et de Recherche Socialistes
PSU	Parti Socialiste Unifié
MRG	Mouvement des Radicaux de Gauche
FGDS	Fédération de la Gauche Démocrate et Socialiste

Communists
PCF	Parti Communiste Français

2 Others

CCCE	Caisse Centrale pour la Coopération Economique
CEA	Commissariat à l'Energie Atomique

CFDT   Confédération Française et Démocratique du Travail

CGT   Confédération Générale du Travail

CIANE   Comité Interministériel pour l'Aménagement de la Nature et de l'Environnement

CIASI   Comité Interministériel pour l'Aménagement des Structures Industrielles

CIAT   Comité Interministèriel pour l'Aménagement du Territoire

CNPF   Confédération Nationale du Patronat Français

CODA   Centre Opérationnel de Défense Aérienne

COGEMA   Compagnie Générale des Matières Nucléaires

DATAR   Délégation a l'Aménagement du Territoire et à l'Action Régionale

DGA   Délégation Générale pour l'Armement

EDF   Electricité de France

ENA   Ecole Nationale d'Administration

FAC   Fonds d'Aide et de Coopération

FDES   Fonds de Développement Economique et Sociale

FEN   Fédération de l'Education Nationale

HLM   Habitation à Loyer Modéré

PEON   Commission pour la Production d'Electricité d'Origine Nucléaire

SGCI   Sécrétariat-Générale du Comité Interministériel pour les Questions de Coopération Economique Européenne

SOFMA   Société Française des Matériels d'Armement

PART ONE

Men and Ideas

CHAPTER 1

The Making of the President – February 1926 to May 1974

The only respect in which Valéry Giscard d'Estaing has not been blessed by providence is in his choice of biographers. Michel Bassi (1969) is the best but out of date. Olivier Todd's account (1977) is the most complete but preoccupied with journalistic trivia, and the excellent book by Jean-Claud Colliard on the *Giscardiens* (1971) is not really a biography. The remaining (and numerous) books on Giscard d'Estaing indulge in sycophantic hagiography of a rather nauseating kind – especially the many accounts of daily life at the Elysée palace of which the contribution of Pierre Pellisier (1978) stands out as an ignominious classic. It is mainly from these unpromising sources that the outline of a remarkable career must be derived.

President Giscard d'Estaing was born in Germany at the time when the Rhineland was occupied by France, in fact at No. 2 Rheinlagen in Koblenz on 2 February 1926. His father Edmond Giscard, who had in 1923 acquired the right by Conseil d'Etat decree to add the noble addition of d'Estaing to his name, was an inspector of finance in charge of finance services in the French commissariat for occupied Rhineland. He was the son of Valéry Giscard, a lawyer at Riom in the Auvergne, who never knew his illustrious grandson. The claim of Edmond Giscard to the title d'Estaing was based on his descent from a female cousin of the famous Admiral d'Estaing who fought with La Fayette in the American War of Independence and was guillotined in the French revolution. Edmond later became the director of a number of companies in insurance and finance especially of the very diversified SOFFO – Société Financière pour la France et les Pays d'Outre-Mer with extensive interests in Africa – and proprietor of the Château de la Varvasse at Chanonat in

Auvergne where his presidential son still goes to vote. In the 1930s Edmond Giscard d'Estaing, a leader of the right-wing Action Française, was a member of the Parti Social Français and even president, in the 8th arrondissement of Paris, of the near-fascist Croix de Feu league. He wrote a lot of anti-parliamentary articles under the name of Valéry de Mories but, as Todd confirms, he was no supporter of Hitler. In France 'the right and the centre preferred the Duce and the Caudillo to the Fuhrer' (Todd, 1977, p. 32). He was anti-British – an almost universal distinguishing characteristic of the right in France, or indeed of nationalists on the left as well. He supported Pétain in the war, though not in a fanatical or pro-German fashion, and was awarded the Francisque, the order of Maréchal Pétain. Todd produces evidence that he did not co-operate with the Nazis in any way (p. 50).

His wife, May Bardoux, came from a distinguished family also connected with the French right. She is a descendant of an illegitimate daughter of King Louis XV, Louise-Françoise-Adelaïde de Montalivet, whose husband was a minister under Napoleon I and whose son Camille was Minister of the Interior under, and enobled by, Louis-Philippe, the last King of France. Geneviève, the grand-daughter of Camille de Montalivet, married Jacques Bardoux, the son of Agénor Bardoux, a minister in the Third Republic and appointed mayor of Clermont-Ferrand under Emperor Napoleon III. Jacques Bardoux was a prolific writer, director of a number of companies, a professor at the famous Ecole Libre des Sciences Politiques in Paris, in the cabinets of both Maréchal Foch and Poincaré and, like Agénor, a conservative *député* for Puy-de-Dôme – a parliamentary seat which his grandson kept in the family after the retirement of Bardoux in 1956. Bardoux in the 1930s, though anglophile, strongly anti-Hitler and anti-communist, and never Croix de Feu, also found himself, like his son-in-law, supporting Mussolini, Franco and Pétain.

In short Valéry Giscard d'Estaing comes from an educated, wealthy and Catholic family, which played a prominent part in public life and whose members had the attitudes and views which were very typical of such a milieu at such a time. Since, as Stanley Baldwin remarked, the secret of political leadership is to have common opinions and uncommon ability, this was not a bad start. Family life was affectionate and well-mannered – his parents used *vous* to address each other – and his childhood was a happy one, his main companions being his sisters Sylvie and Isabelle, brother Olivier (a future *polytechnicien*) and cousins François and Jacques Giscard d'Estaing (both later at ENA). He was educated in Paris (except for a brief period at Clermont-Ferrand during the 'phoney war' of 1939–40) where the family lived most of the time at 101 avenue Henri-Martin in the fashionable 16th arrondissement, attending the Lycée Janson-le-Sailly and, after the war, Louis-le-Grand to prepare his Polytechnique entrance. Valéry was too young to play a really active role in the Resistance but he seems to have tried to make himself useful – distributing leaflets and so on. After the Liberation in 1944, however, he joined up in the 2e Dragons, a reserve unit unattached to a division. The 2e Dragons participated in the advance into Germany, occupied the city of Konstanz and eventually took part in the victory parades in Paris. Giscard d'Estaing was decorated with the Croix de Guerre and the Bronze Star medal.

If one of the important elements that compose President Giscard d'Estaing is his traditional cultivated bourgeois family upbringing accompanied by this youthful wartime experience, another is his education as a technocrat. At Polytechnique, which trained the elite of the public service, he passed out second of his year in 1948. At that time the top graduates of Polytechnique had the automatic right to enter the other recently formed training school for the public service elite, the Ecole Nationale d'Administration. After the almost obligatory few months in North America, Giscard d'Estaing went to ENA, completed a brilliant *stage* in the Saar, and passed out third of his year (Marceau Long, in 1980 Secretary General to the government, was first). Like his father, he chose the Inspectorate of Finance, the most prestigious of the *grands corps*, and began his career at the Banque de France under the direction of his father's friend (another inspector of finance) the bank's director Wilfrid Baumgartner. In 1951 he joined the Ministry of Finance and in 1952 he married Anne-Aymone de Brantes, daughter of a Resistance colonel who had died in the war, and descendant of the extremely wealthy steel family the Schneiders of Le Creusot. It was at this period too that he met Michel Poniatowski, another Ministry of Finance official, who was to become his political right-hand man, and Edgar Faure, future Prime Minister. This is when he is reported to have said 'France wants to be governed by the centre-right. I will place myself centre-right and one day I will govern France' (Lancel, 1974, p. 42). When he became President over twenty years later the formula had become 'France wants to be governed from the centre'.

In 1953 he began that move from administration to politics which, almost unique to France, has become such a feature of French political life in the Fifth Republic since 1958. Edgar Faure became Minister of Finance and he asked Giscard d'Estaing and his colleague from ENA, Jacques Duhamel, also a future minister and centrist party leader, to join his private office, his *cabinet*. His ability so impressed Edgar Faure that when he was appointed Prime Minister in 1955 he took Giscard d'Estaing with him in his *cabinet* as *directeur-adjoint*. In a *cabinet*, as the personal collaborator of a political leader, a civil servant is on the borderline between politics and administration. Indeed, much of the technical and administrative work is concerned with seeing that the minister's political will prevails over departmental reservations. In 1956 grandfather Jacques Bardoux was persuaded to retire and Giscard d'Estaing stood as a candidate for Parliament in the Puy-de-Dôme. Edgar Faure, an expelled Radical at the time – though of the right-wing rather than the left-wing *Mendèsiste* variety – would not endorse him and Giscard stood on the 'Indpendents and Peasants' list under his grandfather's label 'Republicain Indépendent', which was later to serve as the title of the party he led. His name was second on the 'Independents and Peasants' list and the proportional representation system in force at the time awarded that list two of the five seats in Puy-de-Dôme – so he was in, with 15·3 per cent of the votes, and not quite 30 years old.

Although he became President at the relatively youthful age of 48, Giscard d'Estaing was an experienced political leader and administrator, as his parliamentary and ministerial career from 1956 to 1974 testifies. He impressed as a parliamentarian. Tall, and of distinguished appearance and intellect, people began to refer to him as destined for high office – 'porphyrogenetic' or born to the purple was the phrase, originally used about Pitt the Younger, that Duhamel applied to Giscard (Bassi, 1968, p. 122). His maiden speech from the tribune in January 1957 was an appeal for Parliament to support the Treaty of Rome. In May 1958 when the Fourth Republic collapsed he spoke on the

Algerian crisis and called for France's parliamentary regime to be radically transformed. He voted for the investiture of General de Gaulle in June and in November, under the new electoral law of the Fifth Republic with single-member constituencies, held his seat as *député* for suburban Clermont-Ferrand. A leading role in French politics requires a strong local base so over his years as *député* he added the roles of municipal councillor in Chanonat, *conseiller-général* in the *département* of Puy-de-Dôme and mayor of a Clermont-Ferrand suburb, Chamalières. Was he pro-Algérie-Française during the Algerian War? There was a scandalous attempt by Jacques Isorni, lawyer for the arrested OAS terrorist leaders, and other OAS members to suggest that Giscard was secret OAS agent 12B! Giscard sued and the affair, for procedural reasons, dragged on and eventually had to be dropped. No one seriously believes it to have been true. Giscard like most Frenchmen, including de Gaulle, was sympathetic to the struggle for Algérie-Française but he backed de Gaulle who had the clarity and courage to realise that French rule could not be imposed where a population rejected it. Addressing his parliamentary group, whose sympathies were mainly, even strongly, Algérie-française, in February 1960, Giscard said 'France is perhaps not on the same side of the barricades as you. Take care': an excellent example of intelligent Giscardian pragmatism.

He was given junior ministerial office in the Ministry of Finance in 1959 under Pinay, that symbol of prudent conservatism, and after Pinay's resignation in 1960, under his old *patron* Baumgartner. In January 1962, still not quite 36, he became Minister of Finance and Economic Affairs, the holder of one of the three leading government offices. He was the first ENA graduate to accede to such high office. His first period of office, from 1962 to 1966, is best remembered for the *plan de stabilisation* to combat inflation and to balance the budget, although the plan owed more to de Gaulle than to Giscard. Giscard d'Estaing became a well-known public figure with his informal pullover-clad television appearances and his brilliant budget expositions in Parliament. After de Gaulle's re-election as President in December 1965, a new government was formed. Giscard was not offered the Finance Ministry and he refused a 'demotion' even to an enlarged Ministry of Equipment. As Jean-Claude Colliard puts it (1971, p. 62):

To be thrown out of the government could have brought the political career of M. Giscard d'Estaing to a full and final stop: he seemed to fear it himself for several days and many observers wondered if a new orphan of Gaullism was not about to disappear from the centre of the stage. In fact this eviction was without doubt a stroke of good fortune . . . henceforth free in his movements the ex-minister could devote all his time and all his energy to the creation of a real political force.

In the three-year 'crossing of the desert' that ensued until he became Minister of Finance again, this time under President Pompidou, in 1969, occurred most of the events that served to make Giscard d'Estaing a leading and distinctive public figure rather than merely a clever, ambitious and successful young technocrat. They were also the events that cause orthodox Gaullists to bear him a grudge to this day. They are mostly connected with Giscard's role as leader of a new party, a rival to the Gaullist UNR, the Independent Republicans (RI). During Giscard's early parliamentary years he, as well as leading conservatives like Pinay, was connected to a loosely knit group of conservatives and moderates called IPAS (Independents and Peasants for Social Action) in Parliament and, confusingly, CNIP (National Centre for Independents and Peasants) in the country. This group split very badly in October 1962 over the issue of de Gaulle's referendum on direct elections for the presidency of the Republic. Giscard, a loyalist minister, and a few others sided with de Gaulle, while most of the CNIP joined the motley crew of Socialists, Radicals and MRP in the ill-fated *cartel des non*. The reform was popular and in the subsequent election electoral slaughter was visited upon the *cartel des non*. Giscard and his surviving friends decided to form a parliamentary study group (not a party – perish the thought) called the Independent Republicans. It promised 'loyal collaboration with the government and its parliamentary majority' of which it was a part. But 'it will be determined to make the political principles to which it is attached prevail'. These principles included 'favouring the construction of Europe' and 'fortifying the Atlantic alliance'.

As a parliamentary group the RI were strategically important to the government because the Gaullists on their own did not have a majority – except from 1968 to 1973 – and skilfully used their position to exercise influence and to act as a ginger group without actually threatening to bring down the government. After his dismissal from government, Giscard d'Estaing came back into Parliament; he was elected President of the Finance Commission in 1967, and the RI became more openly critical of the government. The RI also organised themselves as a party. In the spring of 1966 Giscard make a Gaullian progress through France – a 'tour of thought and action' inaugurating branches of a Giscardian club, Perspectives et Réalités. 'You are', he told the first national convention of these clubs that year, 'the future cadres of the great moderate party to which *après-Gaullisme* will give birth. You have suddenly broken the monotony of French political life.' They still refrained from supporting censure motions. Even in the 'Events of May 1968' when France was in the grip of a general strike, Giscard, in his famous 'Pygmalion' speech in which he declared that the French people, like Eliza Doolittle, wanted a little more 'consideration', did not call for the defeat of the government: 'we do not wish to add adventure to disorder'.

In these three years Giscard d'Estaing became quite well known, made a good impression in TV appearances and, above all skilfully cultivated the art of attracting maximum attention for his criticisms of General de Gaulle. In a celebrated phrase, on 10 January 1967, he described his attitude to the government as 'oui . . . mais' – support but not unconditional support. After de Gaulle's extraordinary outburst in Canada, shouting 'Vive le Québec libre' from the balcony of Montreal town hall, Giscard on 17 August 1967 attacked 'the solitary exercise of power', a phrase that has come to be used again and again about his own presidency. By this time Gaullists already considered Giscard an enemy: they ran an official candidate against his closest associate, Poniatowski, in 1968 and the Gaullist Minister of the Interior classified the results of Giscard and some of his friends as 'other right' and not as pro-government *majorité*! The cruellest cut came, however, when he publicly opposed de Gaulle's referendum proposals for the reform of Senate and the regions in April 1969. To a packed and expectant press conference in his town hall at Chamalières on 14 April he declared that 'with regret but with certainty' he would not be voting yes. The referendum was narrowly defeated and the General resigned. 'In relation to the General, founder of the Republic', writes Alfred Fabre-Luce

(1974, p. 30), 'Giscard – the man who in 1967 shook him with his "oui ... mais" and in 1969 overthrew him with his "non" – appears to "historic" Gaullists as a parricide. When, the morning after the first ballot [of the 1974 presidential election] he laid claim to their votes he seemed to them like Richard III in Shakespeare's play paying court to his victim's widow.' Incidentally, of course, he won their acquiescence, as did Richard that of the Lady Anne.

The presidential election of June 1969 which followed the resignation of General de Gaulle began with some uncharacteristic hesitation on the part of Giscard d'Estaing. He appears to have considered being a candidate himself against General de Gaulle's former Prime Minister Georges Pompidou, then later to have said he would support a candidate 'whose name begins with a P'. This could have been Pinay, the conservative elder statesman, Poher, the centrist Senate President and temporary President of the Republic during the vacancy of the president, who did in fact stand as a candidate, or Pompidou. He finally threw his weight and that of his group behind Pompidou in exchange for a more liberal approach than de Gaulle's in some areas of policy, notably European integration. After Pompidou's victory, Giscard d'Estaing became once again Minister of Finance with, incidentally, as his junior Secretary of State for the Budget, an ambitious young protégé of Pompidou called Jacques Chirac.

During this second period at the rue de Rivoli, 1969 to 1974, Giscard d'Estaing, a loyal Finance Minister to Pompidou, had more the air of a deputy Prime Minister. These were years of very rapid economic growth for France in which some of its industries, like the motor industry, became European leaders. Huge sums were invested in public infrastructure like highways, the telephone service, or Paris public transport, so that France rapidly acquired a modern and dynamic air. Skyscrapers appeared everywhere – not always to the satisfaction of the Minister of Finance who could see the towers of la Défense ruining the skyline at the top of the Champs Elysées from his office window! Gaullists by contrast were impressed: concrete equals *grandeur*.

The 1974 presidential election

President Pompidou, whose health had been deteriorating for

some time, died suddenly on 2 April 1974. When he was barely in his grave his former Prime Minister Jacques Chaban-Delmas (dismissed by Pompidou in 1972), a 'historic' Gaullist and Resistance hero, declared himself the candidate of the Gaullist UDR Party. A few days later Giscard d'Estaing, choosing Chamalières again as the setting for solemn pronouncements declared: 'here, in this town hall of the province of Auvergne, I announce that I am a candidate for the presidency of the Republic. I want to look deep into the eyes of France, tell her my message, listen to hers.' How pompous it sounds translated into English! A third Pompidou supporter – Edgar Faure, President of the National Assembly and Giscard's old *patron* – declared his candidature, then a fourth, Prime Minister Pierre Messmer. Messmer, expressing the fear that such a division in the ranks would lead to a victory by the left, invited all to withdraw in favour of himself. Chaban-Delmas refused. Giscard said he would have withdrawn if Chaban-Delmas had, so he refused. Faure withdrew. Messmer himself withdrew. Then Jean Royer, mayor of Tours, and the minister appointed to look after small shopkeepers, declared himself a candidate on behalf of decency, family life and the small firm. He did not withdraw but his campaign never recovered from his first televised public meeting during which a number of nubile students undressed before the cameras. The Royer candidature from the outset, however, cut into the support for Chaban-Delmas and allowed a gap to open in the opinion polls between him and Giscard d'Estaing. The gap never closed and Giscard emerged more and more convincingly as the candidate best able to beat François Mitterrand, the Socialist leader who was supported by Socialists and Communists as the candidate of the Union de la Gauche.

There are two rather unusual features in a presidential election in France. The first is, as we have seen, the phenomenon of the self-declared candidature. In America, where parties are far less cohesive and organised at national level than the big European parties, it would be inconceivable for the Democrats or Republicans simply to ratify a self-declared candidate for a presidency. Even incumbent Presidents, if they wish to be re-elected, have normally to campaign at primaries and the nominating conventions for adoption. Yet in France candidates, on the centre and right anyway, follow a Gaullian unwritten tradition that, despite the urgent need for party organisation and electoral muscle during a campaign, a would-be President must be somehow above mere parties. So they declare themselves and then seek endorsements. On the left it is slightly different. The Bureau Politique of the French Communist Party decides whether to have a candidate, and if so, who should be nominated. The Socialist Party comes the closest to having a nominating convention where the rank and file choose the presidential candidate. Gaston Defferre was launched on his disastrous campaign in 1969 – he got 5 per cent of the votes – in this democratic way. In 1981 the rank and file will have played a part in determining whether Mitterrand or Michel Rocard or some other contender should be the Socialist presidential candidate. But in 1974 the special party congress, which is required by party statutes to choose the candidate, was really only the first election rally. The decision to back Mitterrand had effectively already been taken because agreement had been reached with the Communists over Mitterrand as a common candidate of the whole left, not just of the Socialist Party.

The second curious feature of French presidential elections is the two-ballot system – or rather its presidential variant. If no candidate achieves an overall majority of all the votes cast at the first ballot, there is a run-off ballot. However, Article 7 of the Constitution lays down that, unlike in parliamentary or other elections in France, it shall be a run-off between two candidates only: the two that had most votes in the first ballot (unless one or other wishes to withdraw for some reason in which case the candidate who came third is eligible). This rule is of great importance. First, it ensures that whoever is elected has the legitimacy that comes from being the choice of an absolute majority of those voting in the final ballot. Secondly, this duel in the final ballot between two champions in single combat has imparted, or at least encouraged, a government/opposition polarisation to the French party system. The losing candidate of 1974, François Mitterrand, for example, filled the role of *de facto* leader of the opposition for the next few years. Thirdly, the nature of this two-ballot contest imposes a tactical pattern on contenders for the crown. The first ballot can be like an American primary: rivals within the two broad coalitions of government and opposition can compete amongst themselves. However, certain tactical imperatives must be observed. First, there must not be such dispersal of candidatures either on the left or the right that the whole of the opposition or the government coalition is eliminated. For instance if there were four or five pro-government candidates of roughly equal appeal, the result could be a second ballot with only the Socialist and Communist candidates left in! Secondly, it means that a successful candidate is of the kind that can out-distance rivals on his own side at the first ballot but obtain their support at the second. This is a particularly difficult problem on the left, when there is rivalry between Socialists and Communists, because a great many Socialist first-ballot voters will not vote Communist at the second.

In 1974 this problem was solved, on the left, because the Communists agreed to support Mitterrand as the 'common candidate of the left' and a climate of unity prevailed. Mitterrand fought an extremely able campaign, was top as expected in the first ballot, and came within 400,000 votes of winning in a turnout of 26 million. On the pro-government side, however, there was a real battle for the succession, and two things helped Giscard d'Estaing to establish his ascendancy over Chaban-Delmas. First, he was able to rally to his banner all the old Christian Democratic and moderate centre associated with Jean Lecanuet. Lecanuet, a centrist presidential candidate against de Gaulle in 1965, was the leader of the Centre Démocrate which, in conjunction with part of the old Radical Party, had been part of the opposition under Pompidou. So the acquisition of Lecanuet was an enlargement of the Pompidou coalition and gave a reforming, moderate image to the Giscard campaign. Secondly, it became clear that not all Gaullists were behind Chaban-Delmas. There had been conflict within the UDR between 'historic' Gaullists like Chaban-Delmas and Michel Debré, faithful to the General's legend, and the more pragmatic technocrats associated with Pompidou and what had become known as the 'UDR state'. The leading Pompidou technocrat was Jacques Chirac, occupying at the time of his master's death the powerful position of Minister of the Interior, with control of the *préfets* and access to confidential opinion polls. Chirac with some other ministers and members of Parliament, mainly UDR, signed the 'Declaration of the 43'. These forty-three called for unity behind the candidate best-placed to safeguard the fundamental principles of the Fifth Republic and to defeat the 'socialo-communist' candidate. This was fairly obviously a call to support Giscard d'Estaing.

Giscard's campaign opened with a rather boring but

characteristically well-structured technical exposition of 'four ideas, three securities and nine changes'. The four ideas were *indépendence* and *puissance* for France, justice and security for the French. The three securities involved protection against poverty in old age, against economic risk, and for women and families. The nine changes ran from equality of rights and opportunities through improved working conditions and reduced inequality of income to improved hospitals and transport and 'the entry of a generation of new men into the institutions of the Fifth Republic'. It was all incredibly detailed − 'today 44 per cent of beds in old people's homes are in non-private wards, these will be closed by 1980' − and an excellent example of the style of the reforming *polytechnicien*. At home the policy was 'to change ... French politics and society'. Europe was 'for me the essential priority': 'union by 1980', 'conserving what exists, that is the common agricultural policy', 'proposing what is lacking', in particular 'renewed progress towards economic and monetary union and the co-ordinated evolution of European currencies'. The European Monetary System is thus the fulfilment of a Giscard election promise.

In its general policy approach the Giscard campaign was very similar to that of Pompidou in 1969: *continuité et ouverture*. He would continue the policies of the late President in the spheres of economic and foreign policy, especially, as we have noted, European integration *à la française*. But, as Pompidou had done in 1969, he would try to attract former oppositionists into his majority, he would be more liberal on constitutional matters like dealings with Parliament or opposition, or on civil liberties. Just as they had done with Pompidou, the questions of covert action by the police (like telephone-tapping) and government control of radio and television came up. Just as Pompidou had done, Giscard promised liberalisation.

The Giscard campaign was rather American in style. It is unusual in French election campaigns, for instance, for wife and family to play a prominent part. Anne-Aymone Giscard d'Estaing, however, was dispatched to win over the French Caribbean, and the four children Henri, Louis-Joachim, Valérie-Anne and especially the youngest, Jacinthe, figured on posters and in the campaign. The smiling family-man (must be a good Catholic with so many children) made a pleasing contrast with the divorced Chaban-Delmas and the mysterious Mitterrand. There

were tee-shirts printed *Giscard à la barre* – 'Giscard to the helm'.
A talented team of advisers handled the themes of the campaign
with great skill, especially slogans like *un vrai Président*, or the
second ballot theme 'change without risk' which exactly fitted the
public mood which wanted a change but felt uneasy about
entrusting it to the left in which the Communist Party was an
important element. The expert behind the publicity campaign was
Jacques Hintzy, a Giscardian militant from the birth of the RI, and
a director of the Havas advertising agency. Policy, campaign
themes and speeches were prepared by teams of associates,
mainly from ENA or Polytechnique or ministerial *cabinets* or, like
Giscard d'Estaing, from all three. Lionel Stoleru, an economist
and author of a very influential book on the way ahead for the
French economy, *L'Impératif industriel* (1969), later to become a
secretary of state in the Ministry of Labour, was one of the most
important. Paul Mentré (Polytechnique, ENA, Giscard's *cabinet*),
Jean Serisé (ENA, Giscard's *cabinet* since 1962 and still in it at the
Elysée) and Christian Bonnet (to be Minister of the Interior in the
Giscard presidency) organised the campaign themes and drafted
speeches. The director of the campaign was Lucien Lanier (to
become regional prefect of Paris in 1975), with the experienced
Giscardien militant Hubert Bassot and Philippe Sauzay (*chef de
cabinet* at the Elysée) to organise tours and meetings. Michel
Pinton, today the organiser of the *Giscardien* party or federation
UDF, was the campaign's opinion poll specialist. Victor Chapot,
another who went from Giscard's *cabinet* in the Ministry of
Finance to the presidential *cabinet*, was the expert campaign
fund-raiser. He was remarkably successful: the Giscard d'Estaing
campaign with its full colour posters and big meetings was not
short of money. The political tasks of building support, lunching
the influential and winning endorsements fell to Poniatowski,
Michel d'Ornano, Roger Chinaud, J.-P. Soisson, and Jacques
Dominati – all to serve as ministers in the Giscard presidency
except Chinaud who is leader of the UDF parliamentary group.

Three factors helped Giscard d'Estaing to pull so far ahead of
Chaban-Delmas as the most credible candidate for the second
ballot duel against Mitterrand: the endorsements of Lecanuet and
Chirac, the effectiveness of his well-run campaign – with its
central theme of 'change without risk' while Chaban-Delmas
struggled to revive the symbolism of the de Gaulle epic – and
television. Giscard is very effective on television, much more so

than as a speaker from a platform where he sounds monotonous, high-brow and surprisingly pompous – rather like a court chamberlain making an official pronouncement. On television he manages to combine the qualities of the technocrat intellectual, like grasp of detail and the capacity to present arguments in an orderly and structured fashion, with a relaxed informality and sincerity of purpose. During the 1974 campaign his most effective performance was in the face-to-face debate with Mitterrand. Just as the handsome, idealistic and vigorous John Kennedy cut down the shifty blue-chinned Nixon on television in 1960 and went on to win a close-run election, so the sincere, polite and competent-looking Giscard smote the sardonic Mitterrand, struggling with facts and figures. He pressed Mitterrand very hard, naturally, where he was most vulnerable. How would he govern without a parliamentary majority? Was it not taking a prodigious risk to give Communists government office?

Well, he won. A presidential election in France attracts enormous interest from the population. The two main candidates addressed immense audiences in city after city – 100,000 in Paris, 20,000, 30,000, 40,000 in provincial cities like Lyon or Nantes. Eighty-five per cent of the electorate turned out for the first ballot and, as happens only when the result is expected to be close and perceived as crucial for the country, even more – 88 per cent – voted at the second. It all goes to show that the central institution of the Fifth Republic – the executive leadership of a directly elected President – has that wide popular assent called legitimacy.

Giscard d'Estaing became the third President of the Fifth Republic and at 48 one of the youngest heads of state in French Republican history. So long as a French President has a parliamentary majority unwilling to overthrow the government he appoints or to reject the laws it proposes, he has more concentrated executive power in his hands than any other Western leader. He is not like the British Prime Minister, accountable day by day to the House of Commons, nor the American President whose executive power is under the doctrine of 'checks and balances' subject to all kinds of judicial, financial and other constraints from Congress, the Supreme Court and the fifty states. The French President is elected for seven years, the longest term anywhere for a democratic political leader, and is re-eligible. What did Giscard d'Estaing want to do with all this power? In a phrase, he wanted to make France a more liberal nation and a more admired nation. Most of the policies of his presidency, as we shall see, from the attempt to build better relations with the opposition, to tackling problems like slum housing, to asserting a French world presence in foreign affairs, were, whatever the varying degrees of success achieved, related to these themes.

Sometimes one is tempted to describe him as the 'philosopher-king', not because of the originality of his political ideas, but because, as in Plato's Republic, he seems to belong to a specially trained, almost specially bred, class of 'guardians' supremely versed in the modern equivalent of philosophy, technocratic administration. His background, not opulent like the Kennedys' but what French call *aisé*, his intelligence, his ambition, the schools from which he graduated with spectacular success, the people he knew, all opened the path to a career of distinction in the public service. A Belgian finance minister summed him up as 'a great technician who possesses in addition a great political sense' (Todd, 1977, p. 413). Some have argued that success has come too easily to Giscard and that he has never had to fight. André Fontaine wrote rather bitterly that such things as the study of economics, a love of Mozart and 'perhaps too easy and sheltered a life' make one believe 'that wisdom and a sense of proportion are instruments within easy reach ... Then, one fine day, one discovers that the rules of the game are not to be found in Descartes or in Keynes, but rather in Shakespeare and in Machiavelli' (*Le Monde*, 7 November 1979). The positive side of belonging to a well-to-do natural public service elite, however, is the *sens de l'état* that observers from de Gaulle down have attributed to Giscard d'Estaing, and the absence of any marked desire for personal financial gain. Giscard, unlike his father, has not moved into the private sector but remained, either as administrator or politician, in the public service. Although there have been various allegations during his presidency that he has made stock-market gains and accepted gifts of valuable diamonds from Bokassa, the 'emperor' of a corrupt and brutal dictatorship, very dependent on France, in Central Africa, the idea that Giscard is corrupt or corruptible is, in the eyes of almost everyone, simply not a credible accusation.

In May 1974 Giscard did have to fight, and he won 'the first great contest of his political life'. 'To reach the Elysée', continues Todd (1977, pp. 482–3), 'Giscard used the sharpness of his intellect, his capacity for farsightedness, his absence of illusion about human behaviour, his vanity, his self-esteem, his courage . . . and his reserves of power. The great cat . . . has advanced slowly and stealthily through the long grass of politics. Now he is in the open.'

CHAPTER 2

The Ideas of
the President

Valéry Giscard d'Estaing has expressed his views on the important themes of political and economic organisation with clarity, coherence and, over a long period of time, consistency. We find him, for instance, saying the same things about political institutions or economic change or social justice in his speeches of the mid-1960s as in *Démocratie française* (1976) or his presidential press conferences. Liberalism, the need for change, the importance of harmony between majority and opposition and between social groups, presidential leadership, France's role in the world, the need for social reform – these are the important elements of the President's political thinking. It has been criticised for not being compellingly original. This is unfair: Giscard d'Estaing is a political leader, not a professor of philosophy (even if there are Platonic elements of the philosopher-king about his background and style of government). It can be criticised as mere rhetoric in that many of the liberal reforms have not been achieved. Indeed, in the field of justice and the freedom of information hardly any progress has been made at all. This is a question we shall return to in a later chapter, bearing in mind that a political leader in a democracy, however generously endowed with powers, cannot always achieve what he wants to achieve. There is a spirit of humanity and reasonableness in Giscardian political thought, but although *l'épanouissement de l'individu* is asserted as the basic objective of social organisation one does not find expressed the passionate attachment to freedom which is the hallmark of the English philosophers like Locke or John Stuart Mill. *Raison d'état* still has a place in the Giscardian scheme of things. The key expressions are 'liberalism' and 'national unity'. In a way, as we shall see, they have the same meaning because national unity means a harmonious, tolerant, and therefore liberal consensus.

Liberalism

The economic liberalism of Giscard d'Estaing is not the economic liberalism of the British Conservative Party or the American business community. The idea that there is something fundamentally unhealthy about state intervention in the economy has never been a feature of French conservatism. Indeed, it has been suggested (e.g. Hayward, 1973, p. 152) that one of the reasons the French economy has developed more smoothly than the British economy in the last twenty years is that we are now living in an age where there is no alternative to state intervention in the economy – especially for investment in high technology – and that this is more readily accepted in France. In Great Britain the myth of the free and buccaneering entrepreneur of Victorian days survives (despite the extinction of the actual species) and an agonised debate continues about the legitimacy of state intervention. France, by contrast, had, during the heyday of the capitalist entreprenuer, a century of economic stagnation characterised by a type of pessimism about the possibility of growth which was called Malthusianism. Since the Second World War, however, there has been no dissent about the French state fulfilling the role it has filled in the past from Colbert to Napoleon, as motor and promoter of economic development. Throughout a good deal of this successful period of growth the Minister of Finance, that is to say, he who represents the principle of economic control in the most *dirigiste* state in the Western world, has been Valéry Giscard d'Estaing.

Giscardian economic liberalism is explained in detail in *Démocratie française*, the little book he wrote while President of the Republic and which has sold nearly 2 million copies (royalites to a charitable foundation). Giscard rejects 'classic liberalism' but recognises that 'we owe to it a decisive share of our progress' (p. 44), both in terms of political liberty and economic success. This is because liberalism 'places the individual at the beginning and the end of social organisation'. Economically, 'the system of free enterprise, of internal and external competition, and of the effective functioning of the market, possesses over authoritarian planning, even that baptised democratic, a double advantage: on the one hand it permits individual needs to orient production directly ... on the other it uses the technical and psychological stimulus of initiative rather than the dead-weight of administrative decision ... Competition, by obliging each to give the best of himself, is by far the most effective of stimulants.' There are, however, two serious shortcomings in the philosophy of 'classic liberalism'. The first is that one of the natural responses of economic man to competition is to accumulate defences against competition. Thus 'liberal society' has in fact seen the development of all kinds of protection, combination, concentration and domination. Secondly, economic man is a 'unidimensional robot' whose actions are explained only by his material self-interest. 'But man engaged in economic and social life cannot be reduced to that component alone.' 'Total and contradictory', he wants 'security and adventure, material comfort and humanism, freedom and order' (p. 46).

Another characteristically Giscardian criticism of 'classic liberalism' which appears from time to time is that a certain distrust of competition and the market is justified 'in so far as democratic society, determined to submit the spontaneous to the considered [*decidée à soumettre le spontané au conscient*] cannot put its trust in blind forces' (p. 116). Insecurity, the subordination of weaker groups, discontent and social upheaval – these could be the results of the working of blind forces. Speaking in 1960, Giscard d'Estaing emphasised the need for a 'synthesis between individual freedom which it is essential to preserve and which will in any case be the basic motor of economic expansion and the definition of a common will applied to both the objectives and the nature of expansion'. This is what Georges Laverdines (*Pouvoirs*, no. 9, 1979, pp. 17–26) calls 'organised liberalism', and is really nothing more than the concept of the 'social market economy' which has been the dominant model of most successful West European economies since the Second World War with an expressed preference for the West German vision in which the roles of state and industry are somewhat more separate than they have been in France. In economic terms Giscard's liberalism has been less *dirigiste* in rhetoric than in practice and, during his presidency, as measures like the relaxing of price controls in 1978 make clear, he has been less *dirigiste* than his predecessors.

Liberalism in its political sense has also been an important

Giscardian theme. In his celebrated press conference of January 1967, in which he declared his conditional support for Gaullism with the formula 'oui ... mais', he called for a 'more liberal functioning of political institutions'. In particular he was referring to the need for Parliament to be given a better opportunity to exercise its function of law-making and control of the executive but the desire for 'a more liberal functioning' of institutions serves well as a general summary of the President's political faith.

A fairly precise idea of what President Giscard d'Estaing means in political terms by liberalism is also to be found in the pages of *Démocratie française*. It embraces social justice, freedom of the individual, pluralist and democratic political organisation, private property, order and civilised political debate based upon agreement about fundamentals. Typically Giscardian, this list contains nothing messianic or revolutionary. It is however animated by sentiments a good deal more generous and humane than those expressed by most political moderates or conservatives. Furthermore, Giscard was expressing these views long before he became President.

'Justice', writes the President (1976, p. 58), 'consists in the elimination of poverty, the disappearance of privilege, and the struggle against discrimination.' 'Solidarity', meaning a preparedness to make an effort on behalf of less fortunate groups like the elderly, the handicapped, widows, or single-parent families, or dwellers in slums and shanty-towns, is a word frequently used by Giscard d'Estaing in speeches and statements. It has been followed through in a range of policies which have been adopted during his presidency. When he talks of the 'suppression of privileges' (p. 60) he does not mean, as those farther to the left might, the elimination of privileged educational opportunities (although there is a paragraph on the socially circumscribed nature of recruitment to top schools like ENA – p. 67) or of inherited wealth or of exceptionally high incomes. He means principally the elimination of abuses like land speculation where 'certain people ... appropriate for themselves the fruit of a collective effort to which they have not contributed' (p. 61). Once again there has been a serious attempt in his presidency to give effect to these ideas. He also recognises in *Démocratie française* (e.g. p. 54) and in speeches that inequality of income in France is too great to be consistent with his principal goal of 'national unity' and that progress needs to be made. The 'struggle against discrimination' is, in the view of Giscard d'Estaing, most necessary in the case of women, of manual workers whose jobs do not enjoy the consideration or the conditions of employment received by others, and of children who do not get proper educational opportunities. Policy, yet again, has been consistent with rhetoric. Other liberal ideas concerning the rights of the individual, like the right to privacy or the right to a reasonable environment, figure in Giscard's speeches and writings. In his presidential campaign much was made of the need to reform justice to give better protection to the rights of the individual and to eliminate abuses like telephone-tapping by security services. We shall look at these in a later chapter. Overall, Giscard d'Estaing has been a committed reformer, except in judicial questions.

Other manifestations of the desire for a 'more liberal functioning of institutions' have included the relaxing of state control over radio and television, the conferring upon parliamentarians of the right to invoke the Constitutional Council, the announcement of 'bold measures' (Elysée communiqué, 30 October 1978) of decentralisation to local authorities. All this comes under the heading of 'pluralism': ensuring that different kinds of power in society, state power, economic power, the power of mass communications, are both separate from one another and free from excessive concentration. The results in these domains have been, as we shall see, rather disappointing: presidential patronage has had much the same effect as direct control on the mass media, for example, and the French state still gives citizens remarkably little opportunity to make their voices heard in such important decisions as the nuclear power programme or the siting of nuclear reactors, decisions in which *raison d'état* is paramount.

National unity

The theme that binds together the different strands of Giscardian liberalism is national unity: the consensus about the fundamentals of social and political organisation, such as freedom or justice, which make pluralism consistent with harmonious and civilised political debate.

Remove injustices and indignities, make people feel less

discontented, afford them more job satisfaction in their role as citizens, and the country will be more united. If it is more united, there will be less risk of upheaval if hard times come and France will have greater standing in world affairs. That in essence is the formula that lies behind the Giscard d'Estaing approach to government. 'My task as head of state', he explained as he distributed awards to the 'best workers of France' in the unlikely setting of the Grand Amphitheatre of the Sorbonne, 'is to unite different men around one common ideal.' The ideas he was putting forward – share-holdings for workers, participation of workers in decision-making at work – would be a reply to those who 'by error had put their hopes in two opposed but equally utopian systems, workers' control (*autogestion*) and collectivism' and would contribute 'to the reconciliation of Frenchmen with each other'.

There is an ever-present danger of disunity in France. As Giscard put it in a television interview on 18 April 1979:

> there are in our political temperament forces, attitudes, interests which make people prefer short-lived and powerless governments to discipline and to the difficulties of sustained government action . . . I know perfectly well that forces of instability or division exist in France, the question is how to prevent them doing damage to France ... It took a great deal of skill and attention this winter, at the time of the most extreme tensions [a reference to rising unemployment and the violent strikes over redundancies in the steel industry] to prevent French society from tearing itself apart, and if it began to tear itself apart in violence, where could that violence have led to?

The road ahead for France would not be easy but there would not be economic decline because France had the intellectual, educational and scientific capacity to develop the necessary new industries: 'we have a long future of development and progress ahead of us, but on condition that we adapt'. Therefore, to quote the peroration from the New Year's Eve presidential message of 31 December 1979: 'In 1980, France needs the seriousness of purpose, the courage, the capacity to adapt, the generosity and the unity of the French people. As for me, I will dedicate myself to that search for unity which is both so necessary and, in their heart of hearts, so longed-for by Frenchmen.'

How does the over-riding goal of national unity square with pluralism – already cited as a Giscardian *mot-clef*? Pluralism in an economy based on competition, pluralism in the mass-media, pluralism meaning not too much decision-making power concentrated in the hands of central government (not a wholly apt description of the Giscard presidency) – these all fit quite easily into the smiling picture of a more liberal, less discontented and hence more united society. Pluralism as competition among political parties, however, while obviously a prerequisite for any society claiming to be democratic, appears at first sight not to fit into the Giscard grand design. After all, do not political parties incarnate these 'forces of division and instability'? Do not some of them seek the dehumanising goal of 'collectivism'? The answer lies in the President's repeated pleas for 'reasonable cohabitation' or *décrispation* – a less tense and hostile relationship between the majority and a more reasonable opposition.

Démocratie française has a chapter called 'A strong and peaceful democracy' in which these ideas are developed. The main problem in French political life is considered to be the 'state of ideological divorce' between political elites.'The style [of political debate] is not that of a deliberation of citizens ... but a war of religion.' This situation is no longer 'sociologically unavoidable': 'the real picture of France is not one of a country divided into two opposing classes but of a society already advanced along the way to unification' (p. 155). There is undoubtedly a consensus about political institutions that has not existed in the turbulent history of France since the revolution. There is no evidence to suggest that any major social group wishes to overthrow the present Republic. H. Mendras (1980, p. 45) asserts boldly that 'the French people as a whole has completely accepted its system of government'. The country is no longer divided by the old conflicts over religion, over political rights, over the nature of the regime, but it has a political elite which behaves as though it still were. 'France', Giscard said once in a 1977 radio interview, 'is not in a state of fever: only the political class is in a state of fever.'

One of the central ideas of the Giscard presidency, therefore, has been the search for reconciliation between rival political elites. He would like to see in France the type of relationship that exists between government and opposition leaders in Great Britain or West Germany: divergences about policies to be followed 'leave intact a fundamental agreement on the principles of the organisation of social life' and 'each team recognises that the other will safeguard what is essential' (p. 154). Opposition leaders can be briefed on foreign policy or defence issues, where there is already a common perception of national objectives; they can participate in talks with visiting leaders. The attempts by President Giscard d'Estaing to bring about this *décrispation* and *cohabitation raisonnable* have not borne fruit: invitations to the Elysée have generally been declined by opposition leaders. The fear of opposition leaders has been that they would in accepting an invitation seem to their supporters or partners to be giving some kind of seal of approval to the President and his policies. They have seemed to suspect that what they were really being offered was political castration. Visits have therefore been rare. After the 1978 election defeat both Mitterrand and Marchais accepted invitations but more to present lists of demands or complaints than to participate in consultation.

Yet Giscard d'Estaing continued to affirm that the alternation of power between government and opposition is 'fundamental to advanced democratic societies' (1976, p. 154). Indeed the only test of a democratic regime is 'does it admit the existence of an effective opposition, which has the real possibility of becoming one day the majority?' (p. 147). The opposition 'exercises a function in France which is a normal democratic function. A democracy without an opposition is no longer a democracy. Therefore not only am I not astonished that there is an opposition in France but I declare that it is part of our democratic life' (television interview, 18 April 1979).

People sometimes therefore wrongly claim that the real problem in France, he said in a post-election broadcast on 22 March 1978, that it is electorally 'cut in two'. On the contrary it is perfectly normal for a democracy to be 'cut in two'. The real problem is the relationship between majority and opposition.

That is why the *décrispation* of French political life is an essential dimension of the modernisation of our democracy. The dramatisation of political life and the hardening of attitudes play into the hands of the enemies of pluralism. By accrediting the idea that what divides French society is stronger than what unites it, they try to justify the excesses and the injustice of their attacks. By contrast, emphasising for Frenchmen that they must get used to living together and respect each other's opinions, that is the way to prepare minds for democratic pluralism. (1976, p. 156)

In an important interview in the magazine *L'Express* (9–15 May 1977) Giscard d'Estaing cast himself in the unifying tradition of General de Gaulle: a national leader 'must go beyond division and appeal to what unites the French people' as de Gaulle did when 'reconstructing the state'. Leaders like de Gaulle 'did not throw one half of the nation against the other'. The idea of pluralism, therefore, must itself be the basis of the consensus:

> the real political debate, in France as in neighbouring countries, will take place within one conception of society common to the great majority of Frenchmen, a tolerant conception, open, respecting the separation of powers and the right to be different: a pluralist conception. This debate will no longer be the mythological combat of Gorgons and Medusas, of good and evil, which still colours our political life with primitive and dangerous violence, but a competition between men and teams who can turn by turn work for the common good. Then France will know strong and peaceful democracy. (1976, p. 157)

Institutions and the nation-state

Although change – social reform, changes in political attitudes, economic adaptation – is, as we have seen, an important Giscardian theme, there are certain features of the political universe where the President does not want change at all. Nothing said by Giscard d'Estaing has ever called into question the institutions of the Fifth Republic or the nation state as the fundamental political entity. The institutions of the Fifth Republic, and in particular the leadership role of the President, have always had his support. Even when, in August 1967, he criticised the 'solitary exercise of power' by General de Gaulle, he made it clear that there was no suggestion of 'calling into question the authority of the President of the Republic'. It was however indispensable that 'authority makes its final decision only after the necessary deliberation'. In *Démocratie française* the Fifth

Republic's Constitution is described as having 'permitted a better balance of power, and assured the stability of the executive ... we have the historic good fortune to possess institutions both effective and democratic . . . everything must be done to preserve them' (pp. 152–3).

As far as the nation-state is concerned, Giscard d'Estaing has never been quite so fervently lyrical about France as General de Gaulle nor so doctrinaire about the state as Michel Debré. Nevertheless, his commitment to both is unequivocal. France respresents not superpower but *rayonnement* – a beacon of culture and enlightenment. His speeches are full of the notion that France must be an 'example' to the rest of the world: an example 'by our social organisation, by our intellectual capacity, by our way of conducting our economic development, by the insistence on justice that we express' (speech in New Caledonia, 17 July 1979). Giscard has never expressed support for federalism – either in terms of the creation of a federal 'United States of Europe' or of internal devolution to autonomous regions like Brittany or Corsica. To quote the 'oui ... mais' press conference of 1967 again, when he called for a more committed approach to the construction of Europe: 'the EEC Commission cannot be the embryo of a European government. The delegation of sovereignty has served to get the European enterprise started, but can lead us no further. What must be done is to organise the systematic collaboration of governments and to assure the convergence of their policies while respecting their prerogatives.' He refers to the objective of 'confederation'. He used the same word as a presidential candidate in 1974 as part of his claim to be continuing the work of President Pompidou and his European initiatives (*Le Monde*, 3 May 1974). As President he repeated on television on 30 June 1977 his objective of 'a powerful confederation of Europe'. 'Why a confederation? Because we must unite our economies, draw together our policies, and at the same time perserve the ancient and vigorous personalities which are those of our countries ... I want to tell you that this is one of the objectives I have set myself personally: a united France in a confederal Europe.'

A united France: the expression can be applied to the President's concept of more harmonious social relations, but it also means territorial unity. Giscard d'Estaing and the *Giscardiens* are sympathetic to the devolution of greater responsibility to local authorites, especially the *commune* and the *département*. As President a certain number of measures, as we shall see later, have been introduced – such as the right of Paris to have a mayor and a city council like the other 36,000 *communes* of France. There has, however, been no concession to the notion of regional autonomy. Corsican violence has not led to Corsican independence – indeed in a presidential speech in Ajaccio on June 7 1978 Giscard d'Estaing referred to himself several times as the guardian of 'the unity of the nation'. Some of the overseas territories, like Djibouti, have acceded to independence where there is a clearly expressed wish, but independence for all is certainly not a Giscardian idea nor French government policy.

Adaptation of existing institutions in a more humane and liberal direction is what is sought by President Giscard d'Estaing, not fundamental change. I once met Giscard d'Estaing long before he was President – in fact at the time of the 1969 referendum – and he said to me: 'France really must adapt: do you know the *préfet* still wears uniform on official occasions?' Notice that he did not suggest the abolition of the *préfet* – that embodiment of the Napoleonic centralised state. Notice also that twelve years later the *préfet* still wears uniform on official occasions: perhaps a more liberal functioning of institutions is difficult to achieve even for a President, even for one with the excessively concentrated powers to which we now turn.

CHAPTER 3

The Powers of
the Presidency

Presidential supremacy in the Fifth Republic

It was remarked in the first chapter that the President of the Republic in France, provided there is a parliamentary majority unwilling to frustrate or to overthrow the governments he appoints, has more concentrated executive power in his hands than any other Western leader. Senator Henri Caillavet, writing in *Le Monde diplomatique* (February 1980), describes the regime today not as presidential (which implies checks and balances *à l'américaine*) but as 'presidentialism': 'that is to say the occult power of one man in his palace, having an idea on everything, assisted by a court, and dispensing with both popular legitimacy and Parliament. The new personage thus created – becoming more and more common throughout the world – is a sort of president-king.' 'Dispensing with popular legitimacy' is a little severe on a President who has been elected by universal suffrage, and where every parliamentary election has been won by the supporters of the President and of presidential leadership. The general aura of the presidency, however, with its disdain for political parties and electioneering, its self-consciously regal style, the absence of direct public accountability, and the increasingly wide range of policies and decisions which come within the personal ambit of the President, gives some validity to the phrase 'president-king'.

The 'president-king' resembles the President of the United States in having the legitimacy of direct election to chief executive office, in having the prestige of being head of state, in having the whole diplomatic and military apparatus of the state under his direct command and in having great powers of patronage including appointment at the highest levels in the judiciary. An American President, however, has the appointments he wishes to make scrutinised in public hearings by the Senate and sometimes quashed, frequently has great difficulty persuading Congress to vote the laws or the money he wants in order to pursue his policies, can have his actions, particularly if there is a suggestion of anything illegal or unconstitutional as in the Watergate Affair, investigated by congressional committees and the courts, has to campaign hard even for readoption as presidential candidate by his own party, has continually to defend his actions in public at press conferences which have none of the respectful and deferential character they assume in France, and can be impeached for 'grave misdemeanours'. No President in the Fifth Republic has had to put up with anything like that. Parliament and the courts do not have such wide-ranging powers of investigation although the Conseil d'Etat and the Conseil Constitutionnel taken together have many of the attributes of the American Supreme Court and have on occasions over-ruled executive acts – notably when the Conseil d'Etat in 1962 annulled the special military courts set up under presidential emergency powers the previous year. There is a procedure for impeachment of a French President under Article 68 of the Constitution but only when the accusation is 'high treason'. There is nothing to prevent the French Parliament or the mass media being less accommodating to the President. They have nearly all the time, however, chosen not to be difficult and, in the case of the National Assembly, this is the deliberate choice of an elected majority which believes strongly in the Gaullist principle of presidential leadership.

In being able in normal circumstances to count on the majority in the legislature not to frustrate his laws or his policies, nor to overthrow his governments, the President resembles a British Prime Minister or other parliamentary leaders. A British Prime Minister, however, has to answer parliamentary questions twice a week, without foreknowledge of the topics that could arise and with replies subject to supplementary questions, has to make statements in Parliament on crises, international or domestic, on major government initiatives or policies and answer questions about them, has to make leading speeches in parliamentary debates on most important occasions, and even has to attend the House of Commons late at night to cast votes. In addition a British

Prime Minister has all the problems of party leadership and party management to contend with. The French President is subject to none of these constraints nor to the accountability that is their object. The French President cannot be called to account at all except by the electors at the end of his exceptionally long seven-year term of office.

Presidential leadership has become the main characteristic of the Fifth Republic but it derives only partly from the Constitution. Besides, as General de Gaulle remarked at a celebrated press conference (31 January 1964), *'une constitution, c'est un esprit, des institutions, une pratique'*. The 'spirit' of the Fifth Republic Constitution proceeded, he explained, from the necessity to ensure the 'effectiveness, stability and responsibility', of the executive, which had been lacking in the previous Republic. The 'practice' of presidential supremacy is what has emerged.

The actual text of the Constitution, however, divides executive power between the President and the government which, under Article 20, 'determines and conducts the policy of the Nation'. Some powers are given to the President alone, some (like fixing the parliamentary agenda, Article 48, or resolving procedural deadlocks in Parliament, Article 45) to the Prime Minister and government alone, and some, indeed most, require the agreement of President and Prime Minister for their exercise.

The most important powers vested in the President alone are appointment of the Prime Minister (Article 8), dissolution of the National Assembly (Article 12) and the exercise of exceptional powers in an emergency (Article 16). In these matters his powers are absolute except that he cannot dissolve the Assembly twice within a period of twelve months, and he has to consult the Prime Minister, the presidents of both houses of Parliament, and the Constitutional Council (though he is not required to take notice of their advice) before he invokes Article 16. Other powers he can exercise alone include nomination of three members (including the President) of the Constitutional Council (Article 56), the power to submit a law or a treaty to the Constitutional Council (Articles 54 and 61) and the right to address a message to Parliament (Article 18). All other presidential acts – including the right of pardon (Article 17) or acts in his vitally important capacity as chief of the armed forces with the right to preside over National Defence Councils (Article 15) – have to be, under Article 19 of the Constitution, countersigned by the Prime Minister.

The powers vested by the Constitution in the President but requiring the agreement of the Prime Minister for their exercise merit a brief examination because they reveal very clearly the fact that presidential supremacy is not inscribed in tablets of stone but depends upon a willing Prime Minister. Ministers, other than the Prime Minister, are appointed by the President on the proposition of the Prime Minister (Article 8). The President presides at the Council of Ministers (Article 9), provided the Prime Minister agrees to a meeting being called; and he can require Parliament to reconsider a Bill before promulgating it into law (Article 10), provided the Prime Minister countersigns the demand. The President can make proposals to reform the Constitution (Article 89) and submit these reforms, or certain proposals over laws and treaties, to a referendum (Article 11). This recourse to referendum is regarded as one of the President's most important powers. The Constitution, however, makes it clear that he can only exercise these initiatives 'on the proposal of the Prime Minister', which means that the true presidential prerogative is the decision to accept or refuse a prime-ministerial proposal! All five referenda in the Fifth Republic have been manifestly presidential in intiatiative though there has always been published in the *Journal officiel* a respectful letter from the Prime Minister beginning 'In conformity with Article 11 of the Constitution, I have the honour to propose ...'. Article 13 empowers the President to sign decrees and regulations decided in the Council of Ministers, and to make the top appointments in all the sensitive areas of the public service like *préfets*, ambassadors, or heads of department (*directeurs*) in the civil service. Under Article 30 he can call special sessions of Parliament. All these acts, however, require the agreement of the Prime Minister.

The joint exercise of all these powers was much discussed before the 1978 election. If the left had won a parliamentary majority the President would have needed a Prime Minister who would not have been immediately censured by the new majority. Such a Prime Minister, presumably a Socialist, would presumably have been less willing to accord supremacy to a President elected against the left in 1974. Had this happened the Fifth Republic would have become less presidential, though the President, endowed with the prestige of universal suffrage, could have used the powers discussed above to moderate the acts and policies of his new government, and to bring its life to a speedy end by a well-timed dissolution of the National Assembly.

If, as de Gaulle said, a constitution is *un esprit, des institutions, une pratique*, the greatest of these is *pratique*. Presidential supremacy has been the practice right from the beginning of the Fifth Republic. The sources of this supremacy are, apart from the powers bestowed by the Constitution, the personality of the Fifth Republic's first President and the circumstances surrounding his return to power, the legitimacy given to the office by direct election, and the emergence of a majority in the country which was strongly in favour of presidential leadership.

General de Gaulle, in the same press conference speech of January 1964, modestly mentioned that as far as the practice of the Constitution was concerned his 'personal equation counted and I doubt if from the outset, this was unexpected'. Georges Pompidou remarked when he was Prime Minister that no one expected General de Gaulle, once recalled to the helm, 'to be content with opening flower shows' (*inaugurer les chrysanthèmes*). De Gaulle, celebrated for his wartime leadership of the Free French and of the post-Liberation government, was recalled to power in 1958 because of the crisis in Algeria. A military *coup d'état* threatened the state. There was strong popular support for a new constitution making firmer executive leadership possible and for continuing action by de Gaulle to resolve the Algerian question. Once it became clear that French rule could no longer be imposed on the Algerians, he had to gain and retain the support of the French for Algerian independence against a prolonged rearguard offensive by Algérie-Française extremists, which included terrorist attacks, assassination attempts on de Gaulle himself and military rebellions. The most serious of these – the Algiers putsch of 22 April 1961 – led de Gaulle to invoke Article 16 and to rule for five months under wide emergency powers, during which time presidential powers were used to discipline civil servants, police, or military personnel, to set up special military courts and to censor the press.

De Gaulle himself, and the expectation of presidential leadership that he aroused, was an important factor in the emergence of presidential supremacy. The President, however, as he characteristically put it in a broadcast in September 1962, 'must have the direct confidence of the nation. Instead of having that confidence – as was the case with me in 1958 for a historic and exceptional reason – it is necessary that henceforth the

President must be elected by universal suffrage.' The people were asked in a referendum on 28 October 1962 if they favoured direct election of the President. The reply, by 62 to 38 per cent, was yes. This reform of the 1958 Constitution (which had provided for the President to be elected by a 'college of notables' like local councillors and members of Parliament) had far-reaching effects. First, it gave, as de Gaulle said, successor Presidents a source of legitimacy from which to continue the exercise of executive leadership. Secondly it made presidential elections the focus of political life. The public takes more interest in presidential elections than any others, as the attendance at meetings and the voting figures demonstrate. The chief preoccupation of political parties is the launching of a credible presidential candidate. There is, in a phrase, a national consensus that political leadership should be exercised by the directly elected President of the Republic.

This consensus, however, could be blurred if ever, as might well have happened in 1978, a newly elected parliamentary majority challenged the leadership of a President whose mandate was several years old. It is in such a situation that the constitutional requirement for co-operation between President and Prime Minister would be particularly significant. However – and this is the third 'extra-constitutional' source of presidential supremacy – there has been at every national election in the Fifth Republic since 1958 a victory for those who supported the President and wished him to exercise leadership. In consequence every President has been able to appoint Prime Ministers who in no way challenged presidential supremacy and who indeed saw their role as faithful executants of presidential policies. Jacques Chaban-Delmas, who of all the Prime Ministers of the Fifth Republic did the most to develop his own policy intitiatives, has been the clearest in enunciating the doctrine of presidential supremacy. The Prime Minister was not on the same level as the President, he explained in an interview in *Le Monde* on 4 September 1970, because he was not chosen by the people but appointed by the President. His task was to direct the government 'along the lines traced by the President' (*dans le sens des orientations présidentielles*). 'The President is captain of the ship, the Prime Minister his first lieutenant.' In the National Assembly on 24 May 1972 he affirmed that 'a Prime Minister worthy of the name could not remain for a moment in office against the wishes [*sentiment*] of the President of the Republic . . . to contest this principle over any issue, however small, would be to fling down a direct challenge to the institutions of the Republic'. Chaban-Delmas was at the time seeking a vote of confidence from the Assembly which he obtained. To underline the doctrine of presidential supremacy, however, President Pompidou dismissed him from office a few weeks later! Another Prime Minister to have differences with his President was Jacques Chirac. He, however, has constantly affirmed his attachment to the Gaullist notion of presidential leadership and once, in a musical rather than a nautical metaphor this time, declared that the Prime Minister was the conductor of the orchestra but that the President composed the music. With Raymond Barre as Prime Minister, the Fifth Republic has probably found the best balance yet between the spheres of responsibility of President and Prime Minister. Barre remained the architect of the economic recovery programme which he was primarily appointed to introduce and implement. He exercises strong leadership over the other ministers in the government but he never threatens the authority of the President by appearing to have rival ambitions of his own.

From the beginning of the Fifth Republic it can be said that the possibility of a Prime Minister exercising his constitutional right to veto presidential decisions has been literally unthinkable. General de Gaulle, to quote that press conference speech yet again, went so far as to define the relationship between President and Prime Minister in these terms:

> While it must of course be clearly understood that the indivisible authority of the state is conferred in its entirety upon the President by the people who elected him, that no other authority exists, ministerial, civil, military judicial, which is not conferred by him, finally that it belongs to him alone to make changes in the area of supreme responsibility and those areas whose management he has delegated to others, it is nevertheless sensible to maintain, in normal times, the distinction between the functions and freedom of action of the head of state and those of the Prime Minister.

When looking at the Giscard presidency, therefore, it must be remembered that he was elected in 1974 to an office which had clearly established itself as the leading branch of the executive, that the people who elected him expected him to exercise leadership and that the parliamentary majority wished him to do so.

The Giscard presidency

One of the extraordinary characteristics of General de Gaulle's presidency is the way it continues to serve as a model for his successors. This is true of the practice of presidential leadership. It is true of the content of policies. As we shall see in the middle chapters of this book, especially the chapters on foreign and defence policy, that continuity of Gaullism – whether in the affirmation of France in a *mondialiste* or world-presence role especially in Africa and the Third World, in declarations of independence from the United States, or in the continuous invocation of France's strategic nuclear force – has been the predominant note of the Giscard presidency. It is true of the somewhat regal style that has become the hallmark of presidential language and behaviour. Indeed, it is as if the consensus about political institutions in France today, which was de Gaulle's legacy to his country, is based on a presidency which conforms to the Gaullist model. The presidency is expected to exercise leadership. In policy terms, especially in foreign affairs or defence, the French President is remarkably free from constraints on his actions. He can do more or less what he likes, intervene militarily in Africa, support the Palestine Liberation Organisation, or continue détente with the Soviet Union after the invasion of Afghanistan, provided he respects the Gaullist consensus on foreign and defence policy: France as a world-ranking nuclear power with a rather nationalistic stance, independent of America. In style, the relaxed informal image that Giscard d'Estaing tried to impart to the presidency in his early days gave way before long to the Olympian sentiments and lofty prose that everyone seems to expect. Giscard d'Estaing would have liked perhaps to be a second Kennedy but has been obliged to be a second de Gaulle.

Leadership style

As far as presidential supremacy is concerned, Giscard d'Estaing declared during his 1974 election campaign his preference for a regime that was 'more clearly presidential'. As a hint of the constitutional changes to come this preference has produced nothing so far, but as an indication of what kind of President he intended to be, it has been amply fulfilled.

In every sphere of public life presidential leadership has been emphasised. Giscard d'Estaing has carried on the Gaullian tradition of the personal conduct of foreign affairs. It is he who defines policies, attends the summits, makes the important declarations 'in the name of France', visits world leaders. His foreign ministers have been career civil servants – indeed, two of the three have been from his own staff, Jean Sauvagnargues from Giscard's *cabinet* at the Ministry of Finance and Jean François-Poncet from the presidential *cabinet* at the Elysée. All major policy initiatives, however, come from the Elysée, not only in foreign policy matters, like sending troops into Zaïre in 1978, but in domestic matters too like the protection of the environment, or the development of nuclear energy, and social reforms like abortion or taxes on property deals or the reduction of the voting age. Although the Constitution (Article 8) says that government ministers are appointed or dismissed 'on the proposition of the Prime Minister', government reshuffles have always been announced by the President in language that made it clear the initiative was his: 'it seemed to me the time had come to ...' or 'I decided to appoint X because ...'. The Prime Minister periodically receives a publicly announced letter giving him his 'mission' for the next six months. Raymond Barre in 1979, for example, received a letter on 21 November reminding him that by the letter of 25 April 'I had assigned four objectives', congratulating him on progress made, and setting out general government priorities for the ensuing months. Giscard has used his constitutional powers under Article 13 to make and veto appointments to a wide range of top public and administrative offices. In order that he may fulfil his constitutional role as head of the armed forces (Article 15), the cellars of the Elysée have been even more impressively set up as a 'war-room' and nuclear command post than before. In electoral matters and relations with the parties of the *majorité*, the Elysée has been extremely interventionist. The President himself once went so far as to appoint the Prime Minister Jacques Chirac as 'co-ordinator' of the *majorité*, but he has striven to preserve the image of the presidency as being 'above party'.

It has so far proved impossible in the Fifth Republic, thanks doubtless to the indelible mark of General de Gaulle, to exercise this vast sphere of presidential leadership in other than a rather majestic style. President Giscard d'Estaing started off as if he intended to impose a radically changed style. He walked up the Champs-Elysées in an ordinary suit on the day of his inauguration. There was a party of schoolchildren present at the ceremony. The official presidential portrait distributed to every town hall and official building in France shows a smiling figure in a lounge suit, slightly off-centre, against the background of a huge and flapping tricolore flag. In contrast to the portraits of his predecessors, there is no official uniform and sash and no presidential desk burdened with the cares of state. The new President strolled down the Faubourg St Honoré with Chancellor Schmidt, was seen driving his car in the small hours (indeed was alleged to have had a collision with a milk van), invited some astonished dustmen in to breakfast, and gave much more informal press conferences and television broadcasts. Then there were the celebrated occasions, on which the President and Mme Giscard d'Estaing accepted invitations to dinner at the homes of 'ordinary' families. These gave rise to great hilarity, cabaret sketches, families being informed by practical jokers that they had been designated as hosts, and even a satirical novel *Diner avec Giscard* by Yvon Audouard (1976).

As Finance Minister, Giscard d'Estaing had been quite successful with this emphasis on informality. His TV appearances wearing a pullover or holding a one-franc coin to explain economic policy or the press photographs showing him travelling on the métro or playing the accordion had helped to make him a popular political leader. Somehow as President it did not work. Before long the lofty pronouncements about 'la France' and the future of the world were being made in the Gaullian style that seems the *sine qua non* of the French presidency.

Nothing reveals the character of French democracy more clearly than the difference between the populist style and tradition of the American presidency and the public expectation in France of regal presidential style. In America the myth survives of the President as an ordinary citizen who has successfully campaigned for the votes of his fellow citizens. In language, in campaigning, in contacts with the public, in policy, he requires the common touch, though he must transcend it too. American democracy has glaring weaknesses – in particular the way that second-rate men are so often the most successful at the political opportunism that wins elections – but they are the weaknesses of democracy itself. Democracy is not a system for ensuring that the wisest man shall rule but a system which enables the people to choose who rules and to be able to get rid of them peacefully by constitutional means. By the same token any state which can claim to be ruled by the wisest cannot be democratic because what is wise and who is wisest would need to be arbitrarily determined and before very long the cry 'the leader is always right' is heard in the land.

The paradox of the Fifth Republic is this: the normal democratic freedoms apply as far as the right of citizens to choose their rulers is concerned, and yet they keep choosing exceptional men to be President. Indeed, two of the three they have chosen, de Gaulle and Giscard d'Estaing, are by their historic stature or their intellect quite noticeably set apart from other men, and all have been expected to behave in a regally 'presidential' manner.

The affair of the 'Bokassa diamonds' illustrates these expectations of the presidency quite well. Why did the allegation, in October 1979, by *Le Canard enchaîné* that Valéry Giscard d'Estaing had accepted costly gifts of diamonds from the particularly odious dictator of the Central African Republic (for a time Empire), a former French colony heavily dependent on France, not create a greater storm? On the day the story appeared the foreign press and Paris political and administrative circles were jittery with fears of a cataclysmic scandal, but the scandal never developed. There are in my view three reasons for this. The first is that Giscard d'Estaing is quite clearly not a dishonest or corrupt man. The second is that radio and television simply do not put on extensive investigative programmes on current affairs and there is, in addition, a kind of political self-censorship which prompts leading broadcasters to steer clear of topics that might be embarrassing in ruling circles. We shall return to that point in Chapter 11. The third reason, not unconnected with the last, is the general uncertainty about how the President should be treated. Is he, as head of state, to be placed upon a pedestal and held like the British monarch to embody national unity and the dignity and prestige of the country? Or is he a political leader in a democracy who, because he exercises power, must expect to be subject to scrutiny and criticism? The French presidency has so far in the Fifth Republic enjoyed the best of both worlds. It has exercised power, it has enjoyed the dignity and prestige of the headship of state and, because of the prestige of the office, criticism of

Presidents has been remarkably restrained. The idea of an investigative television programme into presidential policy initiatives, presidential patronage, or, especially, presidential finances is somehow as unthinkable as a programme investigating royal affairs would be in Great Britain. Over the diamonds, therefore, the presidency reacted with frosty dignity: 'In reply to a question concerning the practice of diplomatic gifts, the Elysée indicates that exchanges of gifts of a traditional character ... have in no instance been of the character or value mentioned by certain organs of the press ...' (Agence France Presse, 10 October 1979); and the matter was more or less allowed to rest there. In a television interview six weeks later the President explained somewhat testily that he had kept his word in never prosecuting any newspaper, as he has the legal right to do, for an attack on the dignity or honour of the presidency, that all diplomatic gifts go eventually to charity or to museums, and that on the value of the reported gifts 'I reply with a denial that is categorical and, I may add, contemptuous'. It is wholly reasonable for any political leader to reject in these terms an untrue allegation, but to wait six weeks is to imply that the President of the Republic should not have to lower himself even to make a reply to such a charge.

The same Gaullian note of lofty disdain has become a characteristic of the President's references to political parties and elections. Hardly a presidential interview passes without some such phrase as 'it is not in the President's role to have dealings with political parties' or 'it is not the President's job to recommend such or such a list in the European election . . . His role is to remind people what, in these circumstances, is the position of France ... to situate these elections in relation to the presence and the role of France but not to indicate a choice or a preference between lists of candidates' (*Le Monde*, 15 May 1979). Questioned on the divisions within 'his' *majorité* he replied (7 March 1979): 'It is not I who have a *majorité*, it is France. I do not seek a personal *majorité*; it is neither my function nor the interpretation of my function.' In another television interview on 18 April 1979 he refused in a very presidential way to answer questions on his own candidature for re-election:

There is no question of my replying to a question of that nature. I am not someone who is a candidate for the presidency of the Republic, I am someone who exercises the functions of

President of the Republic, and my problem is to act in such a way as to exercise these functions for the good of France and the good of the French ... I want the French people to use their own conscience and judgement, for it is a popular election not a party election. The 1962 reform had as its object the extraction of the election of President from party politics ... I do not wish to enter all this political discussion. The President of the Republic does not involve himself in the hurly-burly [*ne se mêle pas au tohu-bohu*].

He made the same point on television on 19 July 1979: 'the day the President announces his candidature he ceases to be President. He becomes a candidate.'

Another characteristic of the Giscard presidency's style that links it to the de Gaulle tradition is the President's emphasis on his role as oracle or prophet. I am not seeking to imply that Giscard d'Estaing was imitating, consciously or unconsciously, the presidential style of General de Gaulle. It is just that visionary pronouncements made by a *roi-mage* who is far enough above day-to-day preoccupations to see farther into history seems to have become a natural expression of the presidency. Georges Pompidou was less given to this style than his illustrious predecessor, but Giscard d'Estaing has taken it up with enthusiasm and with his training and reputation as a super-technocrat. 'Amazing fellow, this Giscard', remarked *Le Canard enchaîné* in the early days of the presidency, after a television interview in which the President had spoken of the future of the world and its huge problems, 'he even knows how to administer the unforeseeable!' It is of course an excellent thing for a country to have a leader who regards long-term consideration of the future and the preparation of the public for its problems as an essential part of his role. It is also very unusual – especially for leaders who exercise so much day-to-day executive power.

Hardly a Council of Ministers goes by without the President expressing his concern that France should adapt to a changing world, but the most celebrated instance of the President in his visionary role was his long interview in *Paris-Match* in September 1979 'on the future of France in the new state of the world'. The great peril stems from 'fantastic growth of the population of the globe', and the world will be one which cannot, unlike in the past, be 'mastered . . . by political and economic organisation and by its civilisation'. 'France must seek the means to adapt to a new state of the world. This idea may seem surprising in our political thinking, which is always short-term.' Question: 'But you, Mr President, have the good fortune to have at least two years before you, perhaps nine. It is a rhythm which can permit you to face this peril.' Answer: 'My role is indeed to see it, to describe it in concrete terms, and, at the same time, to assure myself that government action goes in this direction.' He went on to range over changing beliefs and religious beliefs in particular, the problem of nuclear war, the end of the perpetual prosperity of the consumer society, the need for France in the future to specialise its economy into sectors of 'very high technology'. In short, to present himself, as the title of an article in *The Times* had it (16 October 1978), 'a leader looking to the third millennium'.

President Giscard d'Estaing sees it none the less as an important part of his role to communicate the big policy choices to the people: 'In his function of President of the Republic, the President naturally takes account of public opinion. I take account of it every day . . . but not in electoral terms . . . I ask myself whether such and such a decision meets the interests of France. At the same time it has to be explained to public opinion' (*Le Monde*, 21 June 1979). One such decision, which we shall examine in Chapter 8, concerns the choice of a vast programme for developing electricity generation by nuclear power. The President has made it his own and explains it to the public in person: what sketchy knowledge I myself possess on how electricity is produced in a nuclear power plant comes from a brief but lucid explanation on radio by President Giscard d'Estaing in January 1980.

Government

A full exposition of the way the presidency works, and in particular of the division of labour between the presidency and the government, would require a research project of its own. The Fifth Republic has not produced any presidential or prime-ministerial memoirs as yet to throw any real light on the decision-making machinery at the top. The institutional starting point of presidential leadership in the functioning of the executive lies in Articles 9 and 15 of the Constitution. By virtue of these the President presides over the Council of Ministers which is the highest formal decision-making organ, and, as 'chief of the armed forces', over the 'higher councils and committees of national defence'. Extending this formal framework, the practice has grown up, and developed under the Giscard presidency, of *conseils restreints* – councils of ministers at which only a few ministers and senior advisers are present. These *conseils restreints* have been considered since long before Giscard's time (see, for instance, Avril, 1967, p. 396) as the place where the 'real decisions' are taken. Françoise Giroud (1977) relates from her ministerial experience that 'the Council of Ministers meetings merely ratified and formalised measures already agreed by President and Prime Minister' (1977, pp. 28–30) in a *conseil restreint*.

Some *conseils restreints* are institutions in their own right. The Conseil de Défense is composed of the President and Prime Minister, a small inner circle of important ministers and the chiefs of staff from the armed forces. It is this body and not the one designated by the constitution – the Higher Council for National Defence, too large to be other than consultative – that directs defence organisation and policy. It has no agenda and rarely publishes a communiqué. The Conseil Central de Planification is another such institution, created by Giscard d'Estaing, which meets every month to consider some aspect of economic planning. In the spring of 1980, for instance, meetings considered the development of the food industry, energy policy, the reduction of social inequalities and the preparation of the 8th Plan. Another institutionalised *conseil restreint* is the Conseil de Politique Nucléaire Extérieure. This was established in 1976, after the departure of Chirac from the government, in an attempt to consider more carefully and to regulate the policy of exporting nuclear technology. The overenthusiastic sales efforts of the CEA (Commissariat à l'Energie Atomique) had got France involved in an embarrassing deal with Pakistan redolent with dangers of military nuclear proliferation.

Other *conseils restreints* meet *ad hoc* either to prepare important decisions coming before the Council of Ministers or to deal with major issues that arise. For instance there were two *conseil restreint* meetings in March 1980 to fix the French position for the summit meeting of the European Council at which the related questions of agricultural prices and the British budgetary contribution were to be discussed. Present at these meetings were a judicious mixture of political leaders and civil servants: the President, the Prime Minister, the Minister of Foreign Affairs, the Minister of Agriculture, the French Ambassador to the EEC, the secretary general of the SGCI (the secretariat of the interministerial committee attached to the Prime Minister's office which co-ordinates all aspects of French EEC policy), the director of the economic section of the Foreign Ministry, two advisers from the President's *cabinet* at the Elysée, and the Elysée spokesman whose role is to brief news media and to advise the President on the public and press reactions he can expect.

Attempts to identify a precise division of labour between presidency and government are, as this brief account of *conseils restreints* and their composition has shown, misleading. It is more helpful to regard the members of the presidential *cabinet* as extensions of the government ministries in the common process of advising the President. For instance, the diplomatic telegrams go to the Secretary General of the Elysée and other foreign affairs advisers on the President's staff as well as to the Minister of Foreign Affairs at the Quai d'Orsay. When any foreign affairs event, such as a visit from a head of state or an international summit takes place, the foreign affairs advisers in the President's *cabinet* who prepare the visit or the summit can call directly on the services of the relevant desks at the Quai d'Orsay for notes and advice. Equally the Elysée adviser who deals with Francophone Africa, traditionally a presidential domain, draws directly on the staff of the Ministry of Co-operation. If it ever arises that the presidency and the government, perhaps as a result of an opposition victory in a parliamentary election, cease to be of the same political colour, the change in the system of government will be felt in the change of these close direct links between the presidential *cabinet* and the ministries.

The President's staff is small. His *cabinet* contains thirty-two people, almost all from ENA or Polytechnique: in 1975 (Suleiman, 1978, p. 108) a third of the *cabinet* were *grands corps* members, with all the prestigious corps represented – Inspectorate of Finance, Conseil d'Etat, Cour des Comptes, the Prefectoral Corps and the technical corps, Mines and Ponts et Chaussées, as well. The single most important adviser to the President – an undesirable innovation since the days of General de Gaulle according to that keeper of the Gaullist conscience Michel Debré

– has come to be the secretary general of the *cabinet*. Jean François-Poncet occupied that role until he was appointed Foreign Minister in November 1978. There are two political advisers concerned primarily with electoral and party support for the President. In 1980 they were Jean Serisé and Jean Riolacci. There is a small team of eight military advisers and a more numerous body of thirteen *conseillers techniques* and five *chargés de mission*. Each major area of policy – the environment, energy, industry, Africa, and so on – has one of these advisers assigned to it. He is in permanent contact with his opposite number in the Prime Minister's *cabinet* and with *cabinet* members and their officials in the ministries and prefectures involved in his sector of policy. He keeps the President informed over any matter that merits personal presidential attention. For instance, when the Brittany coast was threatened in 1978 by oil slicks from the shipwrecked tanker *Amoco Cadiz* the officials in the President's and Prime Minister's *cabinets* concerned with environmental questions prepared and co-ordinated the necessary measures so that the President could make visits, statements and the final decision on the military bombardment of the stricken vessel.

The role of the Prime Minister's office in interministerial co-ordination is of capital importance. There is an elaborate hierarchy of committees and councils through which this is accomplished and in which the Prime Minister's *cabinet* plays the leading part. Under the Prime Minister comes the Secretariat of the Government, which presides at all interdepartmental committees held at civil servant level, and the staffs of all the institutionalised *comités interministériels*. Some of these *comités*, whose meetings are chaired by the Prime Minister with a member of the President's *cabinet* in attendance, are extremely important. It is the *comité interministériel* for European Community affairs and its secretariat-general (SGCI) which directs and co-ordinates the activities of all French officials from ministries engaged in any dealings or negotiations within the EEC. Other important *comités* include CIASI (industrial reorganisation), CIAT (regional action and the *aménagement du territoire*), CIANE (nature and the environment) or the committee which deals with the exports of armaments, and all are under the chairmanship of the Prime Minister. Not all *comités interministériels* are institutions with staffs; they are, like *conseil restreints*, held when there is no consensus at civil service level or when a matter is particularly important. If a *comité interministériel* cannot resolve a matter or if it is even more particularly important it goes to a presidential *conseil restreint* or *conseil interministériel*.

In uncontested authority at the apex of this machine for the preparation and execution of decisions is the President himself. President Giscard d'Estaing, who, it will be recalled, has been trained as an administrator and who has been almost continuously in the corridors of power either as a *cabinet* member, or as a senior government minister, or as President, for a quarter of a century, has a 'serene and methodical' way of working. He consults a lot of people, he has frequent personal conversations by telephone with foreign heads of government, he makes decisions on the basis of a 'convergence of options' rather than the presentation by his advisers of a single recommended course of action, and he leaves himself plenty of time for thought. This enables him to fulfil the role described earlier of 'President for the third millennium'. There are certain fixed points in the week's routine: two private meetings with the Prime Minister, one with the Minister for Foreign Affairs, one with the Minister of the Interior, one with his *cabinet* team, a visit every evening from the Secretary General of the *cabinet* who brings the day's diplomatic telegrams and any notes that the President needs, and the Council of Ministers' meeting every Wednesday.

The President's budget is not particularly large and most of his expenses are not met from it. There are 548 staff in total at the Elysée – the vast majority of them police, secretaries, chauffeurs, or *huissiers* – mostly on the payroll of other ministries. The budget is also spared most of the cost of the President's rather opulent official visits abroad. On these occasions there is a large entourage from government ministers to chefs and even, according to the admiring account of Pierre Pellissier (1978), the mushrooms for the *bœuf aux girolles* to be served (in breach of us import laws) at a Washington banquet. The President's budget of 7 million francs in 1978 included personal and household expenses of 2·2 million francs (including a 288,000 franc salary), 2·5 million for *cabinet* and secretariat expenses, 1·5 million for travel and representation, and 0·7 million replacement costs for the presidential fleet of thirty-five cars and eight motorcycles. The President has a number of official residences available to him – the Château de Bregançon on the Mediterranean coast, Rambouillet for rather grand conferences or meetings, Marly near

Paris which the President sometimes uses for private parties, and occasionally the historic palaces of Versailles, Trianon and Chambord (where political supporters are invited for shooting). On normal working days, the President and his family usually do not sleep at the Elysée but at their own Paris apartment in the rue de Benouville, spending weekends sometimes in their private *château* at Authon.

The prestige of presidential receptions by one who combines the roles of political leader and head of state is an important weapon in the French political armoury. An extraordinary number of foreign heads of state and political leaders are received at the Elysée and the President travels a great deal too. The receptions and travels reflect the particular preoccupations of French diplomacy which we shall examine in a later chapter: the *mondialiste* or world-presence approach to foreign policy, the preoccupation with stability in areas like the Middle East or Africa from which come vital supplies, Franco-German leadership of the European Community. Giscard d'Estaing has taken pains to build personal relationships in the central areas of his foreign policy: with Chancellor Schmidt of West Germany, for example, or with the monarchs and emirs of the Arab world, and the presidents of French-speaking Africa. It appears (Jonas and Nourry, 1978, pp. 97–103) that the most assiduous visitor of all to the Elysée is President Omar Bongo of Gabon. Presidential receptions occupy an important place too in domestic politics. There are lunches and dinners for UDF and RPR parliamentarians. Large banquets are given for different groups. war veterans, teachers, small firms, or once, in Lyon, for 7,000 retired pensioners. These occasions illustrate once again the political advantage of being a President. A British Prime Minister would be severely criticised if she proposed to entertain 7,000 guests to dinner at public expense.

There are various communications systems at the disposal of the President. A direct line connects him at all times to the Elysée where a member of the *cabinet* is always on duty, at night, at weekends, or during holidays. There is the special *interministériel* telephone network, that coveted status symbol described by Françoise Giroud (1977, p. 79), with only 160 names in a directory issued only to those 160, REGIS, the *réseau électronique gouvernementale interadministratif spécial*, and of course the special defence communications systems including the 'hot-line' direct teleprinter connection to Moscow. The President of the Republic, chief of the armed forces, is the man who has to press the button if France's nuclear arsenal is to be used. The communications systems which make this possible are in a basement war-room at the Elysée, with duplicate command posts outside Paris if the Elysée has to be evacuated. The President is in direct communication with the Taverny strategic air force command located underground in an old gypsum quarry in the Paris suburbs. Taverny is linked to CODA (Centre Operationnel de Défense Aérienne), to the Mirage IV bases, to the nuclear forces at Plateau d'Albion and at sea in submarines. Frequent rehearsals take place. The real problem with the French nuclear deterrent, however, is not the effectiveness of the communications system but of the strategic theory on which it is based. That will be examined in Chapter 5.

In the Fifth Republic France has acquired the practice of presidential leadership of the executive, the habit of electing exceptional men to fill that office, and a certain reluctance to submit presidential actions to much scrutiny or criticism. In consequence the French presidency has become a marvellous instrument for political action. It has the legitimacy of direct election and it is expected by the nation to exercise leadership. Spectacular presidential initiatives on the world stage, as we shall see in the chapters on foreign affairs, have become part of the national consensus about Fifth Republic institutions, can be afforded by the national economy without too much strain, and are subject to remarkably few constraints from parties or public opinion. The President's almost unlimited powers to make appointments to all important posts in the public service, to direct every aspect of public policy, to make all important declarations, are contested neither by the Prime Minister nor by Parliament. In any case he is not responsible to Parliament which cannot in any real sense control the actions, the policies, or even the expenditure of the presidency, diffused as it is among so many ministries. Interest groups have not, generally speaking, the power of veto over public policy they have acquired in the more pluralist Anglo-Saxon democracies. The opportunity therefore for coherent personal direction of affairs by one outstanding individual is unparalleled. The questions with which the rest of this book is concerned discusses whether, even with this unfettered authority, the president-king has really been able to impose his own ideas and his own direction on events, and whether a system of government which gives such unrestricted powers to one person can really be characterised as democratic.

CHAPTER 4

The Continuous Election Campaign of the Giscard Presidency

Although a French President is elected for seven years at a time it does not mean he can govern with Olympian disregard for the electoral skirmishes going on below. He does not have the fearful burden of an American President who has to start campaigning for his own re-adoption as party candidate more than a year before his four-year term is up, and then battle it out in primaries and caucuses instead of governing the world's most powerful country. Nevertheless, he does have electoral preoccupations. First, there is the problem of parliamentary elections, which are important because if a majority opposed to the President were elected to the National Assembly he would find it difficult to have the government and legislation he wanted. Furthermore, it is he, the President, who has to decide when parliamentary elections are to be held. The constitutional term is five years but the President, under Article 12, may dissolve the National Assembly and call for earlier elections. He has to employ this weapon carefully because Article 12 excludes any further dissolution for at least twelve months. Secondly, there are local elections which give the opposition a chance to raise its morale and occupy some important and influential political roles of town halls and *conseils généraux*. Thirdly, there are the next presidential elections. One may not wish re-election for oneself, but one does not want to hand the country over to one's opponents – particularly if it means bringing the Communists or their allies into power. During the Giscard presidency the election campaign has been permanent. The campaign for the 1978 parliamentary election (of which the 1976 and 1977 local elections were a sort of 'first ballot') started immediately after the presidential election was out of the way in 1974. The 1981 presidential election filled the columns of political comment and preoccupied all political parties from mid-1978 on!

Political parties

The years of the Giscard presidency have seen, on the one hand, the completion of the Fifth Republic's trend to a bipolar government and opposition party system and, on the other, a growing tendency to rivalry and division in both government and opposition camps. The Giscard campaign in 1974 tidied up the system by drawing into the *majorité* the last remaining centrists who had been in opposition (but not allied with the left) under Pompidou: the Centre Démocrate of Lecanuet and the official Radical Party led by Jean-Jacques Servan-Schreiber. However the departure of Jacques Chirac from the government in 1976 and the formation of a new Gaullist party, the RPR (Rassemblement pour la République), in December the same year were the signals for the opening of hostilities within the *majorité* between Gaullists and *Giscardiens*. On the left the long attempt to build an alliance, a Union de la Gauche, between Socialists and Communists as the only possible response to the electoral dominance of the Gaullists from 1958 to 1973, an alliance which had brought the left to within an ace of winning the presidency with a record vote in 1974, broke down in 1977. The Communist Party (PCF) directed all its fury and all its organising skills in the vital period before the 1978 parliamentary elections not against the *majorité* but against its Socialist partners. Yet the government/opposition polarity is unchanged. The Gaullists huff and puff but they have not, as yet, blown the house down. In late 1979, for instance, they refused to support the government's budget and various other legislative proposals but they did not vote for the censure motions which followed when the government made these matters quesions of confidence under Article 49 of the Constitution. Similarly, despite the bitter antagonism between Communists and Socialists, the latter have given no sign whatever of quitting the opposition to enter into some arrangement with centrist elements in the *majorité*.

One final point in these differences within each camp: on the left they involve matters of real substance – wholly differing conceptions about society, about democracy, about freedom – but in the *majorité* they have much more the character of personal or territorial rivalry. *Giscardiens* and Gaullists resemble each other in innumerable ways. The social composition of their electorates, for instance, has become identical. The belief that Gaullism had a working-class electorate while the *Giscardiens* did not was disproved in 1978, when if anything slightly more workers voted UDF than RPR (Frears and Parodi, 1979, p. 76). In the elites of each top civil servants predominate and their leading figures have been in each other's governments or ministerial *cabinets*. Above all, their policies are very nearly identical. Gaullists are supposed to be more nationalistic in foreign affairs and in preoccupation with French prestige and influence. As the chapters on Foreign and Defence Policy will show, there is no practical difference at all to justify the Gaullist fulminations against President Giscard d'Estaing and his governments. There is perhaps slightly more substance in the argument that Giscard and Raymond Barre have been less interventionist or *dirigiste* than Gaullists of the true faith would have been in the matter of economic or social policy – but the difference is marginal. On questions such as civil liberties or freedom of information, the Gaullists adhere more strongly to the Jacobin conception of a strong centralised state while *Giscardiens* favour a more liberal approach. In practice, however, as we shall see, the Giscard presidency has produced very few liberal changes of real substance. The essence of the Giscard presidency has been *continuité* – carrying on where Pompidou left off. The difference between Gaullists and *Giscardiens* is essentially a difference of style and of personal animosities.

The Giscardiens

Any party identified with the President of the Republic seems, in the Fifth Republic, to possess an immense electoral advantage. When de Gaulle and Pompidou were Presidents, the Gaullist party was the dominant party in French politics. Even within the opposition the years of Mitterrand as a 'presidential' figure were the years of greatest success for the Socialist Party. The *Giscardiens*, however, though they have caught up with the Gaullists in popular votes and parliamentary seats and have passed them in some elections like those for the European Parliament in 1979, they have not emerged as a dominant presidential party. This is largely attributable to the fact that of the four main political 'families', the *Giscardiens* are the only one without a mass membership and mass party organisation. This deficiency, in its turn, is largely attributable to the 'non-party' origins and character of most of the groups that taken together compose the *Giscardiens*.

The UDF (Union pour la Démocratie Française), named after the book in which President Giscard d'Estaing set out his vision of a liberal consensus in French politics and society, groups together the different strands of the President's political support. It was formed a few weeks before the March 1978 parliamentary election to provide, in the best tradition of the Third or Fourth Republics, an election *étiquette* – a label under which non-Gaullist candidates of the *majorité* could be endorsed. Elaborate negotiations had been going on about *majorité* candidatures: in which constituencies there was to be just a single candidate of the *majorité* (for instance where prominent political leaders or ministers were standing), and in which could 'primaries' be permitted? Where a 'primary' was to be permitted, it was agreed that the whole *majorité* should rally in the second ballot behind whichever candidate had done best in the first. It became clear to the non-RPR elements of the *majorité* that if each little party – Republican Party (ex-RI), CDS (ex-Centre Democrats and others) or independents – presented candidates in a 'primary' against the RPR very few of them would succeed in becoming sole candidate of the *majorité* at the second ballot. It was therefore decided, in a series of meetings held in the Pavillon de Musique in the garden of the Prime Minister's residence, that the non-RPR groups would present a common front, a single set of candidates, against the RPR.

The UDF had quite a successful election in 1978. In terms of first-ballot votes (21·4 per cent) and parliamentary seats (137) it practically drew level with the RPR (22·5 per cent and 150), ending twenty years of Gaullist dominance. It remained in being with an organisation structure and staff. It presented a list of candidates (called UFE – Union for France in Europe) in the 1979 European Assembly elections which easily topped the poll (27·6 per cent). However, it still does not look like a dominant political party. Indeed, if there still exists anywhere a 'cadre party', which in Duverger's famous classification is a term for parties which have little in the way of numbers or rules or policies but which function as electoral committees for a few notables, the UDF is it. It made clear at its 1979 parliamentarians' congress that 'the UDF will not prepare a programme for 1981. It is not its role. The presidential election is the election of a man' (*Le Monde*, 26 September 1979). Many of the leading figures associated with it do not really belong to it – they are either 'above party' or 'non-party' or classify themselves simply as *majorité présidentielle*. Giscard d'Estaing himself, by virtue of the lofty traditions attaching to the presidency in the Fifth Republic, does not belong to it. Raymond Barre, the Prime Minister, and Simone Veil, a very popular Health Minister who headed the UFE list in the European elections, though they campaign for it, are not really part of it.

Its most important element, that is to say, the group with the largest number of parliamentary and other notables, is the Republican Party (PR). French political parties seem to remain as strongly drawn to perpetual changes of name as British parties to keeping them, though unsuitable, the same. The PR is simply the RI (Independent Republicans), with which the electorate was beginning to become familiar, after a change of name in 1977. The RI were the original *Giscardiens* – indeed it will be recalled that the label was one used by Giscard's grandfather, Jacques Bardoux.

The Independent Republicans were, as was recounted in the first chapter, a parliamentary group formed in 1962 by the few Independents that survived the Gaullist landslide at the November 1962 elections. They became a party in 1966 after the departure of Giscard d'Estaing from ministerial office. By dint of skilful negotiations with Gaullists over which constituencies they could contest, and benefiting no doubt from their image as a moderate group within the *majorité*, they improved their parliamentary position as the years went by. The ratio of RI *députés* to Gaullists was one to six in 1962, but one to three by 1973.

Associated with the party were the *Perspectives et Réalités* clubs. These clubs, for which a national membership of around 20,000 is claimed, recruit largely among top civil servants, intellectuals and professional and business men. 'Like a non-socialist Fabian society, the clubs see themselves as contributors of new progressive ideas to political debate' (Frears, 1978, p. 62), and as a nursery for political talent. The clubs played an important part in the 1974 presidential election when they formed the nuclei of the local and national committees that organised support for Giscard d'Estaing. After Giscard's victory, the party intensified its efforts to build a mass presidential party, with youth movements, rallies, renewed efforts to 'prospect' for and train suitable election candidates, and above all to organise a *comité national de soutien pour le Président de la République* (national committee to support the President). None of these efforts has been very successful. The important political figures associated with the party are those battle-scarred *Giscardiens* Michel Poniatowski (former Minister of the Interior), Michel d'Ornano (Minister of the Environment), or Roger Chinaud (Group Leader in the National Assembly) but the organisation and public relations are in the hands of bright young *fonctionnaires* many of them on secondment from ministerial *cabinets* or elected to Parliament in March 1978 – like Bertrand de Maigret or Gérard Longuet. At the time of writing the Secretary General is Jacques Blanc – a doctor specialising in the handicapped, a *député* at 34, and junior minister at 38.

Another important part of the UDF is the Centre des Démocrates Sociaux (CDS). The CDS, formed in 1976, represents a reunion of various groups of centrists that had gone different ways in previous years. In particular it includes those centrists who had joined the Pompidou *majorité* and those like Lecanuet who had remained in the opposition until the presidential campaign of Giscard d'Estaing. Most of the CDS stem originally from the Christian Democrat branch of French centrist politics which had its heyday in the Fourth Republic as the MRP (Mouvement Républicain Populaire) which was one of the main governing parties and once (June 1945) had 28 per cent of the popular vote. The leading political figures of the CDS are Lecanuet (former Minister of Justice) and Jacques Barrot (in 1980 Minister of Health and Social Security).

In two respects the CDS people are not ideal bedfellows for the PR. First, their political background is different. Many CDS activists – such as van Lehrenberghe, a leading party organiser, for instance – are Christian trade unionists who as members of the CFDT or the tiny CFTC (Confédération Française des Travailleurs Chrétiens) are used to battling for working-class support against both employers and the Communists in the CGT. They have little in common with the elegant ENA graduates and the fashionable Parisians who predominate in the PR.

Secondly, and related, their ideas are different. They are in a sense more *Giscardien* than the *Giscardiens*. That is to say that the ideas for social reform, with which President Giscard d'Estaing is identified, find much more of an echo in the CDS than in the PR, many of whose leading members are conservative to the point of being reactionary. On European Union, another Giscard theme – on the level of rhetoric at any rate – the CDS are the most enthusiastically integrationist of the *Giscardiens*. The word in the Giscard lexicon that most unites CDS and PR is probably 'liberal'. Both support the President's vision of a more humane and more tolerant society with emphasis on freedom and a less authoritarian style of government. Neither, from the evidence of Lecanuet as Minister of Justice or Michel Poniatowski as Minister of the Interior, or indeed of the President himself in such areas as judicial reform or freedom of information, has been in too much of a hurry to effect liberal reforms. However, both parties have largely backed the President and his government, the major successes of which, as we shall see in a later chapter, have been in the areas of social policy. The one big exception was over the reform of the law on abortion – and on this the majority of both PR and CDS *députés* voted against, and the proportions of each which did so were identical.

The 'delegate general' of the UDF or main organiser, Michel Pinton (one of the election specialists who played a leading part in the Giscard campaign of 1974), summed this up in his speech at the UDF parliamentarians' congress quoted above. He said that the tone of the group must be 'centre-left' because that was the critical position to occupy in the 1981 campaign, but he acknowledged that the UDF was made up of different strands of opinion not all equally reformist. The aim therefore was an 'atmosphere' not a programme. Thus the diversity of its components for whom it acts as an electoral committee and its conception of itself as being entirely at the service of President Giscard d'Estaing combine against the idea of giving the electors anything like a party manifesto.

In addition to the PR and the CDS there are other minor groups affiliated to, connected with, or at elections endorsed by, the UDF. There is the Radical Party, or at least what is left of the Radical Party, the oldest political party in France, after its left wing split away and sided with the Socialists in the Union de la Gauche. The Radical Party, whose leading figure is the wealthy former owner of the weekly magazine *L'Express*, Jean-Jacques Servan-Schreiber, is not actually part of the UDF any more but played a part in its formation. Its candidates received UDF endorsement in 1978 and its *députés* sit in the UDF group. It had however its own rival list (1·8 per cent of the vote!) in the European elections of June 1979. Other components include the old CNIP (National Centre of Independents and Peasants), the loose grouping of conservatives and independents which can claim to be the ancestor of the Republican Party, and two groups of dissident ex-Socialists – the MDSF (Democratic Socialist Movement of France) and the PSD (Democratic Socialist Party). The latter, organised by Eric Hintermann, who used to be secretary to the Socialist Group in the National Assembly, includes among its parliamentarians some well-established local figures like Alduy and Muller, mayors of Perpignan and Mulhouse respectively. Also connected to the UDF are a number of independent personalities, like the Prime Minister Raymond Barre, who identify themselves as *majorité présidentielle*. The president of this diverse but important organisation, the UDF, is Jean Lecanuet (CDS). It may not be an army with many armoured divisions, but it is a vital provider of political management and expertise for election campaigns like 1981.

The RPR

The other half of the *majorité*, both partner to and rival of the UDF, is the Gaullist movement Rassemblement pour la République led by Jacques Chirac. To find Jacques Chirac at the head of a Gaullist movement is at first sight somewhat surprising. He was a protégé of Georges Pompidou and really belonged to the group of ambitious technocrats sometimes called pragmatists who had little time for the true Gaullist elite, the 'barons' like Jacques Chaban-Delmas or Michel Debré who had been faithful apostles of General de Gaulle from the days of the French Resistance on. Indeed, Chirac's opposition to 'heroic' Gaullism was made clear at party congresses during the Pompidou presidency and, above all, during the 1974 election campaign when his 'Declaration of the 43' did more to defeat Chaban-Delmas and to help Giscard to victory than almost anything else. Chirac, however, appointed Prime Minister by Giscard d'Estaing, was able fairly quickly to gain control of a rather demoralised Gaullist movement and assure it that he was the man to lead it back to the heights.

There are different Gaullisms and different Gaullists. There are, as we have said, 'heroic' Gaullists and 'pragmatic' Gaullists.

There is Gaullism as an authoritarian mass movement and there is Gaullism as a moderate party of government. The latter has been the predominant mode in the Fifth Republic. The UNR (Union for the New Republic) was formed to back General de Gaulle and the governments he appointed. The UDR (Union of Democrats for the Republic), as it came to be called at the end of the 1960s, carried on the tradition under President Pompidou. France under Pompidou was even called the 'UDR state' because Gaullists dominated all areas of public life – ministerial office, Parliament, the administration and public corporations. When Chirac resigned as Prime Minister, after reports of growing dissension between himself and the President, the signal was given for the return to a more ancient and muscular form of Gaullism. The new RPR, formed at a huge rally in December 1976, was in name and character much more like the RPF, a vociferously nationalist and anti-communist mass movement with an unpleasantly hectoring and thuggish atmosphere, which gathered to support General de Gaulle when he was out of power in the late 1940s.

The big difference between the RPR and the UDR is in the position of its leader. The UDR never had one – it responded to the authority of the Prime Minister of the day or the President of the Republic. When, therefore, there was no Gaullist President and no Gaullist Prime Minister there was undoubtedly a vacuum. There was also a mood of doubt and frustration natural in a party used to being dominant in the state. Chirac, with his energy and his rather arrogantly messianic claim to be the man who would rally the French people and free France from the threat of communism or be a *recours* – a saviour to whom France would turn if things went wrong – filled the need. The December 1976 rally, which was attended by 50,000 hero-worshipping militants wearing 'I believe in Chirac' badges, got the RPR off to a resounding start and vested absolute powers to appoint to leading executive and advisory positions in its leader.

The first few years of the RPR were of rather mixed success. Chirac succeeded in a boldly opportunistic bid to become mayor of Paris in the 1977 municipal elections, which provided both a boost to morale and access to a strategic and well-endowed base for future operations. In 1978 Chirac succeeded in fulfilling the promise he made to the demoralised Gaullists in 1975 that he would lead them back to Parliament after the elections as the largest group. However, the 1978 election is also the moment when Gaullists ceased to be the dominant part of the *majorité* – the UDF now has 137 parliamentary seats. In the period preceding the European elections in 1974 Chirac redoubled the nationalist fervour of his appeals to the voters. The culminating point was a slashing attack in February 1979 on the President of the Republic and his supporters – *le parti de l'étranger* – for selling out French national interests. This stirring call to the French people was given the idiotic title of the *appel de Cochin* because it was delivered from Chirac's bed at the Cochin hospital in Paris where he was recovering from a motor accident! The *appel* went unheeded and the Chirac–Debré list only managed to gain 16 per cent of the votes in June.

There followed a period of unusual silence broken in the late summer and autumn by the sound of heads beginning to roll. Of particular significance was the departure of Pierre Juillet and Marie-France Garaud. These former close advisers of President Pompidou were reported to be the *éminences grises* behind Chirac. Indeed, Jacques Chaban-Delmas, who bitterly claimed (1976) that these two had persuaded Pompidou to dismiss him as Prime Minister because he was too radical a reformer, had persuaded Chirac to campaign against him in 1974, and had programmed every move by Chirac ever since. There was a feeling, expressed by Gaullist ministers in the government like Peyrefitte and even by party apparatchiks like Yves Guéna, that the RPR was becoming too much of a secret society round Chirac and organisers like Charles Pasqua. An analysis of opinion polls by Jean-Luc Parodi (*Pouvoirs*, no. 11, 1980) illustrated the steady and dramatic decline of Chirac in public estimation since his departure from the premiership in 1976. In September 1979 the Central Committee listened to a Chirac *autocritique* which called for all true Gaullists, including Chaban-Delmas, to return to the fold and announced a 'change of course', a 'new departure', a 'new way'. Chirac, it was explained, was no longer a *recours*, just a 'bringer of hope'.

The 'new way' consisted of making fewer speeches but making life more difficult for the government. The RPR refused to vote for various laws including, in November 1979, the 1980 budget. Whenever this happened the Prime Minister rather contemptuously employed the constitutional artillery of Article 49, subsection 3. The passage of a Bill can be declared a matter of confidence and is automatically adopted unless a censure motion is carried. So the Gaullists continually find themselves condemning government policy but abstaining from bringing down the government: in the stinging phrase of the poet Alexander Pope, 'willing to wound and yet afraid to strike'.

So great has the importance of the directly elected presidency become in the Fifth Republic, so indispensable for the success of any party is the possession of a credible presidential candidate, that the key to all the actions of the RPR is the attempt to create an electoral space for a Chirac presidential campaign. The RPR must be part of and yet distinct from the *majorité presidentielle*. The attempt failed in June 1979 and there was no reason to suppose that it would succeed in 1981. The RPR has some strengths, however. In particular it has a large and active membership – though not the half or three-quarters of a million claimed. It is still the largest parliamentary group. It has the apparatus of Paris City Council. It has a news sheet, *Lettre de la nation*, which, though it has virtually no circulation of its own, has its bitter anti-government comments relayed by all the mass media. Finally, the whole world of Paris journalism and the political elite waits with bated breath for every pronouncement of the RPR's leader – just as they used to do with Valéry Giscard d'Estaing in the period of 'oui … mais'.

The Left

There is not much about the left in this book, not because it is unimportant but because the focus is on the government of France during the Giscard presidency. In any case there are far more books and articles on the parties of the left than on the *majorité*. The left in France has received the fascinated attention of the whole world because France, like Italy, is one of the rare Western democracies, and a large and important one at that, where the only possible alternative majority government includes a large Communist Party.

The most important figure on the left in the Fifth Republic so far has been without doubt François Mitterrand. The Mitterrand strategy for the left, pursued with single-minded vigour since before his first presidential campaign in 1965, has been based on three propositions. First, the only way for Gaullism and its satellites to be defeated was by an alliance of the non-Communist left and the Communist Party. An alliance with the Communists, however, can be electorally a poisoned chalice because of the fears of Communist domination it arouses. The second proposition therefore was that the non-Communist left could be built into a political force large enough, cohesive enough and electorally attractive enough to be the senior partner in the alliance. Thirdly, the Communist Party could, by the offer of full partnership, be persuaded to change.

The Mitterrand strategy of Union de la Gauche was nearly an immense success. As far as the first proposition was concerned, events in the 1960s proved Mitterrand right. Various people – Gaston Defferre the Socialist leader in 1964–5, Alain Poher the centrist candidate against Pompidou in 1969 – tried to put together a 'third force', an alliance of the centre which grouped together all but Gaullists on one extreme and Communists on the other. They failed because Gaullism was not an extreme at all and it had already absorbed much of the centre itself. Mitterrand had the support of all the left, Socialists, Radicals, Communists and miscellaneous, for his presidential candidature in 1965. His second ballot score (10·5 million votes, 45·5 per cent), though it was perhaps more of a vote against de Gaulle than a vote for the left, was at all events the first sign of recovery for the left in the Fifth Republic in which it had been a dwindling, ageing and progressively less inspiring force.

The subsequent electoral history of the Fifth Republic, confirming incidentally the lessons of the Popular Front victory in 1936 and the post-Liberation successes of the left in 1945–6, demonstrated that the left only performs well in an election when it is united. Gains were made in the parliamentary elections of 1967 and 1973 and, above all, Mitterrand's second presidential attempt in 1974, supported by a united left, brought the left to its highest vote since the war – almost 13 million votes – and 49·3 per cent in the second ballot.

The second aspect of the Mitterrand strategy has also had considerable success. The first attempt to build a large and cohesive non-Communist left followed the 1965 presidential campaign. Socialists, Radicals and various left-wing political clubs were loosely amalgamated in the Federation of the Democratic and Socialist Left (FGDS) which presented election candidates in 1967 (with conviction and success) and in 1968 (with less conviction and less success). The FGDS did not survive the setbacks of 1968. The celebrated student revolt and general strike, followed in August by the Soviet invasion of

Czechoslovakia, brought out the defensive, isolationist reflexes in the PCF. This had its effect upon the FGDS because it revived the anxieties felt by its more moderate elements about a strategy based on alliance with the PCF. In 1971 the time was again ripe for a renewed attempt at Union de la Gauche. Some renewal of the Socialist Party had taken place in 1969 following the winding-up of the arthritic SFIO, which had served as France's Socialist Party since 1905 but, under the leadership of Guy Mollet, had become little more than an association for socialist municipal councillors and municipal employees. In 1971 a congress at Epinay brought together Socialists of different hues, including the left-wing clubs that had been in the FGDS, and fused them into a single party – the PS – with François Mitterrand as First Secretary. The strategy of Union de la Gauche was immediately relaunched. The Communists were in a receptive mood. The *programme commun* – a joint manifesto for a Socialist–Communist coalition – was signed in 1972 and included commitments to preserve democratic freedoms, such as the right of opposition parties to exist. The left wing of the Radical Party – that is to say, those that rejected the alliance with centrists favoured by the leader of the Radical Party Jean-Jacques Servan-Schreiber – allied itself with the PS to present common candidates at the 1973 parliamentary election. A large part of the PSU (United Socialist Party – the initial 'U' in French politics often indicates a split), a fragment which had broken away from the SFIO in the 1950s and had become increasingly revolutionary after 1968, rejoined the PS in 1974 – in particular the PSU leader, Michel Rocard. The leaders of the rapidly growing non-Communist trade union CFDT also identified themselves with the new PS. By the mid-1970s opinion polls and local elections made the PS the leading party in France, and in 1978 it obtained more votes than the PCF for the first time since the Second World War.

It was Mitterrand's third proposition – that the Communist Party could be persuaded to change – that proved the most fallible. The PCF throughout its history has oscillated between hard-line and conciliatory phases. In the hard-line phases it has been intransigently pro-Soviet and violent in its denunciation of the non-Communist left. This was particularly true of its initial 'Bolshevisation' period (1920–34), the Cold War period of 1947–62, the period after the events of May 1968 and the Soviet invasion of Prague (1968–71). At other times world events, like the rise of fascism in the 1930s, the international posture of the Soviet Union (for instance, as an ally of the democracies, 1941–7), or its own perception of the French political context have authorised a more conciliatory approach. Communists were part of the victorious Popular Front in 1936, served in government after the Liberation under de Gaulle and others from 1944 to 1947 and supported electoral alliances with the Socialists from 1962 to 1968 and 1972 to 1977.

In the mid-1970s there were grounds for supposing that the Communists had engaged on a process of change which would be very difficult to reverse. If the PCF wanted to become a government party – an objective which is the defining characteristic of political parties – it could only do so in France through the ballot box. The year 1968 had proved, if proof were needed, that in a country where industrial workers have a high standard of living and there is no systematic oppression proletarian revolution is a fantasy. Electoral success in a democracy requires a comportment that attracts rather than repels voters. Deep changes seemed to be taking place. Criticism of persecution in the Soviet Union became more frequent. The Soviet regime was declared to be no longer a model of the kind of socialism the party wanted to see in France. The party strove to make itself less of a secret society. At the 22nd Congress in 1976 the commitment to a pluralist form of democracy – for France, not for the party – was underlined by the abandonment of the old Leninist doctrine of the dictatorship of the proletariat – the phase which was supposed to follow the revolutionary seizure of power. A conciliatory approach by the PCF is normally electorally profitable. In the periods of Union when the left makes gains, the PCF makes gains. In the 1977 municipal elections there were Union de la Gauche lists in all major cities and towns. As a result there were more Communist mayors than ever before, and Communist councillors in important roles in Socialist-dominated cities like Lille.

However, the growing popularity of the PS contained a double threat to the PCF. New votes attracted to the left went to the PS and, with the PCF less distinctive, the PS started to bite into the Communist electorate too so that gains made by the left were mainly Socialist gains. This is very important in a two-ballot electoral system. Socialist gains could be made not at government but at Communist expense. For instance, in the first ballot of a parliamentary election the Socialist candidate could actually run ahead of a Communist *député* seeking re-election, compelling the latter, under the terms of the Union de la Gauche alliance, to withdraw. Secondly, and in consequence, though the PCF might through a strategy of Union de la Gauche become a partner in a coalition government, it risked becoming the junior and dominated partner. 'Liberalisation' in mid-1977 was slammed into reverse gear. A series of meetings to update the *programme commun* was broken off and the PCF turned its guns on the Socialists. When the March 1978 elections came, the elections which the left a year earlier had seemed almost certain to win, the Union de la Gauche was no longer a credible or attractive alternative government.

Since the great hopes of 1978 were dashed, the left has continued in disarray. Indeed, matters have grown worse. At municipal level, where harmony had lasted a little longer, friction began to break out between Communist and Socialist councillors in more and more Union de la Gauche towns and cities. Hardly a day goes by without an account in *Le Monde* of Communist *adjoints* (committee chairmen) being dismissed by Socialist mayors because the Communist councillors have refused to vote for the budget, supported municipal employees on strike, or even, in the case of Nantes (*Le Monde*, 5 February 1979), objected to a move to suspend municipal aid to church schools! There was bitter and damaging hostility between the two parties in the preparation of separate candidatures for the 1981 presidential election.

Both parties continue to proclaim their attachment to Union de la Gauche. On the Socialist side this merely means that, despite what the PCF may say, they have no intention of seeking alliances on the centre or the right. The Communists are for Union too, but *union à la base*. That, in communist jargon, means trying to rally the working class around the workers' party, the PCF, and denouncing the Socialists as ready to join forces with the bourgeoisie. The 1972–7 period of *union au sommet* has left its imprint on the party, though not perhaps as indelibly or irreversibly as was supposed at the time. In the first place there has been a lot of dissent about the change of line. Well-known Communist intellectuals like Jean Elleinstein have kept up, and received some grass-roots support for, their criticisms – especially of the party's reluctance to break with the Soviet Union, and of its refusal to allow greater freedom of expression. This has been maintained even after a public reconciliation with the leadership. Yvonne Quilès, editor of the party weekly *France nouvelle*, left to join a new weekly, *Maintenant*, which offers a platform to party dissidents – though she remained a party member. In particular the powerful Paris federation, which had been the 'laboratory' of the liberalising movement, has become the principal forum for conflict. The Paris party secretary and Paris city council group leader, Henri Fiszbin, and eight senior Paris secretariat colleagues resigned in a battle that lasted over a year, went to Central Committee, and involved principally the right to more open information, and a general approach more appropriate to a Parisian population which was becoming less manual working class. It was clear from reports that they had a great deal of support from party activists in Paris. Curiously enough the 'purge' has not affected only relative liberals like Fiszbin. At the 23rd Congress in 1979, which was not nearly so far-reaching in ideological terms as the 22nd, certain leading hardliners like Roland Leroy, editor of *L'Humanité*, and Madeleine Vincent lost leading places in the PC hierarchy. The vast and effective organising power of the party was directed exclusively to the task of regaining control of its working-class electorate and its traditional bastions in industrial areas so that it could beat off the Socialist challenge in 1981. The PCF vote has remained constant – or stagnant – at about 20 per cent for a number of years. Recent heavy losses in its area of greatest strength – the Paris industrial suburbs – are deeply worrying to the party.

The severity of the Stalinist ice age to which the PCF has returned was dramatically emphasised by the visit of its secretary general, Georges Marchais, to Moscow in January 1980 and his successive appearances on Soviet and French TV. The attitude of the PCF to international events is very often the weathervane which indicates whether the Soviet Union is in a hard or conciliatory phase of foreign policy and whether the PCF itself is in an intransigent or co-operative phase of its relations with the non-Communist left in France. Indeed, the two go together – conciliatory 1936, 1945 and 1967, intransigent 1939, 1947 and at the time of the invasion of Czechoslovakia in 1968, for example. The year 1980 began with the Soviet occupation of Afghanistan with 80,000 troops, which was condemned by many Eurocommunist parties including those of Italy and Spain, and which caused a number of French intellectuals to leave the PCF. Georges Marchais, however, saw fit to underline the intransigent nature of the PCF's current phase by the most extravagant possible support for the Soviet action. External imperialist forces were undermining the 'new democratic regime' in Afghanistan. 'The Afghan people, its government, and its statesmen appealed for help to the Soviet Union.' Viewers of the Marchais interview in *Cartes sur tables* on 23 January were staggered to hear the most aggressively Stalinist utterances for thirty years: 'In 1939 the French Communist Party was right' (when it supported the Hitler–Soviet pact), or his brief reply 'of course' to the question 'for you, peaceful coexistence just means the right of capitalist regimes to be overthrown?'. In addition there was a long vilification of the Socialist Party and of François Mitterrand, during which he altered in a strongly pro-Soviet direction a polite diplomatic statement Mitterrand had made in Moscow in 1975 and read it out as authentic! (For a comparison of the two texts see *Le Monde*, 26 January 1980.) A few days after this episode news came from Moscow that the dissident Sakharov had been arrested and expelled from Moscow. The PCF, somewhat respectfully, regretted this development and the resort to what its spokesmen repeatedly referred to as 'administrative measures', but fell far short of the condemnation such an action would have incurred in 1976.

The effect of all this on the electorate is hard to judge. *Le Matin* published an opinion poll on 24 January 1980 showing that only 9 per cent of people considered that the PCF had changed greatly since Stalin's time (20 per cent in 1977). However, the same poll showed that Communist voters were fairly steady behind the party, and there was evidence that party activists were 'rediscovering with satisfaction their traditional vision of a Manichean world in which, to escape from the threats of imperialism one can count only on the strength of the socialist camp' (Thierry Pfister, *Le Nouvel Observateur*, 28 January 1980). However local by-elections (for instance at the traditionally Communist Paris suburb of Issy in February 1980), which depended on second-ballot support from Socialist voters, began to be lost.

The increasing emphasis on the word 'revolution' by Communist leaders when defining the party's aims suggested a strong attempt to win over for the 1981 election the relatively large number of voters – 3 per cent of the total electorate but 9 per cent of those aged between 18 and 24 – who voted for the extreme left fringe parties in 1978. The loss of the support of the revolutionary young is something that greatly worried the PCF during the years from 1968.

The Socialist Party has been by no means free from disputes and the principal question involved the candidature for 1981. Since the failure of Mitterrand's bid to lead the left to power at the head of an alliance with a changed and liberalised Communist Party, there was a steadily expressed preference in public opinion polls for Michel Rocard to be the Socialist candidate. Formerly leader (indeed in 1969 presidential candidate) of the PSU and exponent in the late 1960s of profoundly revolutionary views, a top civil servant by occupation – inspector of finance, in fact, like President Giscard d'Estaing – *député* in the suburban *département* of Yvelines, Rocard today is associated with a more innovative and less dogmatic approach to economic and social issues than other leading Socialists. This reforming social-democratic image does not go down so well inside the PS (where he has been referred to as 'Rocard d'Estaing') as it does with public opinion generally, and he is of course heartily disliked by the PCF. Before the 1979 Socialist Party Congress at Metz Rocard was part of the 'majority' group round Mitterrand, and the party's left wing – the CERES group (Centre for Socialist Education and Research) led by Jean-Pierre Chévènement – was in the minority. At Metz this was reversed. To conserve the leadership Mitterrand built a new majority with CERES that excluded Rocard. Rocard enjoyed some ambiguous support from another would-be party leader Pierre Mauroy, mayor of Lille, and a growing number of party activists.

Since Metz the ideas of the PS, as enunciated in the 'New Socialist Project' of November 1979, have become less messianic and more 'realistic' than earlier programmes. There is no more talk of suppressing private education, private hospital treatment, or even the French strategic nuclear deterrent, and there is a more nationalist approach to 'national independence' and free trade. The PS wants to see France less dependent on international trade and more prepared to be protectionist. In short the PS, with a programme virtually identical to that of the *Giscardiens*, Gaullists and Communists, spent 1979 and 1980, like these rivals, busy getting ready for 1981.

Elections

The 1974 presidential election

The campaign that brought Giscard d'Estaing victorious to the Elysée has already been recounted in Chapter 1. The three most interesting aspects were his own emergence as the champion of the *majorité*, the singularly close result in the run-off with the single candidate of the left and the immense public interest in the campaign. The real loser in the election was Jacques Chaban-Delmas. The legend of heroic Gaullism was spent as an electoral force – especially so since so many leading figures in the Gaullist movement (like Jacques Chirac and 'the 43') had clearly thrown in their lot with Giscard d'Estaing. For convenience the results, together with the results of the Fifth Republic's other two presidential elections under universal suffrage, are shown in Table 4.1.

The most interesting electoral indicators for the future are to be found in the progress of the left in urban areas, and among working-class voters in those parts of the country, Brittany or Lorraine, for example, where traditionally the left has been very weak.

The 1978 parliamentary election

The election to the National Assembly was the most important political event of the 1974–81 presidency and the occasion on which the President best revealed his qualities as a national leader.

It was an important election because if the left had won it would have raised constitutional problems which would have tested the Republic's institutions, it would have meant Communist participation in government for the first time in any big Western democracy since 1947, and it would have shown whether the Fifth Republic had the legitimacy and democratic strength to survive its first change of government. In the event it only showed that the left can win any election in the Fifth Republic except those that give it political power. One pointer to this could be perceived in the gap between voting intentions, as revealed in opinion polls which gave the left a significant and practically uninterrupted lead from 1974 on, and answers to the question 'in your heart of hearts (*au fond de vous-même*) who do you hope will win?'. Replies to the latter question in the ten

Table 4.1   *Presidential Elections in the Fifth Republic*
(metropolitan France only)

| | December 1965 | | | | June 1969 | | | | May 1974 | | | |
| | 1st ballot | | 2nd ballot | | 1st ballot | | 2nd ballot | | 1st ballot | | 2nd ballot | |
	m. votes	%	m. votes	%	m. votes	%	m. votes	%	m. votes	%	m. votes	%
Abstentions (% of electorate)		15·0		15·5		21·8		30·9		15·1		12·1
Majorité	de Gaulle 10·4	43·7	12·6	54·5	Pompidou 9·8	44·0	10·7	57·6	Chaban-Delmas 3·6	14·6		
									Royer 0·8	3·2		
									Giscard d'Estaing 8·3	32·9	13·1	50·7
Opposition centre	Lecanuet 3·8	15·8			Poher 5·2	23·4	7·9	42·4				
Left	Mitterrand 7·7	32·2	10·6	45·5	Defferre (ps) 1·1	5·1			Mitterrand 10·9	43·4	12·7	49·3
					Rocard (PSU) 0·8	3·7						
					Duclos (PCF) 4·8	21·5						
Extreme left					Krivine 0·2	1·1			Krivine 0·1	0·4		
									Laguiller 0·6	2·4		
Extreme right	Tixier-Vignancour 1·3	5·3							Le Pen 0·2	0·6		
Others	Marcilhacy 0·4	1·7			Ducatel 0·3	1·1			Dumont (ecol) 0·3	1·3		
	Barbu 0·3	1·2							Muller 0·2	0·7		
									Renouvin 0·04	0·2		
									Sébag 0·04	0·2		
									Héraud 0·02	0·1		

months preceding the election revealed either equality between the two sides or, more frequently, a significant lead for the *majorité* (Frears and Parodi, 1979, p. 29).

The constitutional issue concerned what would happen if the voters chose a parliamentary majority that was opposed to the President of the Republic and his policies. Comment and analysis of the different presidential options almost permanently filled the columns of the press for several years before the election (for a full summary of options see Frears and Parodi, 1979, pp. 111–12). Would the President resign? What would be the disadvantages of such a course? Would he be able to do other than choose a Prime Minister supported by the new majority? Who would exercise executive leadership, the President (as had been the case throughout the Fifth Republic) or the new Prime Minister? Giscard d'Estaing made it clear on several occasions that he would not resign. The regime would have doubtless been a little less presidential but the constitution gives the President plenty of powers to exercise a moderating influence on his government. He can block undesirable nominations to senior posts in the public service, for instance, by withholding his countersignature. He could go on holding the centre of the stage by giving presidential television interviews. Above all the Constitution gives him the power to operate the sword of Damocles – dissolution of Parliament and new elections – which would hang above the head of his Prime Minister. The real constitutional lesson of it all is this: for the opposition really to win power in France it must win a presidential election.

There was also a great deal of speculation about whether the civil service or the military would be loyal to a government which included Communists, whether Western defence would be compromised, whether democratic freedoms would be threatened, or whether the economy would be ruined either by capitalists taking their money abroad or by inflationary programmes of social expenditure or by ill-considered nationalisations. We shall never know the answers to these questions, though the apocalyptic hypotheses advanced seem a little exaggerated. Although the attachment of the Communist leadership to Western democratic values is tenuous to say the least, it would presumably have been dismissed from government at the first sign of any unconstitutional, illegal, subversive, or, *a fortiori*, traitorous act. The PCF does not have enough support in the country for its dismissal from office in such circumstances to be the cause of a grave regime crisis.

Some years after the defeat of the left, what features of that election still stand out as significant? The first, staggering still, is the Communist decision to choose election defeat rather than be eclipsed by the Socialist Party. The second is the two speeches of President Giscard d'Estaing declaring there would not be a constitutional crisis if the opposition won.

The PCF had been worried about Socialist electoral gains at its expense for some time. Parliamentary by-elections in 1974 and local (cantonal) elections in 1976 had demonstrated this trend. In February 1977 the first salvo announced the barrage that was to follow. Just before an eagerly awaited television confrontation between Mitterrand and the Prime Minister, Raymond Barre, the PCF published and gave maximum publicity to its version of the cost of the left's economic programme and how it could be financed. So alarming were the figures that Barre had no trouble in ensuring that the focus of the debate was the lack of credibility of a left-wing government! Throughout the spring and summer acrimonious meetings were held to update the 1972 *programme commun*. On 22 September a relatively trifling detail about the full nationalisation of partly owned subsidiaries of nationalised firms served as the pretext for a breakdown. The next six months were spent, not in creating the climate of unity which is indispensable for left-wing success at the polls, but in redoubled accusations of treachery against the PS and a refusal, even on the eve of poll, to give assurances about the respect for the normal left-wing arrangements for a second-ballot pact. The menacing and vindictive tone of the Communist campaign served neatly to reinforce the anti-Communist propaganda which was the dominant, indeed almost the exclusive, theme of the *majorité*.

The role of national leader, above the battle but by no means indifferent to the result, was played with distinction by President Giscard d'Estaing. He had refused to be panicked by his first Prime Minister, Jacques Chirac, into calling early elections, threatening to resign if the left won, or pursuing a government programme which favoured supporters of the *majorité*. Two of the most effective speeches of his presidency were made during the 1978 election. In the first at Verdun-sur-le-Doubs, on 27 January, six weeks before the election, he addressed himself warmly to 'mes chères françaises et mes chers français' and asked the country to make the right choice (*le bon choix*) and to renew its confidence in the present government. He added that the public had of course the right to choose the *programme commun*: 'but if you choose it, it will be applied. Don't think the President of the Republic has, under the Constitution, the means to stop it.' The second speech, on the eve of the first ballot, refrained from the kind of crude anti-communism that President Pompidou had invoked in his broadcast to the nation before the 1973 election. It recognised the desire for change and renewal and greater justice expressed by electors. He warned of international dangers: 'an enfeebled France would be a France that slipped backwards in the competition of nations … assuring at a stroke the economic and monetary preponderance in Europe of our powerful partner – Federal Germany . . . Your choice, as I have told you, will be respected with all the consequences it entails. That is the democratic rule, but it is also the measure of your immense responsibility.' This was a very characteristically Giscardian declaration: the Gaullian themes of national prestige and *grandeur*, which Giscard never fails to evoke, mixed with his own personal themes about reason, good sense, responsibility and democratic choice.

As far as the results of the election are concerned there are three main points to retain. First, the left, with 49·3 per cent at the first ballot, reached its highest-ever share of the vote in the Fifth Republic – though a share well below the 51–3 per cent which had been predicted in the opinion polls. The share of Socialists (combined with the MRG wing of the Radicals) was up from 21 per cent to 25 per cent, making them the 'first party of France' – though a long way from the 28 or 30 per cent they regularly achieved in opinion polls. The Communist share of the vote was slightly down overall, and badly down in its heartland, the Paris region. In Paris itself – as in the country as a whole – for the first time since the 1930s more people voted Socialist than Communist. The second point is that supporters of the *majorité* showed much greater discipline in the second ballot than supporters of the left. A two-ballot election requires this discipline because, in the Fifth Republic, the second ballot has become a duel in each constituency between a single candidate of the *majorité* and a single candidate of the left (Communist or Socialist depending on who did best in the first ballot). In contrast with previous elections, there had been *majorité* 'primaries' in almost

every constituency as *Giscardiens* and Gaullists competed for the
right to represent the *majorité* in the second ballot. This rivalry,
however, in no way prevented a closing of the ranks – and even
the gaining of extra votes. In constituencies where a second ballot
was held the *majorité* increased its share of the vote from 45 per
cent at the first ballot to 50·5 per cent at the second (Frears and
Parodi, 1979, p. 88). The left, on the other hand, in many cases
lost votes, especially where first-ballot Socialist voters declined to
vote for a Communist candidate at the second. In particular,
where the second-ballot choice for Socialist voters was
Communist or *Giscardien*, nearly a quarter voted *Giscardien*
(Frears and Parodi, 1979, p. 91). The third significant aspect of the
result was the ending of Gaullist dominance of the *majorité*. The
Giscardien UDF emerged from the election almost equal to the RPR
in terms of the popular vote (21·4 against 22·5 per cent) and of
parliamentary seats (137 to 150). In addition it revealed itself to be
stronger at winning extra votes, especially from Socialists, at the
second ballot. When one considers that in 1968 85 per cent of the
vote for the *majorité* was for Gaullist candidates, one realises the
achievement of the UDF and also the tremendous electoral asset it
is for a party in French politics to be identified with the President
of the Republic.

Local elections

There have been three rounds of local elections so far in the
Giscard presidency. All have been regarded as a barometer of
political opinion and all have been greater or lesser successes for
the left. It is often said that, in so centralised a state as France,
local elections do not allocate much political power. This is
untrue. Although local authorities are under the *tutelle* of the
préfet, an official like a colonial governor appointed by central
government, there is real scope for local initiative. The mayor of a
town is a figure of real local importance, and, once elected, has six
years to exercise 'presidential' power over his council. Provided
he remains within the law and can obtain the necessary loans he
can be a real innovator in fields like housing, economic
development, or transport. A mayor of a large city is well placed
for a national political role as *député* or minister. The national
importance of Chaban-Delmas, Lecanuet, or Gaston Defferre is
largely connected with their local power as mayors of Bordeaux,
Rouen and Marseille respectively – not to mention the

(% first-ballot vote – metropolitan France only; National Assembly seats – metropolitan and overseas)

	October 1958		November 1962		March 1967		June 1968		March 1973		March 1978	
	%	seats	%	seats	%	seats	%	seats	%	seats	%	seats
Abstentions (% of electorate)	22·9		31·3		18·9		20·0		18·7		16·6	
Left												
Communists (PCF)	19·2	10	21·7	41	22·5	73	20·0	34	21·4	73	20·7	86
SFIO (Socialist Party pre-1969)	15·7	44	12·6	66								
Socialist/Radical alliances FGDS (1967–8); UGSD 1973; PS/MRG 1978					19·0	116	16·5	57	20·8	101	25·0	114
Radicals	8·3	32	7·8	39								
PSU, extreme left, other left			2·4	—	2·1	4	4·7	—	3·6	2	3·6	—
(Total left)	(43·2)	(86)	(44·5)	(146)	(43·6)	(193)	(41·2)	(91)	(45·8)	(176)	(49·3)	(200)
Centre												
MRP	11·1	57	9·1									
Independents	22·9	133	7·7	55								
Opposition centre (CD/PDM)					13·4	41	10·3	33				
Réformateurs (CD + Radicals, 1973)									13·1	34		
Majorité												
CDP (pro-majorité centrists, 1973)										30		
UDF (Giscardiens + centre, 1978)											21·4	137
RI (Giscardiens pre-1978)			5·9	35		44		64		55		
Gaullists	19·5	199	31·9	233	37·7	201	44·7	296	36·0	183	22·5	150
Other majorité									0·7	5	2·0	3
(Total Majorité)			(37·8)	(268)	(37·7)	(245)	(44·7)	(360)	(36·7)	(273)	(45·9)	(290)
Other	3·3		8·6	13	5·4	8	3·5	3	4·4	7	4·8*	1

Note: *Includes 'Ecologists' – 2·1%.
Source: Frears and Parodi, 1979, p. 5.

chairmanships of *conseils généraux*, regional councils and other bodies which have a tendency to accrue to such prominent local figures.

Two of the three local elections since 1974 have been elections to the *conseils généraux* which govern the 101 metropolitan and overseas French *départements*. There is a cantonal election, as these contests are called, every three years though involving only half of the seats on the council each time. There is a single-member two-ballot electoral system as for parliamentary elections. The 1976 cantonal elections proved to be a high point of support for the left – approximately 53 per cent and the gaining of control in a number of *départements*. The Socialists in particular made gains. The government and the President appeared greatly demoralised by this setback. In 1979, despite the breakdown of the Union de la Gauche, the 1976 pattern was almost exactly repeated: 53 per cent for the left, exceptional gains for the Socialists, admirably disciplined second-ballot voting by the supporters of the left. In short, it was like the good old days. The left made a further net gain of six *départements* and now controls forty-two of the ninety-five in metropolitan France. Presidencies of *conseils généraux* were occupied in 1980 by the principal political parties as follows: Communists five, ps/mrg thirty-six, rpr eleven and the udf (which groups together a lot of the conservative and moderate notables firmly entrenched on this type of council) thirty-one.

More important than cantonal elections are the municipal elections which take place every six years in all the 36,000 villages, towns and cities of France. The elector votes for a list of candidates rather than just a single councillor, and the head of the victorious list normally becomes mayor. In towns under 30,000 population the voter may cross-vote between lists; in the 221 towns and cities with a greater population he may not. The victorious list wins all the seats on the council so that, in the large towns and cities at any rate, no opposition is elected to the council. The exception to this rule is that five of the very largest cities – Paris, Marseille, Lyon, Toulouse and Nice – are divided into sectors each of which operates for electoral rules like a town of over 30,000 population. The opposition wins some sectors and hence representation on the city council.

The great importance of the 1977 municipal elections as a political event in the Giscard presidency stems first from the successful way the Union de la Gauche strategy was put into operation and secondly from the reform of Paris City Council's statute and the great battle to become the first mayor of Paris since the Commune in 1871.

The composition of joint Union de la Gauche lists instead of rival Socialist and Communist lists was the most original feature of 1977. Negotiations were difficult, some old Socialist–Centrist alliances as in Nantes or Lille had to be undone, but Union de la Gauche lists were almost universally presented. The left gained 56 large cities to control 159 of the 221 with a population over 30,000 including some in Catholic areas of the country like Rennes or Reims where the left has always been weak. Important town halls (seventy-two of which now have a Communist mayor and eighty-one a Socialist) constitute important bridgeheads for the political campaigns to come. Many of these new mayors presented themselves, for instance, at the parliamentary elections in 1978.

The reform of Paris to make it like the rest of the 36,000 *communes* of France is one of the most important reforms of the Giscard presidency. So many governments have been overthrown in the streets of Paris and Republics proclaimed from the Hôtel de Ville that it was always felt too dangerous to let the city have its own mayor who might become an alternative focus of political power. The 'Battle of Paris' was therefore the highlight of the 1977 elections. The government, at the behest of the President, had rather clumsily designated Michel d'Ornano, Minister of Industry and a leading *Giscardien*, to be the candidate of the *majorité*. However, the battle was won by the recently dismissed Prime Minister and leader of the new Gaullist RPR, Jacques Chirac, who astonished everyone by proclaiming his candidature. He had the advantage of a vigorously aggressive style and the presence on his lists of well-established councillors from the old Conseil de Paris, and the fact that Paris has been a Gaullist city throughout the Fifth Republic. The resources and the power base represented by the Paris Hôtel de Ville have been invaluable in Chirac's subsequent attempt to launch himself as a potential President. As mayor of Paris he tours the world and holds mighty receptions as if he were a head of state.

The European Assembly Elections, June 1979

The European elections should have had a wider significance

than a live domestic opinion poll but they unfortunately did not. The electoral system chosen in France – proportional representation by national lists – denied the voter the right to choose his own regional representative in the European Parliament. There was no need for alliances between parties because there was no second ballot and no government to form. As it was a live opinion poll with presidential overtones, political leaders like Mitterrand, Marchais and Chirac headed their lists. So each of the four main political parties campaigned hard with the sole intention of maximising its own vote and the personal audience of its leader in relation to the party that was normally its partner. Communists strove to catch up the Socialists, Gaullists to outdo *Giscardiens*. Gaullists and Communists both ran intensely nationalist campaigns – the 'hysterical compromise' as a Socialist *député* put it. That France was being sold out to the foreigner was the main theme for both. The *Giscardiens* fought the most successful campaign. Simone Veil, the Minister of Health whom opinion polls had consistently revealed to be the most popular member of the government, was designated to head their list – Union for France in Europe. Raymond Barre campaigned for it; the Minister of Agriculture, Pierre Mehaignerie, was a prominent (and elected) member of it; indeed it was in reality the official list of President Giscard d'Estaing and his government. Its campaign was in fact just as nationalist as the others in terms of the French national interests it stressed, but it seemed less strident and negative. It emerged as the principal winner with 27·6 per cent of the vote – a considerable increase compared with 1978 – and this was regarded as a vote of confidence in Giscard d'Estaing. The Gaullist campaign, led by Chirac and de Gaulle's former Prime Minister, Michel Debré, was a failure. The score of only 16 per cent caused Chirac and his party colleagues to re-think their whole strategy and image. A less frenetic Chirac was produced in the autumn for the eighteen-month run-up to the presidential election. The PCF nationally was steady – though its haemorrhage in the Paris region continued. The PS was slightly down on 1978. Only 60 per cent of the electorate voted – low for France but much better than in some European countries like Great Britain. (For a breakdown of the voting figures see Table 4.3.)

What happened after the election was in some ways more interesting than the election itself. The full diplomatic resources of the French state, especially Michel Poniatowski, the President's

Table 4.3   *European Assembly Election, 10 June 1979*

Registered electorate:	35·2m.		
Abstentions:	39·3%		
Spoilt votes:	2·9%		
		m. votes	*%*
Extreme left (Arlette Laguiller)		0·6	3·1
PCF (G. Marchais)		4·2	20·4
PS/MRG (F. Mitterrand)		4·8	23·4
RPR (Défense des Intérêts de la France en Europe, J. Chirac/Debré)		3·3	16·2
UDF (Union pour la France en Europe, S. Veil)		5·7	27·9
Ecologists (S. Fernex)		0·9	4·4
Emploi, Egalité, Europe (J.-J. Servan-Schreiber)		0·4	1·8
Défense Interprofessionelle (Ph. Malaud)		0·3	1·4
Euro-droite (J.-L. Tixier Vignancour)		0·3	1·3

(Région Europe, 337 votes, and PSU, 332: no voting papers distributed)

roving ambassador and an elected member of the Assembly on the Veil list himself, were applied to the task of getting Simone Veil elected President of the European Parliament. The Gaullists were not very pleased because the British Conservatives had to be given the chair of the Agriculture Committee as the price for their support of Mme Veil. Next François Mitterrand resigned his seat in protest at a judicial ruling in France which declared that where electors had put Mme Veil's declaration (coloured blue) into the ballot box instead of the official ballot paper (coloured white) bearing her name their votes were valid. This, until the decision was reversed on appeal, increased her list's total sufficiently to give it one more seat and the Socialists one less.

In the Assembly itself the Gaullists, like the British Conservatives, have their own group which they share with a few Irish Fianna Fáil. The rules of the Assembly had to be bent to allow them to form an official group, so small were their numbers. Chirac had decreed that Gaullist members were to retire in rotation so that other people whose names were too low on the list in 1979 to be elected by the voters would nevertheless have a chance to serve. In May 1980 he accordingly withdrew to the obscurity of the French National Assembly, the mayoralty of Paris, the *conseil général* of Corrèze, and the presidential election campaign. The *Giscardiens*, in the best traditions of the loose-knit collection of notables that the UDF really is, were elected as one list but went separate ways to join two groups in the European Parliament. Lecanuet and the CDS members joined the Christian Democrat group, Poniatowski and the PR joined the Liberal group. The Socialists and Communists joined their respective groups and one of the Socialists – Jacques Delors, a former member of the Chaban-Delmas *cabinet* – became chairman of the Parliament's Economic Committee. French *Giscardiens*, Gaullists and Communists were about the only members of the European Parliament to support the Community Budget when the Parliament threw it out in December 1979 because too much was being spent on subsidising agricultural surpluses.

The seven years of the Giscard presidency from 1974 to 1981 were a continuous election campaign. Much of it was in preparation for 1981, the election that would determine whether there was to be such a thing as a 'Giscard era' in French politics.

PART TWO

Actions and Policies

CHAPTER 5

Foreign Policy and Defence
I: Bombs and Oil

A trained and refined intelligence, years of political and administrative experience, a generous and far-sighted set of ideas emphasising liberalism and change and, to crown these attributes, presidential power virtually untrammelled, far less subject at any rate to the checks and balances of other Western democracies — surely the reign of Plato's philosopher-king had come at last. In the next few chapters the policies of the Giscard presidency in four broad fields — foreign affairs and defence, economic and social policy including energy and the environment, political institutions and civil liberties — will be examined. The main conclusion, on the basis of seven years in office, is that where technocratic decision-making, albeit humane and enlightened, suffices — for instance, in industrial policy or housing, or social welfare — the results have been good. On the other hand, where one might have expected to find the political expression of a more liberal and enlightened attitude — for instance, in the extension of liberty of the individual, or in a less chauvinistic foreign policy — the results have been most disappointing.

The first field of policy to be examined is, appropriately enough, the most presidential and the one most marked by *continuité* with the policies of General de Gaulle. The personal conduct of foreign affairs and defence by the head of state has become an established tradition in the Fifth Republic. All the important initiatives, all the important visits are made by the President himself. The Quai d'Orsay and the Ministry of Defence are the executants of policy made at the Elysée Palace. This identification of foreign affairs and defence with the President, and the rather grandiose themes of national independence and nuclear power that have been associated with them, are of course a direct inheritance from General de Gaulle. Philip Cerny has argued in his book *The Politics of Grandeur* (1980) that de Gaulle's grandiose foreign policy directly served the function of building a national consensus that would give legitimacy to the new political institutions of the Fifth Republic and to the office of the President. This theme is often reflected in the language of President Giscard d'Estaing: there is a wide consensus in France over 'the independent action of France' (television interview on foreign affairs, 26 February 1980) which reflects national unity in the pursuit of proclaimed ideals like peace, human rights, or the reduction of inequalities between rich and poor nations. It is a noble ambition − if that is what is being done. However, sentiments like these too often cloak something else: vainglorious gestures which foster consensus merely by flattering nationalistic pride, or self-interested actions which purport to be for the good of humanity. France's policy towards NATO for the last twenty years is an example of the one, French policy with regard to the Middle East is an example of the other. One would take the nobility of French foreign policy ambitions more seriously if the initiatives pursued ever cost France anything. As the Socialist *député* Jean-Pierre Cot put it in April 1978 apropos Giscard's disarmament proposals at the United Nations: 'the President avoids any proposition (over nuclear tests or arms sales or whatever) that would be a constraint for France'.

Defence

The starting point of foreign policy in general and of defence policy in particular is the oft-repeated proposition that France, though part of an alliance, is independent. Unlike other signatories of the North Atlantic Treaty, which are also independent sovereign states, France feels the need to assert this independence in the form of refusing formal integration in the command structure of NATO. A particular expression of independence has been the decision to develop and deploy its own strategic nuclear weapons and, indeed, to maintain its own armaments industries in all fields in a high state of technological development.

The strategic nuclear deterrent

The development of the French strategic nuclear force has been a great technical success. The difficulty is to know what purpose it actually serves. Its defensive role is limited, as will be apparent if one tries to list possible answers to the question 'why does the Soviet Union not attack France?'. 'Because it is deterred by the threat of French nuclear retaliation' comes a long way down the list after such replies as 'because it would serve no purpose' and 'because an attack on Western Europe would be a *casus belli* for the United States'. In any case, if NATO failed to deter or contain a Soviet invasion of Western Europe and refrained from the use of nuclear weapons, France, as the enemy forces approached the Rhine, would be faced with the difficult decision of making the first nuclear strike which would bring about in retaliation the instant obliteration of France. Of course other potential aggressors exist, if not now then in the future, at least in the fevered brains of defence planners. During de Gaulle's presidency, General d'Ailleret enunciated the doctrine of French defence: 'tous azimuts' – that is to say, against anyone and everyone (including, one presumes, the United States). During the Pompidou presidency it was whispered that West Germany was the potential future aggressor it was necessary to deter – and indeed the French Pluton missiles (of which more later) can, from where they are based, only be fired at targets in West Germany. It is hard, in all seriousness, to see the deployment of nuclear weapons as a serious factor in the regulation of Franco-German relations, however they might one day deteriorate. More and more the French nuclear deterrent becomes, in the phrase of a retired French diplomat, 'a Maginot line in the air'. More and more one is compelled to see it as a political symbol and a psychological comfort rather than a real instrument.

It is a political symbol with which national prestige and national pride can be identified – rather as the British nuclear deterrent was in British political debate in the early 1960s. 'It gives us a seat at the top table', the British people were solemnly told by leaders like Macmillan and Douglas-Home. It has been maintained since then, it is independently targeted, and though part of NATO, under sovereign British command, but it dropped out of use as a political symbol – at least until Mrs Thatcher's government threatened to revive it by embarking on the Trident submarine programme. The nuclear deterrent as a symbol has never dropped out of French political usage. Any lack of commitment by Giscard d'Estaing to the deterrent *force de frappe* is considered to be the one point on which a break between him and the Gaullists would be a certainty. Indeed the merest suggestion of an end to, or even a reduction of, the number of missile-launching submarines to be built – even though the deterrent is no more credible with eight or ten than it is with four or five because the lower number permits two to be at sea at any time – raises hackles and frantic reproaches. The strategic nuclear force is a political symbol to which President Giscard d'Estaing returns again and again. There are constant visits to the launching sites and the submarines, journalists are invited to marvel at the underground strategic command centres, and the phrase 'the world's third greatest nuclear power', whether true or not, is used like an incantation in almost every presidential utterance. As a symbol of national independence and security, the bomb is now firmly entrenched in public opinion. No political party advocates its abandonment. All agree on the dubious proposition that it reduces dependence on America. It is politically unthinkable for France to give it up.

The French nuclear weapon programme, and all the political, military and prestige incentives that it expresses, preceded General de Gaulle and the Fifth Republic. The nuclear reactor at Marcoule which provided plutonium for the atomic bomb went critical as early as 1956. General de Gaulle formally notified Eisenhower and Macmillan of his intention to deploy the atomic bomb in September 1958. There was a symbolically successful test in the Sahara Desert in March 1960 at the time of Khrushchev's visit to Paris. The bomb was deployed in Mirage IV bombers which depended, for what little credibility they had, on the American KC-135 refuelling tankers. This first generation was succeeded by a second generation of land- and sea-based IRBMs (intermediate range). The land-based ones are housed in silos on the Plateau d'Albion. Fixed land-based missiles are now considered to be too vulnerable to surprise attack to have real credibility as a deterrent. It is therefore really on the sea-based missiles launched from nuclear submarines that the effectiveness of the French strategic nuclear force depends. Because it is virtually impossible, and likely to remain so for many years, to find and track a submarine in all the oceans of the world, an enemy could have no certainty of being able to prevent a missile fired from one from hitting its target. So the French, like the United States, the Soviet Union and Great Britain, have turned to the submarine for their principal nuclear deterrent. So long as one submarine is maintained at sea all the time, the capacity to make a strike against an enemy city, inflicting huge loss, exists.

In addition to the strategic nuclear force there are tactical nuclear weapons. These, called Pluton, became operational in May 1974 just before the election of Giscard d'Estaing. They are deployed on the French-built AMX-30 tanks and due also for the highly praised Super-Etandard carrier-based aircraft. NATO has a lot of American tactical nuclear weapons, the aim of which is to deter conventional attack without resorting to an apocalyptic strategic exchange. If the Pluton missiles were part of NATO they would, within the framework of this rather dangerous theory, make some sense. However, what an 'independent' Pluton is for is by no means clear. Indeed, as Jacques Isnard wrote in *Le Monde* (11 May 1974): 'so far the French people have no idea of the circumstances in which military commands would be authorised, in their name, to open tactical nuclear fire'. Their range is 120 kilometres which means that if they remain in France they can only hit an eastward target in West Germany! This has not unnaturally aroused some protests from this friendly ally as well as the ironic comment 'let's hope they land on the enemy'. If they are not to be used against targets in West Germany they have to be transported. If transported, they would have to be part of some allied battle plan and indeed the important speech of General Méry in 1976, which we shall consider in a moment (and which is one of the rare examples of a major declaration being made by someone other than the President), suggests that that would be the case.

The debate, however, continues, not just in relation to the French Pluton, on whether tactical nuclear weapons are in fact usable or whether they would merely light the powder for a major nuclear war. In a letter to the *Guardian* on 24 June 1974, Admiral Flohic said, on behalf of France, that 'we will fire tactical nuclear weapons at an early stage as a signal that we have no other choice than to fire our strategic nuclear weapons'. After six years of Giscard presidency this crude theory had at least been refined and clarified. On 4 February 1980 General Claude Vanbremeersch, Commandant of the 1st Army and a former member of the President's personal military staff at the Elysée, said in an interview with *L'Aurore*:

If the 1st Army is fighting alongside the Allies, and if, the cohesion of forces being broken, the Americans use their nuclear weapons on time, the engagement of our Plutons will have no essential significance. It will have at least had the merit of placing our forces on the same 'nuclear footing' as the others ... On the other hand, if the forces of the Alliance do not fire nuclear weapons when the front is broken the French government could take the decision to use atomic weapons when it considers the country is directly threatened. My problem is to see that the missiles are as effective as possible ... in order to give a signal to halt [*coup d'arrêt*] that will be highly significant and very clearly distinguished.

The ghastly weakness of this position is that defence means the French President thinking it worth the risk of being the first to press the button for a nuclear war.

The French arsenal (or panoply as they prefer to call it) of nuclear weapons is under continuous modernisation and development. The M4 missile, which has a range of 4,000 km and carries multiple independently targeted warheads (MIRVs), will be deployed on submarine No. 6 due in 1985, and then progressively on the others, so that each submarine will eventually have ninety-six separate nuclear warheads. Work is also going on to reduce the noise, increase the speed and harden the missiles of the submarines. Testing of nuclear devices continues – formerly in the Pacific Ocean, to the indignation of Australia and New Zealand, now underground but still in the Pacific Ocean – and successful results are proclaimed to the world as part of the deterrent's deterrence. The old Mirage IV and the newly modernised Plateau d'Albion missiles will probably be replaced by a mobile version of the M4 carried around on a truck. Another possibility under study (for which 2 million francs was committed in 1978) is a low-altitude cruise missile which can evade radar screens. On the tactical side there are the Super-Etendard aircraft, in service from 1981, and an air-to-ground medium-range missile which can be fired from the recently ordered Mirage 2000. There was in 1980 considerable debate over whether France should develop the neutron bomb as a tactical device. A bomb which destroys people and leaves property and equipment intact – it sounds like the ultimate in inhuman cynicism. In fact because it emits less blast and heat it has great practical advantages: it can destroy a military target without causing devastation for miles around. The French Minister of Defence confirmed (*Le Monde*, 19 January 1980) that France could have neutron bombs operational in five years. President Giscard d'Estaing, in his February 1980 television interview, said that French nuclear capability had nearly quadrupled already during his period of office and would total 90 megatons (Hiroshima × 4,500) by 1985. Nuclear forces cost 12·4 billion francs of a 1980 budget of 89 billion.

Sanctuarisation élargie

In terms of basic nuclear strategy and development Giscard d'Estaing has continued along the path traced by his predecessors. Any hint that he might do otherwise – for example, by reducing the share of the budget spent on the nuclear deterrent or by cancelling the sixth submarine (hastily reinstated after protests) – has aroused sufficient Gaullist clamours to cut it short. The originality of Giscard's defence policy has been the redefinition of France's role in respect to NATO 'in a world which is a very unstable world' (speech on board the *Terrible*, 8 November 1974), the concentration on conventional forces, and in particular a 'mobile, special force' (ibid.) for intervention overseas or the protection of vital supplies. The redefinition of France's role was sketched by the President on television on 5 May 1976 and explained by General Guy Méry, Army Chief of Staff, the President's closest military adviser, and chief of the Elysée military staff in 1974–5, in a speech on 1 June. Hitherto French defence had reposed on the notion of *sanctuarisation* of French territory. No matter what happened beyond its frontiers, French defence policy was to ensure that France itself was not directly threatened. This policy, quite apart from showing little solidarity with allies, was unrealistic because France could not ignore destabilising events in neighbouring countries. Also threats to supply-lines of oil or raw materials are just as direct as a threat to the territory. General Méry developed the idea of *sanctuarisation élargie* – France still a sanctuary but considered in a wider context. This means a change from a strategy based on massive nuclear riposte to a direct threat to French territory to participation in defence of NATO's eastern frontier. A 'non-battle' strategy changes to a battle strategy: France would take part in a battle in forward areas (though, to still Gaullist fears of a sell-out, it would not occupy a *créneau* or be permanently responsible for a section of the front as part of NATO's strategy). However, it is an important change: *sanctuarisation élargie* means that France participates in NATO joint planning. The French departure from NATO in 1966 was to a large extent a symbolic gesture of independence. In fact participation and co-operation has been maintained in most NATO agencies (Goodman, 1975, pp. 121–3). Non-co-operation was confined to 'key symbolic areas' (Cerny, 1980, p. 235): on the military nuclear programme and on the commitment to commit French forces in a European war or to strengthen NATO's front line. The Méry speech represents a real change in this policy, and the 1976 French Parliament approved a Defence Programme Law which committed the armed forces to the mission, among others, of 'participating in the defence of Europe including the northern and southern approaches'. There are now smoother relations between France and NATO. France takes part in the independent Programme Group (mainly in weapons procurement collaboration) but has no access to NATO targeting.

There has been since then a steady increase in defence budgets (in 1980 it reached 89 billion francs), 15 per cent up on 1979, and 3·8 per cent of GNP compared with 3·4 per cent in 1974). A lower proportion of capital spending now goes on the strategic nuclear deterrent (25 per cent in 1980 against 34 per cent in 1976) and there has been considerable development of conventional forces with the aim of making them comparable to those of West Germany. In the period of the Programme Law the army will have some 500,000 men in sixteen divisions, 1,200 main battle tanks and sophisticated anti-aircraft equipment, the navy 140 warships (including small conventionally armed nuclear submarines and ships that fire Crotale short-range non-nuclear missiles) and 100 combat aircraft, and the air force 450 combat aircraft especially Mirage F1s, Jaguars and Mirage 2000s (NATO *Review*, June 1979, pp. 11–13). These forces are widely deployed: France has a very large naval presence in the Indian Ocean (where the tactical nuclear weapons arguably fulfil a deterrent function in a less dangerous manner than they do in Europe) and has already shown its capacity to intervene rapidly in distant trouble spots like Zaïre. Indeed the Zaïre intervention gave the kiss of life to the French-built troop transporter the *Transall* and led to the reorganisation of 'external action forces'. Attention has been given to the problem of low pay, low morale and even a certain amount of open dissidence, which affected the army in the mid-1970s.

Arms sales

From the point of view of world peace, French foreign policy presents two problems. The first, already discussed, is the irrationality of French nuclear weapons not properly integrated into NATO. The other is the problem of French sales of armaments, being a fundamentally and urgently pursued part of foreign and economic policy. France has a large armaments industry and has struggled successfully to make it, like its nuclear forces and for similar reasons of prestige and virility, the third largest in the world. This is first of all a problem for France. According to some experts (e.g. *Armed Forces Journal International*, October 1978) the policy of arms exports (which are necessary if development costs are not to be absorbed wholly by the national defence budget) means that relatively unsophisticated material suitable for the Third World has to be developed and the French, for sales purposes, then have to use it themselves! It was even alleged that the Palestine guerillas were better armed than the French paratroops in the UN forces in Lebanon! However, the French have some good and highly saleable equipment: Mirage F1s for example or the missile-firing ships which are fast and modern. The greater problem is that the sale of arms *tous azimuts* becomes a policy goal in itself and can be a dangerous factor in international relations, in the Middle East, for example. Alfred Fabre-Luce (1974, p. 105) argued that French arms were supporting repression (South Africa) and aggression (Libya), so what does a good liberal like Giscard do when the balance of payments depends on such sales? The ingenious solution was to lift embargos and sell to all, not just Iraq and Libya, but Egypt and Israel too: 'a festival of arms in an atmosphere of good conscience rediscovered'.

Immediately after his election Giscard d'Estaing declared (30 May 1974) that France would 'refrain from arms sales that would run counter to our mission [of support for the cause of freedom and the right of peoples to self-determination]'. The cessation of sales to South Africa was announced in August 1975 but this was criticised first as being symbolic, since French arms were already being manufactured there under licence, and secondly as cynical since France was abandoning one saturated market in order to sell arms to other African states! In the Giscard peace initiative in the Middle East in February 1980, which included recognition of Palestinian rights, there was more than a suspicion that the real motives were connected with oil supplies and arms sales. When Chirac was Prime Minister he was alleged to spend as much as 10 per cent of his time on arms sales (*Sunday Telegraph*, 7 September 1975), the Defence Ministry was known as the *ministère des pots de vin* (Ministry of Bribes – allegedly to Arabs) and *Le Monde* (5 June 1975) reported a budget of over 13 million francs for 'travel and reception expenses'. The General Inspector of Finance issued a warning (29 June 1976) that the state was getting too involved in arms deals. Jacques Isnard (*Le Monde* 31 March 1978) complained that the state was doing too much, arranging design, manufacturing, banking and insurance, controlling companies, issuing guarantees, providing after-sales service, training overseas users and getting into shady deals with dictatorships of all sorts. The main state agency is the Délégation Générale à l'Armement (DGA). Through it the state owns a quarter-share of the Société Française des Matériels d'Armement (SOFMA) to which civil servants and military personnel can be seconded. The sales effort has been very successful: orders worth 25 billion francs were received in 1978, a steady progression which has multiplied arms sales by five at constant prices since 1970, and the arms industry keeps 287,000 people (4·5 per cent of the working population) employed – 155,000 of them in the private sector, 73,000 in the DGA itself (National Assembly 1980 Finance Law reports). Arms exports have to be authorised by the Interministerial Committee for the Study and Export of War Materials on which the Ministries of Defence, Foreign Affairs and Finance are represented. The DGA, through its Directorate of International Affairs, presents all requests to this interministerial body.

Kolodziej has argued (*International Affairs*, January 1980) that the French policy of arms exports is linked both to its foreign policy philosophy and to internal economic imperatives. 'The foreign policy of the de Gaulle regime, carried forward by its successors, rejected the notion of regional or global security systems (based on superpower dominance).' There should be a 'multipolar international system ... composed of states possessing sufficient military capabilities to resist superpower threats and to decrease, if not eliminate, that dependence on one superpower or the other for their security or foreign policy goals. French arms sales promoted such a fluid and decentralised system' (p. 57). However, 'the inability, or unwillingness of the Giscard d'Estaing regime to decrease arms sales provided additional evidence of the economic pressures motoring French transfers. When he was campaigning for office in 1974, President Giscard d'Estaing intimated that selling arms would be a lesser priority: "I do not think it is a sector in which we ought to accent our effort", he said. The pledge was never kept' (p. 61). Arms exports from 1974 to 1978 almost doubled from 4·8 to 8·4 billion francs (an increase of over a half in volume terms), helping to offset France's trade deficit to some extent. Furthermore 'France's ability to gain access to oil is tied to its role as an arms supplier' (p. 63). The largest arms contracts have been with France's largest oil suppliers, Iraq and Saudi Arabia and, a decade earlier when relations were better, Libya. Finally, decision-making over arms sales is 'a model of closed bureaucratic politics, but one in which the principal actors share a common interest in selling arms', a striking feature being 'the absence of broad public or inter-party debate' (p. 68). 'Decreasing exports would hardly ease the government's problems of maintaining solvency, access to oil, employment, social stability, and popular support' (p. 70). So 'the support structure for France arms transfers ... rests solidly on a tripod of security and foreign-policy considerations as well as domestic economic and political requirements' (p. 72).

In the Programme Law for 1977–82, to which reference has already been made, the task of French forces were defined as being to counter five kinds of threats: the threat from the East from the growth in Warsaw Pact forces, the threat of instability in the Third World (sources of essential French supplies), the threat from control by an adversary of a European neighbour state, any threat to the security of a country to whom France is tied, and a threat to indispensable sea-traffic of supplies. This is a reasonable list and shows much greater solidarity with neighbours than previous French defence policy. The problem is that the use of military force is often counter-productive in the modern world. Great Britain, for example, found that after the Six Day War in 1967 it was the only state in Europe to have its oil supplies cut off by the Arabs. It was also the only European state with a military force in the area. The role of that military force was to safeguard oil supplies! The lesson is clear: one sometimes defends one's interest better by political and economic, not military means, as powerful states like West Germany have found.

The other big problem which faces the defence policy of France and other European states, a problem about which a debate has begun to develop, is the general problem of European security now that the Soviet Union has nuclear parity with the United States, the deadly SS20 missile targeted on Western Europe and not covered by SALT agreements on arms limitations, and vast conventional superiority over NATO. Trial balloons about joint Franco-German, or Franco-British, or trilateral nuclear programmes have been floated and denied by the Elysée. Fears continue about whether the United States, with its concentration on a 'graduated response' which begins with a strike against military targets, will in the 1980s be, to quote former Secretary of State Kissinger, 'any longer in a strategic situation to reduce a Soviet counter-attack to tolerable levels'. The political rhetoric of 'independence', repeated like a ritual chant for the last twenty years, which has had its effect abroad, by creating distrust among allies, as well as on public opinion at home, has made it very difficult for the French to get down to collaborating in the difficult task of preparing an adequate defence for Europe. There are signs, however, that under Giscard d'Estaing the effort has begun. He has certainly had the intelligence to see that the 'all or nothing' policy of massive retaliation or neutrality had no credibility whatsoever, and has done something positive to change it.

Foreign policy – 'mondialisme'

The defence policy of President Giscard d'Estaing started by being Gaullian and, remaining so in style, progressively became less so in content. Foreign policy on the other hand has become more and more Gaullian as time goes by. The key word in French foreign policy has been *mondialiste* – French presence worldwide. In the Middle East, in Africa, in Europe, even to some extent in relations with the superpowers, the United States and USSR, *continuité* with Gaullism has been the predominant note. When he was explaining foreign policy on television (26 February 1980) Giscard d'Estaing declared that France's 'international action' had four objectives: to defend the interests of France and especially its security, to try to maintain peace because France was a peaceful country with no territorial ambitions, to make Europe regain the influence in world affairs it used to have, and to contribute to 'an organisation of the world which takes account of new realities and corrects injustices'. The 'new realities' are the emergence of 'new powers' and the importance of non-aligned countries; the injustices are the 'excessive inequalities' between rich and poor nations. In pursuing these objectives France is animated by three considerations: loyalty to its alliances, the pursuit of an independent policy and certain 'solidarities'. These 'solidarities' tie it first to democratic regimes in general, notably the Western democracies, secondly to its partners in Europe in particular, and thirdly to countries which by language or by history have special links with France. This applies especially to French-speaking African countries 'to whose development and stability we bring our contribution'.

Apart from the general defence of French interests and the *mondialiste* conception, the most visible parts of French foreign policy during the Giscard d'Estaing presidency have been the development of exceptionally close Franco-German relations and the interventionist French role in Africa. In his conduct of foreign policy Giscard has become progressively more confident, that is to say, able to process round the globe like a world leader. He is greatly helped by the fact that there are virtually no domestic constraints on French foreign policy – so long as he stays within the domestic consensus, which can broadly be called Gaullist, that France is a world-ranking nuclear power, independent of the United States, and with an assertive foreign policy. In Great Britain or America, public opinion, lobbies, political parties, Parliament, press and television are frequently mobilised over a whole range of foreign policy issues – Vietnam, Iran, South Africa, Chile, arms sales, Israel – and this becomes a tangible constraint on government action. In France, the lack of regular critical comment on television, the restricted role of Parliament in foreign affairs and the much smaller share of interest groups and political parties in influencing public policy all help to make life easier for the executive.

Much of French foreign policy in the Fifth Republic has been concerned with 'reaffirming France's rank in the world'. According to Philip Cerny (1980) a foreign policy based on *grandeur* was for General de Gaulle an indispensable condition for the cohesion of the French nation around the institutions of the Fifth Republic. The Giscardian word *mondialisme* is just another synonym for *grandeur*. The principal attempts by France during the Giscard d'Estaing presidency so far to assert a worldwide presence have been (not counting the African initiatives which we shall examine in the next chapter) the North–South conference on energy and development, the French proposals on disarmament and the pursuit of détente, the attempts to gain privileged relations with non-aligned and oil producing countries and the French peace initiatives in the Middle East. The essence has been to adopt over the whole field of international affairs a line distinctively different from that of America without engaging in the anti-American excesses of the de Gaulle era or of Pompidou's Foreign Minister Jobert.

The North–South conference was a French initiative which grew out of French objections under Pompidou to American domination of the Washington conference on oil in February 1974 and the French refusal to take part in Kissinger's International Energy Agency. President Giscard d'Estaing, in his press conference on 24 October 1974, proposed an oil conference that would be tripartite: producer countries, industrialised consumers and non-industrialised consumers. The Americans and the European countries were cool, but after various preparatory meetings the idea finally got off the ground in December 1975 as a bipartite North–South conference between the industrial nations and the developing nations. It was a 'ministerial conference on international economic co-operation'. The committees of the North–South conference – energy, raw materials, finance and development – carried on work until June 1977 when the conference ended with rather limited and disappointing results. There was agreement on financing bigger stocks of raw materials and of increasing development aid. There was nothing, however, for the Third World on indexation of raw material prices or on a moratorium for debts, nor for the developed countries on energy supplies and prices. Though it was considered a failure by everyone else, the French regarded it as a successful attempt to replace 'confrontation [of 1973–4] with dialogue'. It often gets a reference in communiqués when Giscard d'Estaing visits Third World countries and there is an official in the President's *cabinet* who specifically looks after North–South matters. After France shifted from support of Pakistan in 1980, India and Algeria became her main non-aligned interlocutors in the North–South dialogue, which as far as France is concerned continues.

Disarmament has rather a similar story – a spectacular initiative giving France some prestige but in other respects having rather modest results. France had been absent from disarmament talks in Geneva since 1962. The Elysée began to consider, under Giscard, whether there would be some advantage to be gained by re-joining. A report was commissioned under the chairmanship of Jean Taittinger, a Gaullist former minister. France decided it would take part in disarmament talks but that between pointless talks on general disarmament and the SALT dialogue between the superpowers there was a third way, a French way. The proposal was for a new European disarmament conference which would include Europe 'from the Atlantic to the Urals', to coin de Gaulle's phrase, and which would replace the talks on multilateral balanced force reductions (MBFR) which had been going on, with France absent naturally, in Vienna for some time. Just as *sanctuarisation élargie* is a formula for getting back into NATO without rejoining NATO, the European conference proposals are a way back into MBFR without joining MBFR. Although Giscard d'Estaing claimed that, unlike President Carter, he did not conduct foreign policy by *déclarations fracassantes*, the other Giscardian disarmament proposal in fact began with a *déclaration fracassante* at the United Nations in April 1978. The theme of the conference was disarmament but France's proposals for a disarmament committee and even for an institute for disarmament research were ignored. The French in any case would not accept the paragraphs in the final resolution dealing with nuclear tests. On nuclear questions in general France has maintained its refusal to take part in any disarmament discussions and has announced its intention to take no part in SALT III, the latest negotiations on strategic arms limitation.

As far as détente is concerned, France has tried to follow a line that preserves relations with Moscow and distinguishes France from the United States. Détente, said the French Foreign Minister, Jean François-Poncet, after the Soviet military intervention in Afghanistan, 'is profitable to all parties, ... has consequences in the commercial ... the political, and above all military domains ... It seems to me that it would require enormous stupidity to sacrifice those gains in a few days' (*Le Monde*, 8 January 1980). In consequence, France, though admitting that Afghanistan 'constitutes a serious blow to the global character of détente', refused to be associated with any of the American reprisals such as economic sanctions or the 1980 Olympic Games boycott. These gestures of 'independence' were not very well received by Western public opinion in general, nor by many in France including the supporters of the President. He was accused of letting down the West and not being firm enough with the Soviet Union. However, he was able to get a substantial measure of agreement from Helmut Schmidt, the German Chancellor, whose country has also reaped substantial benefits from an Ostpolitik based on détente but is both more vulnerable than France to any deterioration in East–West relations and more closely tied to America in its defence. The other important source of approval for a French line that was distinct from that of America was the non-aligned countries – in particular India, which Giscard visited in January 1980, and the Islamic oil producing states which he also visited two months later.

The Afghanistan affair illustrates very well both the French policy on détente and also the way that the French government is not prevented by domestic, public, or party opinion from pursuing a grand design for increasing French influence in key parts of the world. In the early years of the Giscard presidency relations with the Soviet Union seemed rather cool. Although Giscard had welcomed Brezhnev to Paris in December 1974, spoken of giving concrete meaning to détente at Helsinki in 1975, strewn flowers on Lenin's tomb in October 1975 and declared in interviews at home the following month that France was the sole embodiment of détente in Europe and that détente not confrontation was its policy (*Le Figaro*, 12 November 1975), France was considered to have become more 'Atlanticist'. However, as the presidency has continued, Giscard d'Estaing has become more and more 'Gaullist' in insisting on an 'independent' stance in East–West relations and more and more exposed to the accusation, levelled against de Gaulle, that France was making diplomatic gains by acting as a 'free-rider' on its Western partners' reluctance to upset, by sanctioning France, a 'delicately balanced framework which guarantees collective security and collective prosperity' (Wallace and Paterson, 1978, p. 38).

The policy of détente is related closely to the contradictions of

Franco-US relations. Has France under Giscard d'Estaing become more 'Atlanticist'? The foreign policy of Giscard d'Estaing towards the United States and its Western allies is as ambivalent as was that of General de Gaulle. De Gaulle withdrew France from NATO, pursued an independent, indeed anti-American line over the Middle East and Vietnam, made war on the dollar with French gold reserves, but backed President Kennedy without reservation in the confrontation with the Soviet Union over Cuba in 1962. Giscard d'Estaing uses a more moderate language than de Gaulle, has developed in *sanctuarisation élargie* a defence policy that shows slightly more solidarity with NATO than before, but when in 1979–80 America had its back to the wall, in terms of trying to find an appropriate response to the seizure of its diplomats in Iran and to the Soviet occupation of Afghanistan, Giscard d'Estaing gave the distinct impression of putting French independence and French trade with the Soviet Union, not to mention Communist indulgence at the second ballot in 1981, a long way ahead of standing by his allies. The contrast with the loyalty of Chancellor Schmidt, who continued to have diplomatic encounters with Soviet leaders and who was prepared to be critical of American policy, is striking. Resentment of American power and fear of American domination are components of nationalism in France that one does not find in West Germany or Great Britain. A Frenchman who worked in the field of international relations, asked about solidarity with America at the time of the Afghanistan invasion, said to me 'solidarity means dependence'. In this fatuous remark is encapsulated twenty years of ambiguity and self-delusion.

With the non-aligned countries, Giscard d'Estaing has been as active and attentive as General de Gaulle. Making full use of the prestige of a presidential reception or visit, Giscard has travelled very widely, received innumerable heads of state in Paris and won a lot of goodwill in the Middle East, in Asia, in Africa and in Eastern Europe. In the early years of the presidency Egypt was, if one excludes the oil producing states, the main non-aligned country to be the object of French attentions. The Pompidou embargo on selling arms to Egypt was lifted with profitable results. However the Camp David arrangements for a bilateral pact between Egypt and Israel, underwritten by the United States, were contrary to French policy for a global solution in the Middle East though for Egypt they were a positive step with a more attractive partner. Chinese leaders Hua Guofeng and Deng Xiao-ping have been received in Paris and relations improved. Raymond Barre and, in re-election year like Nixon, Giscard d'Estaing visited Peking. However, as a sign that détente with the Soviet Union takes a higher priority in French eyes, Jean François-Poncet declared in the National Assembly on 3 May 1979: 'France has no intention of playing on the divergences between China and various other countries, notably the Soviet Union.' Pakistan was a privileged interlocutor for a time. The sale by France to Pakistan of a uranium re-processing plant (which could have a military application) was agreed but then in December 1976 suspended. Finally the two 'founder members' of the non-aligned club were visited. President Tito of Yugoslavia gave Giscard valuable support for his *mondialiste* diplomacy at a time – December 1976 – when the latter was receiving a lot of criticism from countries like Algeria for being 'imperialist'. Above all there was in January 1980 the visit to India, 'the most important non-aligned country' (television interview, 26 February 1980). Giscard d'Estaing was the first head of state to visit Mrs Gandhi after her re-election as Prime Minister. The French position on Afghanistan – opposed to the presence of Soviet troops but not prepared to support American measures like sanctions against the USSR and military aid for Pakistan – was much appreciated by India. Giscard's 'great idea' was, according to *Le Point* (28 January 1980), 'to develop with India the project for a "Third World way", equidistant from the two super powers, which would regroup Algeria, Yugoslavia, India, all the "true" non-aligned countries, plus certain Europeans'. Fanciful perhaps, but very much in the de Gaulle tradition of 'independent' grand designs.

Relations with Islam in general and with the Arab oil producing states in particular have been marked by a progressively closer alignment with Arab views on the Palestine question. France is totally dependent on imported oil and, although its nuclear power stations are growing rapidly in number, has at present little in the way of energy alternatives. Almost 80 per cent comes from Arab countries and 66 per cent from Iraq and Saudi Arabia. There have been attempts to diversify sources of supply. Some comes from Mexico (visited by Giscard in 1979), the Soviet Union (more than from Iran, according to the Foreign Minister – *Le Monde* 8 January 1980),

Nigeria, or Venezuela. The stability of Arab countries and French trade and relations with them remain the main preoccupations for France. Furthermore, the enormous increases in the price of oil during the 1970s set the French economy and balance of payments a major problem. France responded to the challenge by an immense effort to improve relations with oil producing countries, to sell them high technology in the form of industrial and transport development, armaments, or nuclear power stations. Iran, Iraq and Saudi Arabia were the main interlocutors. France was not alone in paying effusive attentions to the Shah of Iran and, despite serving as a refuge in exile for the Ayatollah, not alone in suffering the economic consequences of his downfall.

A pro-Arab policy in the Middle East is nothing new for France. After the Six Day War in which Israel, armed with French bombers, moved quickly to pre-empt an Arab strike and occupied Sinai, the West Bank of the Jordan and the Golan Heights on the Syrian border, General de Gaulle condemned Israeli aggression and placed an embargo on arms sales. France had the advantage of being the only Western country where public opinion would swallow such a dish. Giscard d'Estaing came to power in 1974 reputed to be much more sympathetic to Israel, and indeed the arms embargo (to everyone in the Middle East) was quickly lifted. However, as early as October 1974 France voted in favour of representation at the United Nations for the Palestine Liberation Organisation (PLO). Foreign Minister Sauvagnargues met the PLO leader Arafat, and Giscard declared at a press conference (24 October 1974) that the Palestinians were not just refugees (as described in the UN resolution 242 of 1967) but a 'people' with 'a natural aspiration . . . to have their own fatherland'. French policy has kept to that line ever since: the problem of Palestine was a reality, not a French invention, as Sauvagnargues told the Israelis in November 1974. In October 1975 the PLO was authorised to open a Paris office. In January 1977 there was the Abu Daoud affair, to which reference will be made in the chapter on justice and civil liberties, in which an arrested Arab terrorist was obligingly taken to the airport and sent off to an Arab destination after the hasty rejection of West German and Israeli demands for his extradition.

France's willingness to act as a policeman of stability in Africa, as demonstrated by the 1978 intervention in Zaïre, was much appreciated by the nervous feudal monarchs of Islam who began in the late 1970s to feel threatened by the tremors of Muslim dissent and revolution. France has a vital interest in the stability of regimes in the Persian Gulf and is contributing to a growing extent to their defence. Tanks and missiles have been supplied to Saudi Arabia and counter-insurgency training which, according to the pro-Giscardian weekly *Le Point* (28 January 1980), proved its effectiveness in the rebel occupation of the Mosque at Mecca. The same journal (1 October 1979) reports French installation of an electronic system for border protection in Iraq. *Le Nouvel Observateur* (12 March 1980) quotes a French government minister comparing France's energy position to 'balancing on a tightrope'. Another rebellion, this time successful, in Mecca, and the wire breaks. 'The stability of the Gulf regimes is a question of survival for France.'

In March 1980, in another bid to secure stability, came the famous Giscard d'Estaing visit to the emirs and the kings in the Gulf states in which he put forward a new plan for a solution to the conflicts in the Middle East. 'Giscard of Arabia', as the *Corriere della Sera* ironically called him (11 March), began to reap the fruits of his various diplomatic offensives: regarded as independent from the superpowers, with the support of powerful states like West Germany, India and Saudi Arabia, his proposals, which contained nothing he had not been saying since 1974, had a considerable impact: that the Palestinians had the right to a country of their own, that Israel had a right to be recognised and guaranteed frontiers but that it could never have peaceful relations with its neighbours if it continued to occupy captured territory, that the Palestinians represented by the PLO should be a party to negotiations, and that the outcome should be guaranteed (this was a new idea) by the five permanent members of the UN Security Council – the United States, USSR, China, Great Britain and France. The difficult word Jerusalem was not pronounced. Nor was that of Afghanistan which had not exactly contributed to a climate of confidence between the great powers. The Giscard initiative became a European Community peace plan at the Venice Euro-Summit of June 1980, a good example of the skilful use of diplomatic resources and of the European dimension in Giscardian diplomacy.

There is of course more to French *mondialiste* foreign policy than this brief survey has covered. There is the active role in Africa which will be examined in the next chapter. There is summitry. Giscard has had frequent meetings with Presidents Ford and Carter. At Puerto Rico in 1976 and in Guadaloupe (on French territory) in 1979 there were summit talks between the United States, Great Britain, West Germany and France and further seven-nation summits in Tokyo (the same four plus Canada, Japan and Italy) the same year and in Venice in 1980. In May 1980, with Soviet troops still occupying Afghanistan, Giscard d'Estaing accepted a dramatic invitation to a personal meeting with Brezhnev in Warsaw. Once again Giscard was accused by Western opinion generally of putting French prestige above Western solidarity and allowing Brezhnev, who made not a single concession, to appear in the guise of a peacemaker. What does it all amount to? By pursuing an 'independent' and *mondialiste* foreign policy, taking no risk with its security, France may infuriate its allies but obtains some prestige and, in a world where trade is awarded by dictatorships from political considerations, some tangible economic benefits. Furthermore a grandiloquent foreign policy is undoubtedly part of the expectation that the French public has come to have, and constitutes an adhesive for French national unity and the legitimacy of the presidency.

CHAPTER 6

Foreign Policy and Defence
II : Europe and Africa

The brief survey of France's world-presence approach omitted the two areas of the world, Europe and Africa, which have a special place in French policy. Both have been the arena for spectacular initiatives during the Giscard presidency. In Europe the main themes, apart from a continued and rather unyielding defence of national economic interest, have been the development of a very close Franco-German relationship amounting almost to a co-directorate of the European Community, the fulfilment of Giscard's idea of regular European summit meetings where the big European questions can be discussed, and the progress towards monetary union through the launching of the EMS (European Monetary System). In Africa the main preoccupations have been to prevent 'destabilisation', to protect supplies of raw materials and to promote that strange cultural entity *la Francophonie*.

Franco-German Europe

Franco-German relations have become the centrepiece of French diplomacy under Giscard d'Estaing. From the rapprochement in the early 1960s effected by General de Gaulle and Adenauer, West Germany has passed in French eyes, to quote *Le Figaro* (7 June 1979) 'from hereditary enemy to hereditary friend'. The path of this development has to some extent been influenced by personal relationships. Pompidou was claimed to be somewhat suspicious of Germany and to prefer Edward Heath to Chancellor Schmidt. In recent years the relationship between Giscard d'Estaing and Helmut Schmidt, both former finance ministers, both technocrats, both liberal in outlook, who became leaders of their respective countries almost on the same day in May 1974, has been an important factor. Their first overseas visits as leader were to each other's countries. They meet frequently, they dine frequently, they talk frequently (in English) on the telephone. Gradually, as *The Economist* put it (26 May 1979), the rest of Europe has come to 'march to the tune of France and West Germany'. The outward aura of Europe's leading statesman belongs to Giscard d'Estaing – a role he could not have assumed if Willy Brandt had remained in power. 'Schmidt likes it that way' because 'Germany dare not be too assertive . . . Close co-operation between Europe's Siamese twins', concludes *The Economist*, 'makes so much sense that the relationship must be seen as permanent.'

The two countries have many interests in common. They are above all each other's principal trade partners, indeed 20 per cent of all French exports go to West Germany. They have suffered greatly in the last hundred years from wars with each other. They both give emphasis to détente, France because of the fiction that its security is related to independent arrangements with the Soviet Union, West Germany because it is more vulnerable than anybody else to an increase of East–West tension. The last few years have brought a considerable increase in the ties between the two countries. Apart from the personal relationship of the two leaders, there are regular six-monthly working meetings, increasing routine contact between ministries and exchanges of civil servants for training periods and of journalists. The 1963 treaty between France and West Germany established a co-ordinator in each foreign ministry to supervise the development of all these links. On the cultural side, the Office Franco-Allemande pour la Jeunesse, which had a budget in 1978 of 54 million francs, claims to have promoted 4 million youth exchanges in fifteen years. There is also a strong bilateral policy of increasing the teaching of each other's languages in schools. The French are able to play an effective part in this struggle against the imperialism of the English language by the neat if authoritarian device of assigning German as a subject for the academic top stream in a growing number of schools. When parents complain, they are told they have a choice: if their child wants to learn English he can go into a lower class!

West Germany does not feel the need for domestic purposes to conduct attention-seeking diplomacy. Furthermore, for historical reasons, and for reasons connected with Soviet fears of German assertiveness, West Germany is happy to take an apparently junior role in the Franco-German partnership and a quiet but effective role on the world stage generally. West Germany has in reality far more weight economically, financially and technologically than its partner. Brandt's Ostpolitik eclipsed by far in importance any diplomatic initiative the French, even under de Gaulle, have ever taken in relation to the Soviet bloc. If the German Chancellor were to emulate French diplomacy around the world, and start airlifting paratroops into trouble spots, cries of genuine alarm would be heard on all sides. Similarly if, as by far the strongest partner in the EEC, the Germans gave the impression of trying to lead the Community, anxieties would be aroused. Giscard d'Estaing has also, at least until the Afghanistan crisis, greatly helped the Germans by no longer playing the Jobert game of trying to force them to choose between Paris and Washington. Germany would like more Franco-German co-operation on defence matters and particularly for the French tactical nuclear weapons to be moved to its eastern border. This Giscard has refused to do for the declared reason that the Soviet Union would consider it provocative.

The arrangements suit the French well too. A Giscard d'Estaing initiative, backed by West Germany, has more weight than a French initiative on its own. Bilateral agreements on a common position before EEC meetings give France powerful support in the defence of its interests. There is the advantage of growing co-operation in the technological and military fields. France and Germany have co-operated with great success on the Rhine–Rhone canal project, the Airbus, the Ariane rocket and space-lab programme, and fast breeder nuclear reactors. The French are touchy about co-operation in certain sensitive areas, especially nuclear re-processing, where France is technologically ahead of its partner in the nuclear fuel cycle and resolved to stay so. The commitment to make France as strong economically as the redoubtable West Germans is the heart of Giscard's ambition for France. It is a theme to which he returns constantly, almost obsessively, in his speeches. Monetary policy, notably the creation of the European Monetary System, and economic policy centre on the attempt to reduce inflation to the German rate, to link the franc to the Deutsch Mark, to achieve *parallèlisme* with

German economic development. Giscard has even expressed the aim (2 May 1976) of having as big an army as West Germany.

Walter Scheel, in his first official visit abroad as President of the Federal Republic, spoke in April 1976 of the 'irreversible character' of Franco-German reconciliation. There have been tangible results during the Giscard presidency in technological and monetary co-operation and in the harmonisation of foreign policy over a number of issues like the crisis in Cyprus, the Middle East, the question of enlargement of the European Community and a joint agreement not to export nuclear re-processing plants. At frequent Franco-German summits important co-operative ventures are broached, from nuclear development to a joint approach to combat terrorism. The two partners feel, with some justification given the virtual absence from the scene of Great Britain, that in the words of the communiqué after their February 1977 meeting, they must take initiatives to 'resume the march towards monetary and economic union, obligatory stage in the road to European Union'. France and the Federal Republic, said Giscard d'Estaing on 7 February 1978, 'never forgot that they had in their charge to a great extent the progress of Europe'.

As far as Europe generally is concerned, the proclaimed ambition of President Giscard d'Estaing is for Europe to recover the influence in the world it used to have. Hence the attempts to secure a joint European Community view on world problems like energy or the Middle East or the Soviet intervention in Afghanistan. The trouble with the achievement of this noble aim is that the French themselves frequently find it to their advantage to demonstrate their independence. Hence the Europeans are either invited to follow along and join in some spectacular French initiative, as in the Middle East in 1980, or simply ignored. The French insisted on voting for PLO representation at the UN in 1974. Despite German entreaties for a common European recognition of the new People's Republic of Angola, France, flying to the aid of victory, acted independently. The French preferred the spectacular and leading part in the Zaïre military intervention of 1978 to joint action with Belgium, the European country most involved. The French and the British have been unwilling to reduce their own diplomatic missions in favour of joint European Community missions. This was proposed for the newly independent Portuguese Guinea but rejected by France. There has been the preference for 'independence' over a co-operative approach to European defence. Alfred Grosser (*Le Monde*, 10 April 1979) quoted a cartoon in the German press which over the caption 'Europe must speak with a single voice' showed a picture of the French cockerel crying 'moi, moi, moi'.

The general view of Giscard d'Estaing on a confederal rather than a federal approach to European integration, leaving the nation-states as separate entities, was discussed in the chapter on the President's ideas. This approach, based on close co-operation between sovereign states, has been pursued during his period of office. The greatest innovation has been the regular summit meetings, invented by Giscard and called the European Council; this meets every four months, normally in the capital of whichever country occupies the rotating presidency of the Council of Ministers. The main political problems, like British renegotiations or the plans for European Parliament elections, are on the agenda for the European Council, which has become the top-level decision-making institution in the Community. The launching in 1979 of the European Monetary System (EMS) which links the national currencies to a European currency unit (ECU) and to each other was an important initiative in which Giscard d'Estaing played a big part. The French also played a diplomatic part in persuading the Irish and the Italians to come into the system even if the British stayed out, and then held up the start of the system until Germany made some concessions on agricultural *montants compensatoires*. On day-to-day community issues France, like Great Britain, adopts a nationalist rather than a *communautaire* standpoint. When in 1975 there were demonstrations by wine-growers in the South of France, France suspended imports of Italian wine. The EEC commission tried to sort out a compromise so that France would not be arraigned before the European Court of Justice. It failed, and in September the Chirac government put an illegal and still unsanctioned tax of 11 per cent on Italian wine imports. The same thing happened over the 'lamb war' with Great Britain in 1979. The French embargo on imports of British lamb were held to be illegal by the Court of Justice but the embargo remained. The French were also the most intransigent opponents of concessions to British complaints about the Community Budget. Despite all this, Europe, and the relationship with West Germany in particular, remains at the centre of French diplomacy and economic activity.

Africa

The Importance of Africa

If the close relationship with West Germany is one good example of President Giscard d'Estaing developing a de Gaulle policy, French policy in Africa during the Giscard presidency provides another. France had, like Germany and Great Britain, an extensive empire in Africa. According to Stanley Hoffman (1974, pp. 19–20), 'no economic drive explains the spread of French colonialism'. It was 'an empire acquired as a means towards rank and as a way of spreading France's universal values rather than as a source of wealth'. After independence was granted to the former colonies in the early 1960s, great importance was attached to the maintenance of French influence there. Under General de Gaulle there was always something of a cloak-and-dagger air about the way this influence was exercised through the intermediary of Jacques Foccart, the Secretary General for African and Madagascar Affairs, attached to the Elysée Palace. Pompidou retained the services of Foccart, while Giscard d'Estaing dismissed Foccart but appointed Foccart's deputy René Journiac as adviser on African affairs in his *cabinet*. When Journiac was killed in an air-crash in Africa in 1980 another former business associate of Foccart, Judge Martin Kirsch, was named as his successor. Africa under Giscard d'Estaing has been a personal presidential domain just as it was under de Gaulle. There are personal links between the President and the Francophone heads of state like Bongo of Gabon, or Houphouët-Boigny of Ivory Coast, and the lines of communication go direct through the *cabinet* at the Elysée. A good deal of secrecy surrounds the policies and the budgets involved. Whatever the means employed, France has managed to retain a paternalistic relationship with most of its former African colonies. Indeed, granting independence has been described as 'the pursuit of colonisation by other means': Michel Debré when Prime Minister wrote to President Bongo's predecessor in Gabon in 1960 that 'independence is given on condition that, once independent, the state commits itself to respect the co-operation agreements previously signed'. France dominates the overseas trade of its former colonies, develops their raw materials, gives them financial and military aid, sends them teachers and *coopérants*, and on occasion removes their leaders and appoints new ones. One reason is that many of these states are small or very poor like Chad or the Central African Republic. Another is that France, to its great credit, did much more than other colonising European powers to assimilate native elites. Leaders like Houphouët-Boigny or Senghor of Senegal, for example, were ministers in the French government before their own countries became independent, and are still listed in *Who's Who in France*. Another reason is that *coopération* – the key word in French African policy – means much more than just aid; it represents as well a whole host of technical and military agreements under which French troops on a number of occasions have been available to restore order or prevent a *coup d'état*.

Africa is important to France for a number of reasons, political, cultural and economic. France's direct historical links with so many Third World states are an important dimension of its claim to a *mondialiste* role in international affairs, an opportunity for France to demonstrate its generosity and efficacy as a partner, and a source of valuable support in international bodies like the Organisation for African Unity or the United Nations. The promotion of the French language is an extremely important theme in French foreign policy and *Francophonie*, a cultural entity of all French-speaking peoples, only has real substance as a concept because so much of Africa is Francophone. Economically, Africa is becoming, in the words of Guy Georgy, Director of African Affairs at the Quai d'Orsay (*Afrique contemporaine*, March/April 1975, p. 5) 'more and more indispensable in Europe which depends largely for its industrial activity on its imports of energy products and raw materials. Africa will be, more and more, the privileged supplier of France and Europe, for its riches are immense and still relatively unexploited.' These riches include uranium, cobalt and oil – strategic materials the supply of which is a central French preoccupation. Readers will recall that among the missions for the armed forces quoted earlier were the countering of any threat to stability in the Third World or to the indispensable sea-traffic of supplies. Indeed, largely for this purpose the French maintain a considerable naval presence in the Indian Ocean with, eventually, carrier-based tactical nuclear weapons. General Méry, the military voice of President Giscard d'Estaing, declared in a speech to the IHEDN Defence Studies Institute on 3 May 1978 that the security of France was closely tied to the security of Africa: it was near French territory (especially French territories in the Indian Ocean), 260,000 Frenchmen were working in Africa, and supply routes for oil and vital raw materials pass very close to the coast of Africa. Africa is an important source of trade today – 20 per cent of French exports (not counting exports to South Africa) – but a source of anxiety for the future. A French background report for UNCTAD and other international conferences in 1979 analysed the threat to the French and other industrial economies of the industrialisation of the Third World (see *West Africa*, 28 May 1979). By 1985 3–7 per cent of French workers in total could be affected and in some regions, in a way reminiscent of the decline of the Lancashire cotton industry in Great Britain, the figure could reach 40 per cent. Hence the French need to guide economic development as much as possible in the Third World, especially where France has influence.

The essential steps by which France, under the leadership of Giscard d'Estaing, has sought to implement an active African policy have included proposals for a Europe-African-Arab 'trialogue', a summit conference to supplement the North–South dialogue which he suggested at the Franco-African congress at Kigali in May 1979, repeated Franco-African conferences attended personally by the President, and considerable support in both financial and military terms for co-operation. France gives about 0·6 per cent of its gross national product in official aid (the highest figure in Europe after the Netherlands and the Scandinavian countries) and has accepted the UN target of 0·7 per cent (Giscard speech, Franco-African congress, 10 May 1976). In cash terms in 1979 this represented some 14 billion francs although the total outflow of resources which would include other investments and loans is, on the basis of the 1976 figures, twice this sum or 1·5 per cent of GNP. The main agencies for development assistance are the Fonds d'Aide et de Coopération (FAC) which is under the control of the Ministry of Co-operation, and the Caisse Centrale de Coopération Economique (CCCE) which handles FAC and other funds. FAC contributes to technical assistance, teaching and education, military co-operation and infrastructure loans. Since a report by Pierre Abelin, Minister of Co-operation, in 1975, French aid has switched from direct help for infrastructure (schools, roads, dams, and so on) to what President Giscard d'Estaing called (Yaoundé, 9 February 1979) 'co-operation of reciprocal interests', which means investment, in conjunction with private and nationalised companies, in industrial development. This finance is organised through CCCE which is a public enterprise but acts like a bank, on a commercial basis with considerable autonomy. Its directors include leading figures from the French banking and industrial sectors (public and private) and the state is represented by the director of the Société Française de Matériel d'Armement (SOFMA) (*Le Monde*, 18 December 1979). In 1979 it loaned 1·7 billion francs, much of it (called the second *guichet*) confined to bilateral or international projects in the most advanced African economies. Half of all CCCE credits go to major French companies or their subsidiaries – often old West Africa trading companies like the Société Commerciale Ouest-Africaine (*West Africa*, 12 March, 1978), and nearly two-thirds go to four countries, Senegal, Ivory Coast, Gabon and Cameroon, which are France's most reliable allies in Africa. Two examples in Cameroon were 120 million francs (in partnership with Elf-Aquitaine, Shell, Mobil and the Cameroon government) for a large oil refinery and 130 million francs to the aluminium producing subsidiary of Pechiney-Ugine-Kuhlmann which is Cameroon's top export-earner. *West Africa* waspishly concludes its article on 'Co-operation French-style' by describing CCCE as 'a means by which France profits from and dictates the nature of political and economic development within favoured African states'. The development of a more multilateral approach to co-operation, for example, the links between Africa and the EEC (Yaoundé Convention, 1963, Lomé Convention, 1974 and 1980) has not affected France's privileged position in the African monetary system – where the former French colonies in black Africa use as their currency the CFA franc (Franco-African Community) tied to the French currency, and French privileged access is guaranteed under defence agreements to strategic raw materials such as oil, uranium, or beryllium. These agreements provide for priority sales to France and embargoes to other countries if required (Pierre Lellouche and Dominique Moiss in *International Security*, Spring 1979, p. 116).

Military intervention

The word that links the economic to the military aspects of co-operation, and offers the best introduction to an understanding of Giscard's African policy, is destabilisation. What worries France, as other powers, is a breakdown of existing political and economic arrangements in any region of the world where vital supplies or other interests might be affected. The Soviet-Cuban penetration of Africa was seen as a threat to stability and, if continued, to France's African clients and hence to French interests. Giscard d'Estaing is also keenly aware that African destabilisation has economic consequences: in a speech at the Franco-African conference of 22 May 1978 he urged that 'we must all today harden our determination and our policies to face up to the uncertainties and risks of the world economy'. This determination is closely linked to the new emphasis in Giscardian defence policy, discussed above, which concentrates on mobile conventional forces in an unstable world.

France maintains quite a large military presence in and around Africa, the greatest after Cuba, in fact, with, according to *Le Nouvel Observateur* (22 May 1978), some 14,000 troops. Over half of these are in French territories in the Indian Ocean (Réunion, Mayotte) or Djibouti which became independent only in 1977. However, there is an important base at Dakar (Senegal), contingents in the other Francophone countries, and (according to *West Africa*, 14 May, 1979) recent agreements to build bases near the uranium mines in Gabon and Central African Republic. The first 'layer' of defence in any incident is supposed to be the national army of the African state (trained and equipped by France). If that fails – and in the three main areas for French intervention since 1974, Mauritania, Chad and Zaïre, it failed very badly indeed – then the second or third layers, French troops in Africa and if necessary, the *forces d'intervention extérieures*, French troops from France, are brought in. Mauritania, a vast area of the Western Sahara in which France has important economic interests in iron ore mining, has been involved since 1975 in a war on its own territory and the adjacent former Spanish Sahara with a movement called the Polisario Front or, as it became more organised and more successful, the Sahari Popular Liberation Army. Another ally of France, Morocco, which under the rule of King Hassan II, has been a firm supporter of France at the OAU and a participant in French military interventions in Zaïre, is also locked in conflict with the Polisario Front, and despite the use of Mirage F1 bombers, had lost ground. France gave open support to Mauritania and Morocco in 1977 and 1978 by sending in its 'second layer' – Jaguar strike aircraft from Dakar – against the Polisario guerillas. The Polisario Front had not made itself popular in France by holding some French hostages for over two years. The Front, however, continued to make military and diplomatic gains, winning the support of an increasing number of radical states, notably Algeria, whose relations with France were not good, which had blocked a number of important French contracts and which denounced all French actions in the African continent as imperialism. In July 1978, despite the presence of French military advisers, the Mauritanian President Ould Daddah was overthrown by an army *coup d'état*, and the new government signed a ceasefire with the Polisario Front. The French position rapidly changed, a solution acceptable to all was called for, and a government minister even suggested that small nations like the Saharis had the right to form their own state (1 March 1979). Help to Morocco was scaled down by both France and the United States who declined to supply military aircraft. In parallel to all this, relations with Algeria rapidly improved and France was awarded a big gas liquefication contract. So France extricated itself quite skilfully from a military failure.

In Chad, another vast and impoverished part of the Sahara Desert south of Libya, and a former French colony, French troops have often intervened to help the government when it was facing disorder. The large French contingent of troops and advisers was withdrawn when President Tombalbaye was overthrown in 1975, intervened again in 1978 at the request of the new provisional government and tried to impose a reconciliation between an incredible profusion of secessionist factions. The northern secessionists managed to make the French government look ridiculous by the kidnap of a French ethnologist Mme Claustre and her husband whom they kept for three years, despite repeated occasions on which France handed over ransom in terms of military equipment and over 10 million francs in cash. One French intermediary was butchered before the hostages were finally released in February 1977. The ransom money was subsequently used to pay the troops of the 'Armed Forces of the North' (*Le Monde*, 13 February 1980) an important component of the instability in Chad. In 1980 the French contingent of 1,200 was still there with the mission of separating rival Chad armies and evacuating European residents.

The French military intervention in September 1978 in the Central African Empire − hastily renamed Republic − was probably the most unashamedly imperialist (and the most redolent with farce) of the Giscard presidency. Central Africa (formerly Oubangi Chari) is very poor except for its diamond mines (twelfth largest producer in the world) and its virtually unexploited 8,000 tons of uranium reserves. The emperor, formerly colonel, formerly corporal, Bokassa, had overthrown President Dacko in 1966, had himself crowned at France's expense in a festival of unparalleled vulgarity in 1977, enjoyed French (and Zaïre) military help to put down a rebellion in January 1979, basked in the warmth of frequent personal contacts with his 'dear relation' Valéry Giscard d'Estaing and distributed, so it is alleged, gifts of diamonds to various highly placed persons in the French government including the present head of state. In mid-1979, however, he began to lose favour in Paris. Stories began to emerge, at first denied by the French government, of the emperor's personal involvement in the massacre of some schoolchildren, even of cannibalism. He is even said to have hit René Journiac, sent by Giscard d'Estaing to persuade him to abdicate, with his gold-topped cane. On 20 September 'Operation Barracuda' brought in several hundred French troops and the former President Dacko. Dacko was installed in power. Bokassa fled to France, of all places, where he claimed right of entry as a French citizen. After twenty-four hours on the airstrip at Evreux this was refused, and he was sent to the obliging Ivory Coast. The operation was bloodless, rapid and successful. However 'while most countries in Africa have welcomed the overthrow of Bokassa', said *West Africa* (1 October 1979), 'there has also been an outcry against the blatant role of France in the affair'. Furthermore it was not easy for France to protest too loudly when the Soviet Union, though much more brutally, did the same thing a few months later in Afghanistan.

The most spectacular instance of French military intervention in Africa, and the one which best illustrates the President's approach to the problem of destabilisation, is the paratroop mission to Kolwezi in Zaïre in May 1978. Zaïre is not in France's traditional sphere of influence in Africa since it belonged before independence to Belgium. However, because it is French-speaking, it is not considered outrageous, by France at any rate, for France to take an interest. Zaïre is a country of vast potential riches – it produces 60 per cent of the world's cobalt, is a huge producer of copper and important in diamonds, tin, manganese, silver and gold. It is governed by a corrupt dictatorship under General Mobutu who in 1963 successfully prevented the secession of the mineral producing Katanga Province. Zaïre's debts to the International Monetary Fund are prodigious but its importance to the West as a pro-Western regime and as a producer of essential raw materials have earned it repeated salvation from collapse. It is in Zaïre that a West German firm called OTRAG, to the consternation of the Soviet Union and East Germany, is developing and testing private enterprise satellite-launching rockets.

The first French intervention, at the request of Mobutu, was in April 1977. French Transall transport aircraft airlifted Moroccan soldiers and equipment to put down an armed rebellion in the old Katanga Province, now called Shaba. The following year the rebels crossed the border from pro-Soviet Angola once again. Once again the Zaïre army was put to flight. The town of Kolwezi, where a lot of Europeans who work in the mining industry live, was occupied. The rebels, apparently popular with the native Kolwezi population (*Herald Tribune*, 21 August 1978; *Le Nouvel Observateur*, 29 May 1978), began looting and killing in European residential quarters. French paratroops were sent in directly from their base in Corsica, with the help of American C141 transporters, with the mission to safeguard lives of French and foreign residents. Order was quickly restored and the rebels melted back into the jungle. Belgian troops, originally intended to go in with the French, were upstaged and arrived to play a secondary role a day later. Belgium was annoyed. The Foreign Minister Simmonet complained that France was 'trying to maintain points of support on the black continent while Belgium wants co-operation with a country not just a regime'. The Flemish press denounced French imperialism. The French expedition, however, was brilliantly executed, was concluded by a speedy and exemplary French withdrawal, was popular among French public opinion largely because of the mission's humanitarian aspects graphically depicted on television, aroused a certain amount of rather envious admiration from other Western countries like Great Britain, and deeply impressed the Saudis as it was no doubt intended to do.

Welcoming African heads of state a few days later on 22 May, Giscard d'Estaing was able to feel proud of a 'gesture of solidarity' to Africa. The Zaïre action, he explained to the French people, had had three wider objectives: to stabilise Africa, to prove that France had the capacity to act and to give confidence to French citizens working abroad. The weakness of the French position in the long run is that to fly to the assistance of regimes that are detested by their populations may only give destabilisation a brief postponement, and may lead to overextended and ultimately doomed military involvements.

Aspects of Africa: South Africa, Ivory Coast, Algeria

This section on Africa concludes with a brief survey of French policy in three countries which each illustrate aspects of the President's *mondialiste* grand design: South Africa, Ivory Coast and Algeria. The first reveals how adroit the French have been at keeping economic and political interests apart and maintaining freedom of action in Africa. Predominant influence with Francophone countries has been preserved all the time that France was the primary supplier of military equipment to South Africa, and incidentally a persistent and unrepentant breaker of sanctions in Rhodesia. As a reward for such reliability, and despite the announcement a year earlier that the supply of arms was to cease, France received a South African contract for two nuclear power stations in 1976. Some notice, at last, began to be taken by African countries. The OAU condemned 'the alliance of mercantilism and imperialism'. The African National Council in South Africa declared that 'France has become the most dangerous enemy of the African continent'. Even the President of Cameroon in Paris in July 1976 denounced all states with links with South Africa. The conference of non-aligned states the following month called for an oil embargo on France for violating UN sanctions on arms supply to South Africa. In October the existence of South African submarine orders and the following year of other vessels from France were revealed. In October 1976 France vetoed a UN resolution condemning South Africa. In August 1977 the French Foreign Minister de Guiringaud, considering the dignity of France was affronted by angry demonstrations in Tanzania protesting at France's South African policy, cut short his visit to Dar es Salaam. For a state wanting influence in Africa it was time to change policy. In March 1978 de Guiringaud announced in Nigeria that 'French policy with regard to Pretoria is now straightforward and clear'. The politics of sport provided the first tangible sign of change. Adroitly protecting itself from the fate of New Zealand, which faced a major African boycott at the 1976 Olympics on account of its sporting contacts with South Africa, the French government in 1979 with no public debate or discussion refused visas to the South African rugby team.

The Ivory Coast is one of the most interesting examples of French *coopération* and the pearl of *Francophonie*. It is probably the fastest growing of the new African economies. Development has been successful, peaceful and sustained, and mainly in agriculture. It is the leading producer of coffee in Africa and the world's third largest cocoa-grower. These products represent two-thirds of exports, France being the leading trade partner. Animated by no nationalistic rancour, respected by other African leaders, President Houphouët-Boigny has willingly accepted French co-operation in development and his country has become the model of stability and progress in Africa. Forty-five thousand French people live in the Ivory Coast; 25,000 work in the private sector and 6,000 in the public sector, including 3,700 French teachers and other co-operative aid project workers. The national language is French – other languages are 'dialects'. Along with the rest of the reliable four, Senegal, Gabon and Cameroon, Ivory Coast has not been 'subservient to any Parisian diktat' but 'there has been a remarkably consistent coincidence of policy between them and Paris in international and African matters' (*West Africa*, 2 July 1979). The Ivory Coast has even been a moderate on South Africa, advocating 'dialogue' and refuelling its aircraft. A model for Africa in every way, it is a peaceful country, single-party but without political prisoners, with less urban crime than in other big African cities. The main road from Abidjan airport into town is the avenue Giscard d'Estaing.

The history of relations between France and Algeria is cyclical in form, alternating between periods of denouncing French imperialism and periods of rediscovered Franco-Algerian friendship. The jewel of the French Empire, Algeria, before independence came after a cruel and lengthy war in 1962, had over a million French settlers. The first few years of the Giscard d'Estaing presidency were a period of cool, even stormy relations. There had been problems over trade. France dominated the Algerian economy until Algeria nationalised the foreign oil companies in 1971, and France reduced its imports of wine and oil from Algeria. In 1978 France bought only 3 per cent of its oil from its former colony. In April 1975 Giscard d'Estaing made the first visit by a French President to Algeria since independence, but events in the Western Sahara where French military and diplomatic weight was deployed on the side of Mauritania and Morocco prevented any improvement in relations. In 1976 contracts for French industry stopped, posters were put up urging 'don't buy French', and America, a large purchaser of oil, became Algeria's largest trading partner. French 'imperialist' interventions in Africa were not the only aspect of French policy to which Algeria objected. There was the problem of the 800,000 Algerian immigrants in France. Algerians live in the worst housing, do the most unpleasant jobs and are occasionally subject to incidents of racial violence in France. In addition, as unemployment rose, the French government restricted immigration, suspended the entry rights of families of immigrant workers, announced that residence certificates, even the large number of ten-year permits granted nearly ten years before, would not be renewed, and offered 10,000-franc inducements for immigrants to return home. In 1978 and 1979 efforts were made to improve relations and a lot happened: France ended her opposition to the desire of the Western Saharis for a homeland; France began to get contracts again – especially the Arzew gas liquefication project; there was progress on a deal to supply 5 billion cubic metres of natural gas to France; and France compromised on the compulsory return of immigrants by giving an extension to the expiring long-term residence certificates. In January 1980 there was a successful visit to Paris by the Algerian Foreign Minister Benyahia. Working groups were established to deal with outstanding differences, notably on immigration. Above all, account was taken of the changed international situation. Algeria, always considered one of the hard-line pro-Soviet Third World countries, did not support the USSR intervention in Afghanistan. This opened the way for her to return, with India, to being part of the Giscard grand design for a common approach by non-aligned countries to important world problems like the Middle East, where France intended to proclaim the rights of the Palestinians. Consequently in the most important of all the Francophone countries on the African continent the 1980s began with a recovery of French influence.

French policy in Africa under President Giscard d'Estaing has illustrated all the aspects of his *mondialiste* approach. There is the preoccupation with stability, particularly where the supply of vital raw materials is concerned. There is the determination to preserve French influence, prestige and cultural *rayonnement*, particularly in the privileged relations with Francophone states. To help maintain French influence, prestige and vital interests there is the self-confident assumption of a military role. There is the rhetoric of humanitarian liberalism, and the adroit management of economic interests, both of which contribute to the capacity to make rapid changes of policy as in Algeria and South Africa. Above all, there is the President's freedom to practise 'the solitary exercise of power' for which he once criticised General de Gaulle. The direct personal dealings between Giscard d'Estaing and African heads of state resemble those of renaissance monarchs. Military actions, diplomatic changes of policy, covert influence exerted through advisers on African policy in the President's *cabinet*, can be decided personally without any public discussion and without generating severe political pressure from public opinion or Parliament or interest group mobilisation of the kind that has made policy on South Africa or Rhodesia so much more difficult for successive British governments. The officially proclaimed policy of France towards Africa is: 'Africa must be left to the Africans, outside the struggles for world hegemony. The only exception is in the help for which its task of development calls.' The fact that those remarks were made in Gabon, a country which does half of its trade with France and which relies on French military and technical assistance and which welcomed as French ambassador in 1980 not a diplomat but a former secret service agent and oil company executive (*Le Monde*, 19 December 1979) who had performed useful services to the Gabon government, underline that the exception is rather large.

Management of foreign affairs

As far as the management of foreign policy is concerned, Chapter 3 explained how advisers in the President's *cabinet* act as extensions of the Quai d'Orsay, or, in the case of Africa, of the Ministry of Co-operation. The really important decisions are taken after meetings of a *conseil restreint* attended by the

President, the Prime Minister, the Foreign Minister, any other minister specifically involved (like Agriculture when the question of the British contribution to the EEC budget was discussed in 1980) and a few senior officials such as the director of the Economic Division of the Quai d'Orsay. The functions of co-ordination and control fall largely to the interministerial committees under the direction of the Prime Minister. Leading examples are the Interministerial Committee for the Study and Export of War Materials to which the DGA (Délégation Générale à l'Armement) makes recommendations, and the one that deals with questions of European economic co-operation. This latter committee has a secretariat general (SGCI) with a staff of over a hundred. No French official may take any action in the EEC without the authorisation of SGCI.

As every paragraph of these two chapters has underlined, the economic dimension of foreign policy is becoming increasingly significant. The intimate relationship between a nation's economy and its foreign policy is becoming a more and more dominant characteristic of international affairs. First, overseas trade objectives or international agreements on agricultural prices, or supplies of oil and essential raw materials, are seen as ever more vital to stability, prosperity and economic activity at home. Secondly, in many international economic dealings the state is itself a principal actor – the trade in armaments or monetary affairs are obvious examples. Thirdly, economic power is the basis of an effective foreign policy. It is from economic strength that come the resources to support ambitious interventions, credible diplomatic initiatives, impressive military might and the high technology that it depends on. As Ernest Bevin once told a Labour Party conference in Great Britain: 'Give me another ton of coal and I will give you a foreign policy.' It is upon the success of Renault, Peugeot-Citroën, Dassault aviation, or of CEA and Framatome in nuclear technology that French pretensions to a world role depend, as well as so much at home. So the traditionally interventionist French state with its need for an active *mondialiste* foreign policy finds itself at one with the objectives of the giant French firms, private and nationalised. This interdependence of the political and the economic has been accentuated in recent years by various factors: the crisis in the Middle East and its effect on oil supplies and prices, the increasing tendency for economic competition to be competition between states each trying to preserve an internationally competitive champion in the important industrial sectors, and the growing propensity in the world for big contracts and trade deals to be awarded for political rather than strictly economic reasons.

The Directorate of Economic and Financial Affairs at the Quai d'Orsay is the main source of advice for the big worldwide and multilateral economic questions. It has sections dealing with commercial, financial and industrial matters, including armaments and the control of strategic products, economic co-operation in international organisations such as the OECD or the EEC, and general matters such as energy or minerals. A lot of other government departments too are involved in the economic sphere of foreign affairs – the Ministries of Industry, of Agriculture, of Overseas Trade, of Co-operation, to name but a few. One of the main actors is the Ministry of the Economy with its important directorates for External Economic Relations (trade relations and negotiations) and the International Affairs section of the Treasury Directorate (monetary matters, aid, etc.). When a number of ministries are involved the task of co-ordination falls to interministerial bodies like the SGCI.

A reorganisation of the Quai d'Orsay, carried out during the Giscard presidency, has to some extent recognised the growing interdependence of the 'economic' and the 'political'. The Economic Directorate, in addition to its responsibility for the big multilateral economic questions referred to above, and the Directorate of Political Affairs, in addition to such weighty matters as the Europe–Arab dialogue, disarmament, or atomic questions, both used to have their own 'geographical' sections dealing with different areas of the world. Now five geographic directorates have been created: African Affairs, Europe, Asia and Oceania, North Africa and Levant, and America. These have responsibility for both political and economic aspects of bilateral relations.

The other big aspect of French foreign policy (and another big directorate at the Quai d'Orsay) is cultural affairs. Most nations devote attention to cultural relations in their conduct of foreign policy because artistic and educational exchanges can generate goodwill. For France, however, the promotion of the French language and culture and the *rayonnement* of French civilisation occupy a central place in foreign relations. As with 'economic' affairs, and 'political' affairs, cultural concerns cannot be isolated from the others. French links through language, culture and history to former colonies and other parts of the world are held to be an important rationale for a *mondialiste* foreign policy. A certain French cultural nationalism is an important foreign policy element. *Francophonie* – the French-speaking world (made up for the most part of African countries in which only about 3 per cent of the population actually speak French) is regarded as a cultural, even a political entity, or at least as a zone of legitimate French influence. It is for France to intervene militarily in Chad or even Francophone Zaïre which was not a former French colony. It is for France to seek representation for the French-speaking minority, defeated at the polls, in the new state to emerge from the Anglo-French condominium in the Pacific Ocean of the New Hebrides. President Giscard d'Estaing may not have shouted 'Vive le Québec libre' from the balcony of Montreal town hall as General de Gaulle did in 1967, but he still continues the same policy of privileged relations with Quebec and aid and encouragement to separatist aspirations. The Prime Minister of Quebec is received in Paris like a visiting head of state. France continues to battle away in international bodies like the EEC or the United Nations to prevent the English language, or Anglo-American as the French sometimes call it, becoming the principal or sole international working language.

This rather aggressive aspect of French cultural foreign policy does not in fact flow from the Cultural Relations Directorate at the Quai d'Orsay. Francophone affairs, with their enormously important cultural but also economic and political connotations, come under a special section of the Political Directorate. Other departments are involved too. French dominance over its former African colonies, discussed at length earlier in this chapter, is exercised mainly through the Ministry of Co-operation, which handles economic and military aid, and by the Elysée Palace itself because Africa is traditionally in the Fifth Republic a personal presidential domain.

The Cultural Relations Directorate, which is responsible for 42 per cent of the whole foreign affairs budget, is mainly concerned with providing French teachers on secondment abroad (8,000 in 1973) and with various forms of co-operation. Traditionally its main areas of involvement have been North Africa, Lebanon and South-East Asia, where historic ties with France are strong, although this tripod has been shaken by recent turbulent world events. In recent years – and this does perhaps reflect the fact that under Giscard d'Estaing there have been some changes – the emphasis of cultural relations has moved away from the rather arrogant Gaullist approach to the distribution of civilisation. A new and more co-operative style, from a state with attractive industrial and technological products on display, has had quite a positive effect in areas where French influence has traditionally been weak such as English-speaking Africa.

Conclusions

When one surveys French foreign and defence policy under the three Presidents of the Fifth Republic, it is Georges Pompidou who appears as the odd-man-out. Pompidou's election slogan, *continuité et ouverture*, coined partly to attract the electoral support of the *Giscardiens*, became reality in foreign policy. There was broad continuity but there were some changes. France stopped blocking British entry to the EEC; the assertion of a world role for France was toned down to an emphasis on France as a Mediterranean power; the nuclear deterrent was maintained but was less flourished as a symbol; the style of the Presidency was less august; there were fewer spectacular diplomatic initiatives with the French President cast in the role of world leader. Perhaps some of this was attributable to the ill-health of President Pompidou. At all events Giscard d'Estaing, who also came to office under the banner of *continuité et ouverture*, who began his presidency with efforts to establish a more informal style, who was presented as being more 'Atlanticist', more 'European' and more sympathetic to Israel than his predecessors, has reverted to a marked *continuité* of the policy and style of General de Gaulle in most aspects of foreign affairs. In defence the nuclear deterrent plays to the full the symbolic role it played under de Gaulle and conventional forces have been greatly strengthened. Gaullian themes like the independence of France from the two superpowers predominate. In accepting the invitation to meet Brezhnev in Warsaw in May 1980, Giscard was pursuing the characteristically Gaullian obsession that France was to be considered a front-rank power in any East–West dialogue. In other parts of the world, initiatives in the Middle East, overtures to the non-aligned countries, spectacular summit diplomacy,

Giscard d'Estaing has been more and more Gaullian in style and in policy.

Even what is most personal to Giscard d'Estaing can in reality be classified as *continuité*, not change: African policy, the Franco-German directorate of Europe, and the defence policy modification of *sanctuarisation élargie*. The neo-imperial role in Africa is in the pure Gaullian tradition, the policy of rapprochement with Germany was begun by de Gaulle in 1963 and the idea of a directorate for Europe (not just Franco-German) was floated by de Gaulle in 1968, while the prestigious notion of Germany and France in a leadership class of their own is pure Gaullism. Gaullists regard the new defence policy of *sanctuarisation élargie* as a betrayal of the true faith but that only shows how ready they are to delude themselves. The idea that France could remain aloof from what happened outside its own borders and retain a defence policy based solely on the threat of a nuclear retaliation only against an enemy who menaced France directly was both absurd and in direct contradiction to any ambitions to play a leading role in Europe, for which some preparedness to take part in common defence is a prerequisite, or in other parts of the world, particularly in a world where threats to France are likely to begin in the Gulf states or the supply-lines of the Indian Ocean. In 1980 the *Giscardiens* of the UDF produced a report calling for French defence policy to be more prepared to take part in a European battle, with a 'graduated response' from a better range of tactical nuclear weapons including the neutron bomb. Jean-Marie Daillet, their defence spokesman, tried to tell the Gaullists that 'we remain faithful to the main lines of the military policy defined at the outset by General de Gaulle' (press conference, 27 May 1980). But the Gaullists were not listening.

If one paradox of French foreign policy is that Giscard d'Estaing, though condemned by Gaullists, is in fact a very Gaullist President, the other is that he cannot escape the embrace of the domestic consensus on foreign policy, which can loosely be called Gaullist, and yet that within it he has more freedom to act than any other Western leader. When Pompidou was President, the Gaullist party was the dominant party of the state – in government, in Parliament, in the public services – a serene and pragmatic party of government. If the President embarked on a big policy change, such as a more sympathetic approach to co-operation in Europe and to the enlargement of the EEC, the

Gaullist party was there in force to back him up, just as it had backed de Gaulle's historic policy change over Algeria. President Giscard d'Estaing, however, as *l'état*-UDF has gradually replaced *l'état*-UDR and as the Gaullists have been driven on to the defensive, finds the Gaullists more sensitive to any policy initiative that can be interpreted as a betrayal of what General de Gaulle stood for. Because the symbols manipulated by de Gaulle – French independence, French nuclear power, France with a rank in the world – are an important part of French national cohesion, the legitimacy of the regime and of French national pride rediscovered, the Gaullist consensus on how a President should conduct himself in foreign affairs and defence is an important constraint. Within this framework, however, a French President has nothing much to fear from lobbies or interest groups or activists in his own party campaigning for a different policy on South Africa or Israel or nuclear weapons, and having a significant effect on support for the President. French Jewry tried to organise itself to oppose Giscard after the President's statement in 1980 in favour of the Palestine Liberation Organisation. Since presidential elections turn, however, on the question of whether the left can really be trusted to govern the country, such initiatives were unimportant. Within the ranks of the UDF there is an important body of opinion which would have preferred President Giscard d'Estaing to take a much firmer line against the Soviet occupation of Afghanistan, in favour of boycotting the Moscow Olympics, or in support of Israel. However the French party system and, particularly, any links there may be between a President of the Republic and any party, are too loose for this opposition to be a strong constraint. Within the boundaries of the Gaullian consensus on foreign policy and defence, therefore, the President is free to roam where he will.

The foreign policy of France is still as unashamedly nationalist under Giscard d'Estaing as it was under de Gaulle. The spectacular world diplomacy of General de Gaulle was an important part of the effort to rebuild the cohesion and self-confidence of the French people after almost a century of humiliation culminating in the defeat and occupation of 1940–4. France is the only big West European state than can indulge in self-confident and assertive nationalism. Germany is handicapped by historical memories, Great Britain by its serious economic difficulties. There are, as William Wallace points out (1978), two points of view on French foreign policy. One is that it is characterised by great international impact, clarity of objectives and realism in bargaining for national advantage. The other is that there is a contradiction between stated aims and capabilities. 'The Pompidolian and Giscardian echoes of Gaullist foreign policy seemed largely to consist of grand but insubstantial gestures, activist in their pursuit of international objectives, but little concerned with the effect of those initiatives on the interests of their allies' (p. 38). There seemed to be a contradiction between the logic of interdependence and the rhetoric of independence. However, Wallace concludes that 'if the over-riding objective of managing foreign policy is to maintain as far as possible the distinction between domestic and foreign policy, and to stamp political objectives on the mass of technical transactions among government, then the French machinery must be judged the most effective [of the major West European states]' (p. 47). International economic policy is expertly managed by the Foreign Ministry's large and powerful Economic Directorate. The leading role of the presidency, which is not subject to much domestic constraint except pressure from Gaullists (and Communists) to be more nationalist, ensures that the *grandes lignes* of foreign policy and the wider issues are kept separate from detail and day-to-day management. The overall aim is to defend French interests, especially against the threat to vital supplies from 'destabilisation' in Africa and the Middle East, and to make France a more admired nation in the world. France is superior, as Giscard d'Estaing announced in May 1975 on the first anniversary of his election: 'my fundamental idea is that the superiority of France is a superiority of the spirit. It is not a superiority of force, it cannot be an economic superiority ... It is a superiority of the spirit, that is to say, that of a country which understands best the problems of its times and which brings to them the most imaginative, the most open, the most generous solutions.' The world's judgement of this 'fundamental idea' will be the test of the success or failure of Giscard d'Estaing in foreign affairs.

CHAPTER 7

The Economy

For de Gaulle there was a link between national cohesion and a foreign policy based on *grandeur*. For Giscard d'Estaing who, as we have seen, has maintained the Gaullist essence in foreign policy, there is also a link between national cohesion and social reform. In May 1978 he defined the three elements of his 'grand design' – French presence in the world, reduction of tension abroad and reconciliation at home. Reconciliation, as we saw in the chapter on the President's ideas, means an end to the unnecessary hostility between elites of opposition and majority, and an end to social injustice that breeds resentment and division. If an ambitious foreign policy is impossible without a successful economy, so too is a reforming social policy. France during the Giscard presidency has, like other Western countries, had to weather the storms of energy crisis, inflation, unemployment, overseas trade deficits and monetary problems. Despite difficulties, however, a reasonable rate of growth has been maintained and determined efforts have been made to maintain the international competitiveness of French industry.

Industry and the economy

There is an underlying strength in the French economy, mainly derived from the great success of a few vital sectors like the automobile industry, that provides the resources to cope with difficulties and pursue ambitious developments. The state has been able to define and pursue technocratic objectives for the restructuring and development of industry without undue interference from interest groups. Management of the big companies has improved beyond measure, drawing in a gifted and highly trained elite from the Polytechnique and ENA, and responding to the spur of international competition provided by the EEC. The French state has done its best to see that in each key industrial sector there is one internationally competitive French firm, using American technology if that is the only way.

This strategy was put forward in an extremely influential book on industrial policy, *L'Impératif industriel*, written in 1969 by Lionel Stoleru, one of the closest advisers of Giscard d'Estaing, a member of his *cabinet* and later Secretary of State in the Ministry of Labour. The prescriptions of this book are valid for other industrial countries in difficulty, like Great Britain. The industrial imperative was the survival of industries exposed to external competition and the will of the state to pursue a coherent policy when faced with falling growth and rising unemployment. Analysing the performance of French industry and the policy of the state in the 1960s, Stoleru drew three conclusions (pp. 147–52). First, 'the competitive economic system in which the Western industrial countries live cannot ... be identified with the liberal regime of economic doctrines: the state no longer limits its action to the creation of a favourable environment for industrial development, leaving to private initiative the task of achieving the necessary balance between different types of activity and structure, but quits this neutrality to intervene directly in industrial structures'. Secondly, 'the sectors the most in difficulty are often those where state intervention has been the the most delayed'. Here he is referring to industries like steel or chemicals where the state had to intervene to impose restructuring and mergers when the industries were already losing out badly to foreign competition. Thirdly, the state did not always have a coherent strategy and its interventions were 'not in general oriented towards the search for productivity'. Government co-ordination, when it existed, was often directed towards other objectives, to ensure orders for flagging industries like shipbuilding, to refuse dependence on America for political reasons (the graphite-gas nuclear power process), or 'to increase national prestige by building the biggest liner, a French racing-car, or the fastest aeroplane ... To dominate the world market for ravioli may not be an objective that inspires the crowds but for all that it is probably a more effective means of guaranteeing employment and growth ...' What was needed was a deliberate economic and industrial policy based on the principle that 'the sole sectors which have any chance of survival are those where the search for productivity is achieved by a deliberate association of the efforts of the state and the private sector'. This of course, as the reader will have observed, fits in perfectly with the Giscardian notion of 'organised liberalism' discussed in Chapter 2. It also fits perfectly into the culture and history of a country where the private sector has not been the motor of innovation and growth and has not developed an ideology which regards state intervention as illegitimate.

The way ahead, argued Stoleru, should be based on two principles. The first was not to be blinded by prestige considerations and to be prepared to accept foreign, even American, participation in key industries, if the alternative was to have none. For instance, in the field of nuclear power: 'the technological contribution of Westinghouse is so far beyond what can be found inside the Common Market that one wonders if it is worthwhile to oppose it' (p. 267). This is exactly the line that came to be followed by French industrial policy during the Giscard presidency. The concentration of the nuclear power industry on the Westinghouse process, and the *Francisation* of the industry by buying out the American parent, has, as we shall see in detail in the next chapter, been the essence of the restructuring of the nuclear industry. Another instance of the adoption of that line was the end of the Plan Calcul in 1974. The *Plan* Calcul was an attempt to preserve an independent computer industry in France by merging small firms to create a national champion cii (Compagnie Internationale pour l'Informatique). John Zysman (in Warnecke and Suleiman, 1975) has described how the desire to have an independent technology arose out of 'simple insecurity' – that is to say, fear of dependence on and domination by the United States, and as a 'symbolic gesture' of French strategic independence (p. 232). However, 'French experience suggests limits on a government's ability to shape the growth of a domestic industry that forms an integral part of an international marketplace' (p. 245). The market share of cii was low, despite internal protected markets like the telephone service or the military, and its components were uncompetitive. Under President Giscard d'Estaing, the government dissolved the state agency responsible, the Délégation à l'Informatique, and promoted a much more viable merger between cii and the American firm Honeywell. A similar policy has been followed in motor components and electronic micro-circuitry – state subsidies, co-operative deals with foreign (especially American) companies and *Francisation* of majority share-holdings. Matra has gone into partnership with Harris Corporation to produce micro-chips, Renault with American motors in the United States in order to increase exports to America.

The second Stoleru principle was that only one firm in an industry should be aided by the state: 'it is necessary for the state to have before it a single centre of decision-making to take responsibility for each of the industrial objectives pursued' (p. 218). Competition in key sectors is no longer competition between domestic firms in a domestic market but competition between a competitive French firm and giant firms from other countries. This has been followed through in sector after sector. Mergers in chemicals, automobiles, nuclear power, tyres, electronic equipment and other industries have ensured that France has one, or at the most two as in the motor industry, internationally competitive firms. Aviation is one exception. Though a lot of mergers have taken place, the state supplies huge subsidies in cash (8·3 billion francs in 1976) and support through orders to Dassault in military aircraft, SNIAS in civil aircraft and rockets and SNECMA in aero-engines. For the Airbus (SNIAS) finance in 1976 was 93 per cent from the state, 7 per cent from the company. Overall, however, for the last few years a dynamic policy of concentration on firms and sectors capable of restoring international competitiveness has been pursued. The greatest French success has been in the automobile industry. In Renault (nationalised) and Peugeot-Citroën it has now two internationally competitive market leaders which have made France the biggest car exporting country after Japan. When a region is in difficulty, it is to the automobile industry that the government turns for investment in new factories. If the automobile industry ever sneezes, France will catch a cold.

The objective of competitiveness has also been pursued in the more traditional declining or struggling industries like textiles or steel. Textiles in France, as in other European countries, have come under great pressure from low-cost Third World imports. The answer has been not to prop up the industry with protectionism but to give regional aid for redeployment of workers in areas affected, like the Vosges, and aid for restructuring. In steel, production had fallen to two-thirds of capacity – from 27 million tonnes in 1974 to 22 in 1977, with a recovery to 23·4 in 1979. Despite a belated policy of mergers the two remaining firms, USINOR and SACILOR, had debts which, at 38 billion francs, were slightly more than the annual sales turnover. The industry was not nationalised but government financial intervention means that it is effectively two-thirds owned by the state. Restructuring, concentrating production on the most efficient plants, notably at Fos (Marseille) and Dunkerque, a reduction of the workforce from 150,000 to 110,000 with financial help for redundant workers, including repatriation grants for immigrants, 3 billion franc grants for new industries in the worst-hit steel areas, especially Lorraine – these have been the main elements of the government's plan for steel. Despite the violence which in the winter of 1979 greeted the threat to jobs in the industry, the industry settled down, has improved its productivity to within striking distance of West Germany's and reduced its losses.

Restructuring of industry, particularly if related to an offensive strategy designed to secure international competitiveness in viable industries in which the nation can specialise, brings great problems of 'adjustment unemployment'. Christian Stoffaes (1978) argues that to achieve such a policy – the only one for survival – there must be effective co-ordination, as through the Comité Interministériel Economique et Sociale set up in 1977, and a strong state that can impose 'arbitration on selfishness' (p. 337), especially against short-term pressure group coalitions in favour of protection. In democracies like the United States or Britain where pressure groups, and in particular trade unions, play a more influential role, the policies that emerge tend to be defensive and hence in the long term ineffective.

State aid to industry is very considerable, though not all of it is guided by the 'national champions' policy outlined above. The state intervenes to save basic sectors which are threatened, as in the case of steel, to aid by diplomatic effort and protection as well as with finance sectors like textiles that have to adapt to new types of overseas competition, and in *contrats de croissance* with the most dynamic firms in sectors like scientific instruments or machine tools where import penetration is strong. 'Defensive nationalisation' of declining industries has been avoided. 'Lame ducks' obtain some help but not very much. Véronique Maurus (*Le Monde*, 23 March 1979) claimed that France today was 'the largest cemetery for bankrupt firms in the world'. Various organisms distribute aid to private industry: CIASI (Comité Interministériel d'Amenagement des Structures Industrielles), which was created during the Giscard presidency in November 1974, IDI (Institut de Développement Industriel) and FDES (Fonds de Développement Economique et Social), to name but three. However, Véronique Maurus quotes the phrase 'heard like a *leitmotif*' in the corridors of these institutions: 'when the firm arrives here, it is too late. The enterprise has already bled to death.' The global sums available for industry are nevertheless impressive. In 1974–5 1 billion francs was made available to bring about the Peugeot–Citroën merger and 450 million for Renault to restructure truck manufacturing in France by taking over Berliet. An action fund for investment of 2·5 billion francs was included in the Barre Plan of 1976, the FDES allocated 1·6 billion francs to reorganise and develop the wood and paper industry in 1977, and the steel industry, as we have seen, received a large amount of aid, also through FDES in 1979. As Charles Debbasch, a presidential adviser, has put it: 'our policy is now *faire faire* not *laisser faire*'.

The bulk of state aid to industry, however, goes to public sector firms – 31 billion francs in 1978 (Victorri, 1979, pp. 72–89), not counting the massive investment in telephone equipment discussed below. France, after Austria, has the largest public sector in Western Europe in terms of its share of investments, employees and value-added. One-third of all industrial investment in France is in the public sector. Much of public sector policy is concerned with support for unprofitable but socially necessary activity – such as railways in rural areas or loans for small farms. In transport alone the 1980 budget provided 10·6 billion francs for the French national railways (not counting a further 7 billion for railway pensions), 2·2 billion for public transport in Paris, and 300 million for the transport services linking Corsica and the mainland. Aid to the declining coal industry, in the form of subsidies, diversification into chemicals and building, and into the 'industrialisation of mining regions', amounted to 5 billion francs in 1976. Unprofitable firms in important sectors like SNIAS (aerospace) can only keep going if the Treasury automatically finances their deficits. SNIAS received over 1 billion francs in state aid in 1978. State investment in the public sector during the period of the 7th Plan (1976–80) was up by 60 per cent at constant prices over the period of the 6th Plan (1971–5).

The 7th Plan and the Barre Plan

Obituary notices on French economic planning frequently appear and even the Prime Minister, Raymond Barre, to whose office the Commissariat Général du Plan is attached, has spoken of the 'disappointments' of the 7th Plan. Planning in France takes the form of a series of five-year economic and social development programmes intended to act as guidelines to supplement market forces and create a climate of expansion. The problem, however, as Diana Green has noted (1980), is that implementation of the Plan depends on the process of preparing each year's state budget. The Plan can be a reference point for budgetary decisions, she says, and in negotiations between spending ministries and the Budget Ministry, but 'in practice there has been a notable lack of co-ordination'. Budgets concentrate on expenditure next year, not long-term investment; they are inflexible because most of the spending is already committed to fund all the government departments and activities that already exist. Finally, even if elements of the Plan are incorporated in the budget, the whole Plan can be blown off course by an economic climate less favourable than the planners hoped for or anticipated.

During the Giscard presidency there has been an attempt to overcome the conflict between budget and Plan in two ways. One is the creation of the Conseil Central de Planification under the chairmanship of the President himself who is, it will be recalled, a former long-serving Minister of Finance and an inspector of finance by training. The second, and the 7th Plan's most original feature, was the designation of Programmes d'Action Prioritaires (PAPs) under which the vast sum of over 200 billion francs was to be concentrated on certain programmes of investment in the economy, in public equipment and services, in reducing dependence on imported energy, on scientific research and on other socially desirable objectives such as training, employment, the family and the quality of life. The largest share by far went to investment in the telephone service – for long an object of derision from foreigners and hence a stain on French prestige – which accounted for about half the entire programme. There was also the vast programme of investment in nuclear power, discussed in the next chapter, and the construction of a canal link from the North Sea to the Mediterranean – essentially the Rhine–Rhône canal (1·6 billion francs). This latter project, however, has cost much more and is considered to be much less economic or useful as a transport system than originally imagined. As an economic planning device, though, as Diana Green confirms, the PAPs indicated a far greater degree of commitment to actual investment plans even if they did still need funds to be specifically allocated to them by the budget.

The overall objectives of the 7th Plan (though not the implementation of the PAPs) was, not surprisingly, blown off course by the worldwide economic foul weather of the late 1970s. The steep rise in the price of imported oil played havoc with the French trade balance abroad and contributed to inflation at home. Economic growth and growth of exports were less than forecast in the 7th Plan, the rise in prices, unemployment and the budget deficit much greater. Raymond Barre was appointed Prime Minister in August 1976 with the specific assignment of producing a counter-inflation policy. The Barre Plan duly emerged on 22 September. The anti-inflation elements included a three-month price freeze, a reduction in value-added tax, wage and salary restraint, a reduction of money supply growth to 12 per cent, and increased income tax, car tax, and bank rate. The Plan also included measures to restore France's trade balance and to support the growth of the economy and employment. Oil imports were limited to a fixed figure of 55 billion francs in 1977, which was satisfactory until the Arabs raised prices again. There was special aid for export investment and indeed all new investments were to be tax-free. An action fund of 2·5 billion francs to aid industry was proclaimed. To offset discontent and any feeling that only rich industrialists were obtaining any benefit, the Plan also included increased state aid for farmers, suffering from the great 1976 drought, and for social security. The salaries of the rich were frozen, 'external signs of wealth' like yachts or golf were taxed, and expense accounts were controlled. It was a determined package, not very popular, and pursued with vigour. The industrial strategy designed to increase competitiveness was maintained so that unemployment tended to rise. After the local election setbacks of March 1977 and as the fateful 1978 parliamentary election drew closer, the Barre Plan No. 2 introduced some modifications in the form of measures to favour employment and to increase family allowances and pensions. There was also a short-lived attempt to enforce stricter controls on certain prices – such as the humble but delicious *croissant*. In the *croissant* war, as this skirmish came to be known, the bakers found ingenious ways of evading controls and making the government appear ridiculous. After the 1978 election the policy of controlling prices was dropped. Indeed, the prices of everyday commodities like bread and rents were decontrolled for the first time for generations. This contributed to inflation and also to industrial profitability. It is probably the most significant example during the Giscard presidency of a more liberal (in the sense of free market) approach to economic management.

Three years after the Barre Plan the press was full of anniversary analyses. Since unemployment was still 1·5 million and inflation over 10 per cent, could it be said that the Barre Plan was a failure? The Prime Minister's own claim was that, thanks to it, France had come through the economic crisis of the 1970s much better than countries like Great Britain or Italy, would have been worse without it, and had continued on course for its main economic objectives of reduced dependence on imported oil and a competitive French presence in all major industrial sectors. In addition the government had maintained public services and continued to shield poorer families and pensioners from the worst effects of inflation. The claim is reasonable.

France is doing well. The rate of economic growth may not be what it was in the golden days of the postwar boom which went on into the early 1970s, and President Giscard d'Estaing has tried to prepare the French people for the end of that era and the onset of 'sober growth'. Nevertheless, growth has continued to average a respectable 3 or 3¼ per cent a year. Incomes, expenditure on public services and social security benefits all rose substantially in real terms throughout the 1970s. The government has also been able to pursue its other ambitions for which a strong economy is needed: increased spending on and modernisation of the strategic nuclear force, for instance. In the late 1960s when the barriers to trade within the EEC were about to be removed, Pompidou as Prime Minister initiated a big campaign to get French firms to face the dangers and grasp the opportunities of foreign competition. By the late 1970s it was clear that the big French firms, benefiting from government aid to restructure their industries, were increasingly geared for overseas markets. Exports have been very buoyant with a strong surplus in 1978 – ready for the next OPEC hammer-blow. Support for French agriculture – 'our oil' as the President called it – has been vigorously pursued in the EEC. Although France, contrary to popular belief, does not have a big overseas trade surplus in the food and drink sector, agricultural exports are vitally important and the dwindling proportion of French people still on the land (9 per cent as compared with 39 per cent in 1939) is no longer behind the rest of the country in living standards.

Economic policy-making is located at a higher level than previously. Giscard d'Estaing learnt from his former incarnation as Minister of Finance just how powerful a great ministerial empire covering both economic policy-making and control of the nation's accounts can be. When Raymond Barre was appointed Prime Minister in 1976, therefore, he became Minister of Economy and Finance too, with a Secretary of State under him to administer that department. Barre, with the full support of the President, was the architect and executant of the economic recovery policy that bears his name. In March 1978, in the new Barre government appointed after the parliamentary election, the Prime Minister gave up the title of Finance Minister but the old Ministry of Finance was split into two: the Ministry of the Economy and the Ministry of the Budget. The rue de Rivoli is no longer occupied by a minister of the political weight of its former occupants like Michel Debré or Valéry Giscard d'Estaing. The tandem of President and Prime Minister, with all the *conseils restreints* and *comités interministériels* which meet under their chairmanship, is the directing force in economic policy. The economic strategy which they attempt to co-ordinate embraces industrial policy, regional development policy, energy policy and foreign policy with its primary economic goals pursued in EEC negotiations, in the preoccupation in foreign affairs with supplies of strategic raw materials and French exports of high technology, especially military or nuclear, in relations with former African colonies, with Middle East monarchies, or even with the Soviet Union. The attempt is impressive and only possible because, in economic as in foreign policy, the executive in France is shielded from those forces like disciplined and well-organised interest groups which, in the more pluralist democracies like Great Britain or the United States, have the capacity to frustrate government objectives. We return to the question of interest groups and economic policy as one of the curiosities of French democracy in the concluding chapter.

CHAPTER 8

The Environment

The policy of President Giscard d'Estaing on the environment has been a revealing and determined mixture of enlightened despotism, *raison d'état* and genuine concern. The President has acted personally to stop the building of skyscrapers and urban motorways in Paris; on his initiative a new policy for mountain areas forbids the construction of vast new ski resorts on virgin sites – 'Sarcelles-sur-neige'; there have been measures to protect the coast-line, to combat pollution and to do away with slum housing. There has also been the West's most ambitious nuclear power programme, pursued, for reasons of national interest as the President sees it, in a singularly authoritarian manner.

The urban environment

Edgar Faure, a former Prime Minister, told me that he considered the outstanding achievement of Giscard d'Estaing to be the 'struggle against *le gigantisme urbain*'. The urban environment in France has indeed seen a number of personal presidential initiatives, only to be expected of the man who, as Minister of Finance, was reported to be aghast when from his office window he saw edging over the world-famous skyline of the Champs Elysées and the Arc de Triomphe the asymmetrical towers of La Défense. President Pompidou was a great supporter of skyscrapers, motorways and any other symbol of dynamic and thrusting modernism. Giscard d'Estaing was no sooner in office than he put a stop to the proposed expressway on the Left Bank of the Seine and a planned 220-metre-high building in the Place d'Italie, and intervened in the development of the former vegetable market site of Les Halles. All these matters subsequently led to conflict with the mayor of Paris, a concrete and expressway man, Jacques Chirac. In the field of housing the emphasis has shifted, as in other countries, to restoration of existing houses rather than wholesale renovation. The Barre Report was commissioned and, in 1975, recommended increased aid to people on modest incomes wishing to buy their own homes. The programme to get rid of the appalling *bidonvilles* or shanty-towns occupied by immigrant workers has been stepped up – indeed, notorious areas like La Digue des Français at Nice have been demolished. Other measures on the urban environment include a law in December 1975 to combat speculative development by putting a ceiling on density of development permitted on any site, a law in December 1976 protecting open spaces and the built-up environment, contracts between the state and medium-sized towns like Rodez, Auxerre, or Chambéry to make them more attractive places to live and work in, and regulations requiring the involvement of an architect in any building work over 170 square metres. Another initiative was the coast-line protection directive issued by the Minister for the Environment and Quality of Life, Michel d'Ornano, in August 1979. Undeveloped parts of the coast are to remain so (except the nuclear power site at Plogoff), no more building is allowed within 100 metres of the coast and town plans are to be revised.

'La politique de la montagne'

Two interesting and contrasting fields of Giscardian policy and policy-making are the measures to protect France's 'natural heritage' (*patrimoine naturelle*) – especially the policy for mountain areas (of which I carried out a small survey in Savoie) – and the nuclear power programme. The policy for the protection of mountain areas was launched by the President in a speech at Vallouise (Hautes Alpes) on 23 August 1977. The policy declaration had been preceded by a long period of preparation, consultation with local representatives, reports from staff in the Prime Minister's office, from the tourism section of the Environment Ministry, and from local prefectures. A lot of the speech concerned aid to mountain agriculture (460 million francs to 150,000 mountain-dwellers in 1979), but it was the section on restricting tourist development that attracted the most discussion. There was no consensus on this policy; it was imposed. A series of post-Vallouise decrees laid down that there were to be environmental impact studies for all developments, that tourist development should be excluded from all areas suitable for agriculture, that it should form part of existing villages and, above all, that it should be strongly discouraged at the high altitudes ski enthusiasts prefer. All development projects were to be submitted to a government office in Paris – the UTN bureau (Unités Touristiques Nouvelles) – which would co-ordinate the views of relevant ministries on environmental, regional economic development, or agricultural aspects.

France's mountainous regions experienced very rapid development in the Pompidou era as ski resorts, under the *plan neige*. Commercial promoters promising windfalls for property values, local employment and communal tax income descended on the Alps and other regions and undertook vast developments with, from an environmental point of view, rather dubious results. Anyone who has driven up the Tarentaise valley in Savoie and come suddenly upon the concrete skyscrapers of Les Menuires or Val Thorens will appreciate the problem. Furthermore the apartments constructed were extremely expensive, only occupied a few weekends a year, provided rewarding jobs almost entirely for outsiders, or 'proletarianised' the employment opportunities for local people. Nevertheless, they undoubtedly met a vast and growing demand for skiing holidays (4 million French people went skiing in 1978) and they attracted an extensive overseas clientèle, and indeed, with their discothèques and fifteenth-floor balconies they seemed to be taking business away from the leather trousers and sleigh bells of the Austrian resorts. They also constituted an essential part of the economic development of departments like Savoie which had, ever since 1945, seen in tourism the answer to the steady depopulation of mountain regions. The financing of these schemes was sometimes extremely shaky, and artful promoters had left local *communes* with tasks beyond their resources. This has now been tightened up somewhat by the state's *trésorier payeur général* in the prefectures, who has to approve the loans involved and negotiates with the promoter his contribution to the communal facilities his development will require.

Opinion was extremely divided over the new *politique de la montagne*. The brief research that I was able to do made it clear that the government's administration services in the mountain areas – prefectures, town halls, technical services and the mountain tourist development office – were basically opposed to the restriction on development. Of course one must be careful not to ruin the environment, but the big tourist developments met a demand and brought prosperity to the region. The *politique de la montagne* was a cynical policy to appease the ecologists and disarm critics of the nuclear programme. It was a 'colonial' policy involving sending all the dossiers up to Paris for decision – the reverse of the President's declared aim of giving more responsibility to local authorities. 'It would be a mistake to stop all urbanisation of the mountains,' declared the Gaullist *député* for the Tarentaise (twenty ski resorts), 'the maintenance of life in these regions demands economic activities, and hence jobs' (*Le Monde*, 31 August 1979). Reports were produced by official bodies in regional tourism development and by skiing associations showing the benefits to the local population – and in particular the arrest in depopulation attributable to the ski resorts.

The government's programme did not have an immediate effect. Promoters had outstanding permissions for large developments – for example, a huge resort of 6,000 'beds' on a virgin site at La Plagne (Savoie). Nevertheless, pressure began to be exerted. Existing plans at Le Mottaret were declared unacceptable for environmental reasons and the promoter had to cede certain rights in exchange for permission to build a part of his original scheme. Four *routes de balcon* – scenic highways – were quashed. Above all, battle was engaged at Val Thorens – one of the original 'skiing factories' – where the government found an ally in the unlikely form of the Socialist-controlled *conseil général* of Savoie (equivalent to a British county council). The original plan for Val Thorens, conceived by the famous promoter Pierre Schnebelen when Joseph Fontanet, a former minister mysteriously murdered in Paris in 1980, was president of the *conseil général* and mayor of the *commune* containing the Val Thorens site, was for 35,000 'beds' – the second-largest town in Savoie! The successor to Fontanet as mayor is, by coincidence, the director of the government's Mountain Tourist Development Research Office and a critic of the new policy. The *conseil général* is involved in the development as a partner in a Société d'Economie Mixte and of course has to provide roads and other services. Despite pressure from the *préfet*, the *conseil général* blocked the development of Val Thorens beyond 12,000 'beds' because it has had enough of tourist development exclusively for the rich and which provides only a few menial tasks for local people. Promoters, however, are learning to adapt, and a new type of resort, which fits in with the norms of the new policy, smaller, more sympathetically designed – architecture Swiss-chalet rather than international airport – with apartments to rent as well as for sale, is being developed. The model village of this type in Savoie is Valmorel.

Another aspect of environmental policy in mountain areas is the creation of national parks. Even in the national parks, however, it is difficult to impose a totally conservationist policy. There are outstanding plans for huge resorts which means that some areas of the newest park, the Mercantour in Alpes-Maritimes, will be 'provisional'. To crown it all and to conjure up an ecologist's nightmare, there is in the Mercantour national park a large deposit of uranium, against the exploitation of which 5,000 demonstrators marched to the park in June 1979, and elsewhere Electricité de France has plans for hydroelectric dams!

The nuclear power programme

To invoke the uranium deposits of Mercantour is to introduce another policy to which the President is personally committed: the development of electricity generation by nuclear power to replace France's dependence on imported oil. France does not have a large coal industry like Great Britain or West Germany and it has scarcely any oil. It has some natural gas in the south-west and the potential for hydroelectric power in some of its rivers. There is a development programme for solar energy, 'green' energy (from agricultural products) and off-shore oil exploitation. There have been measures to conserve energy: the clocks are now advanced an hour for summer daylight-saving, a maximum permitted room temperature has been introduced, public buildings like schools have restricted budgets for fuel, industry and local authorities receive a rebate on energy-saving investments. The government is helping to finance the development of a petrol-saving car, speed limits have been introduced and there has been an intensive anti-waste campaign. Coal imports (main suppliers West Germany, South Africa and Poland) have been increased and some coal reserves in Provence are being exploited, with, by the way, no prolonged public debate and inquiry about the effect on the countryside as in Great Britain's newly discovered coalfield in the Vale of Belvoir. Gas imports from Algeria and the Soviet Union have increased. The problem of oil, however, remains – still meeting 58 per cent of the nation's energy needs in 1978 – and it is oil that has to be imported from the world's most unstable region.

A vast programme of nuclear power development has been adopted as the solution and vigorously pursued at a rate of 5,000 megawatts per year. The aim is to have 40,000 MW by 1985, producing half the nation's electricity, one-fifth of the total energy requirement, and leaving oil to meet only 40 per cent of national needs. The implementation of this policy shows the French state at its most cohesive, its most effective and its most undemocratic. The policy involved two overlapping stages, the technological development and the restructuring of the nuclear supply industry, and the development of the sites for nuclear power stations with the accompanying problem of public relations. At the risk of a slight digression from the specific question of the environment, I shall first explore the interesting story of the former.

On the technical and supply side, the French nuclear industry presents, once again, the picture of a closed bureaucratic model of decision-making, with relevant interests on the inside and subject to no interference from external pressure groups. The main agencies, which go back over twenty years to the Fourth Republic, are the Comissariat à l'Energie Atomique (CEA), the PEON Commission (Production de l'Electricité d'Origine Nucléaire) and Electricité de France (EDF), the public corporation responsible for producing and selling electricity. The directors of CEA and EDF are members of PEON as of right, as is the DGA (the government's delegate for armaments) and officials responsible for regional development (*aménagement du territoire*) and anti-pollution measures. Membership of PEON, whether from government, public industry, or private industry, is highly technocratic. According to Philippe Simonnot (1978, pp. 24–5) twenty of the twenty-eight leading members went to Polytechnique and sixteen of the twenty belong either to the Corps des Mines or the Corps des Ponts et Chaussées, the two most prestigious technical *corps* in the French public service. PEON brings together administration, industrial and financial experts with the object of making recommendations to government. The important nuclear decisions of recent years have been the vast growth of the nuclear programme and the decision to drop the idea of an independently French system of generating nuclear power. A leading role in this was played by André Giraud, formerly director of CEA, later in the government as Minister for Industry.

The decision to drop the French graphite-gas process, which had been functioning at Marcoule for many years, and to restructure the industry on the basis of the American Westinghouse pressurised water reactor (PWR), is an interesting one. The Gaullian belief that the state could, and indeed should, always ensure French presence in a key industry ran into difficulties in the 1970s. The Plan Calcul which was supposed to ensure an independent French computer industry was dropped in 1975 and the French CII was merged with the American firm Honeywell to make a much more successful and viable company. In nuclear power, it was clear that the French process was not exportable, so, since exports are the basis of any high-technology industry, the vast purchasing power of the EDF as the monopoly consumer of electricity supply was deployed on the *Francisation* of a nuclear industry based on Westinghouse PWRs.

The licensee for the Westinghouse system was Framatome. The American company owned 45 per cent and Creusot-Loire the rest. In 1975 the *comité interministériel restreint* for nuclear policy authorised CEA to take a share in Framatome and, in accordance with a general industrial philosophy of ensuring that in each key industrial sector resources should be concentrated on the one potentially competitive enterprise, laid down that Framatome should be the sole constructor of nuclear power stations. This meant that CGE, the other main firm in the nuclear construction industry, was excluded but its subsidiary Alsthom was designated as the sole supplier of turbo-alternators for Framatome. How was Westinghouse persuaded to sell its shares in this potentially profitable venture? According to *Le Monde* (28 November 1975) the American firm needed access to the vast supply of uranium in France and Africa controlled by CEA (100,000 tons of reserves). A deal was done (1,200 tonnes of uranium 1975–83) and CEA acquired a 30 per cent stake in Framatome for $16·7 million and three representatives on the Framatome board (one of whom is Jacques Giscard d'Estaing, the President's cousin).

In 1976 CEA created a subsidiary COGEMA (Compagnie Générale des Matières Nucléaires) which is responsible for the production of combustible material from mining to enrichment, and even to retreatment of spent materials in the re-processing plant at La Hague. So France now has an industry that controls the whole nuclear cycle. In order to reduce dependence on American supplies, it is developing very advanced technology in uranium enrichment (the 'Eurodif' diffusion process jointly financed by France, Spain, Italy, Belgium and until the revolution – since when it has withheld its payments and had its $1 billion deposit retained by France – Iran). In waste disposal, French technicians are developing the vitrification process, which solidifies the waste into black glass deposited in boreholes beneath the pilot plant itself. France is also, with German and Italian financial support, constructing the world's most advanced fast-breeder reactor Super-Phénix which produces its own plutonium. Power stations, nuclear fuel, waste processing and re-processing plants are being marketed worldwide, although the French are now more sensitive than they were to the dangers of proliferation – especially of re-processing technology which can produce weapons-grade plutonium. The sale of a re-processing plant to Pakistan, vigorously pursued despite American pressure by the Chirac government, was revoked in December 1976. In May 1977 France claimed to have a new process, in which the Americans are co-operating, that enriches uranium enough for a power station but not for a bomb. The following month the Franco-German summit agreed not to sell any more plants which could make combustibles for bombs.

'There can be no question', concludes David Fishbrook (*Financial Times*, 18 June 1979), 'that France has taken the world leadership in exploiting nuclear energy and in developing the advanced technologies needed to sustain its progress far into the future.' The nuclear power industry is an excellent example of an industrial policy based on 'the abandonment of projects conceived in a specifically French framework in order to aim at the constitution of enterprises which are competitive in a world context' (Stoffaes, 1978, p. 256).

To return to the environment, the nuclear programme was held so strongly to embody the national interest in terms of reduced dependence on oil imports, of industrial and technological development and of export promotion that of course it could not possibly be allowed to be impeded by a few ill-informed and parochially self-interested conservationist groups. So far the French authorities have been able to pursue their objectives more rapidly and more ambitiously than those in any other Western democracy. There have been some protests against the nuclear programme in general and against certain sites in particular. The biggest demonstration was at the Super-Phénix site at Creys-Malville in 1977 when one person was killed. The most sustained resistance so far has come from the mayor and citizens of Plogoff, a village on the remote and wild Breton cliffs.

An official in the Prime Minister's office told me, when I asked him why France, unlike West Germany or (before its referendum) Sweden, was able to pursue such a large and apparently accepted nuclear programme, that there were three factors: the personal commitment of the President, the EDF as a monopoly supplier with a clear policy and the *préfets* as an effective local administration able to handle any objections. The President is certainly committed; indeed, as was noted in the chapter on presidential style, he gave a personal interview to the Europe 1 radio station on the nuclear programme, its necessity and its safety. He has even announced, over the reservations of the EDF, that people living in the vicinity of the power stations will, to compensate them for the inconvenience of the long construction period, receive a substantial discount on electricity. The EDF and the *préfets* collaborate in the choice of potential power station sites and the impact study. The *préfet* then organises what is laughably known as a public inquiry. This consists not, as in Great Britain or the United States, of a hearing at which objectors can present their case, through a lawyer if necessary, produce expert witnesses and cross-examine those of the applicant, but simply of making plans available in the town halls of surrounding *communes* and a book in which individuals may write their point of view. These are then examined in private by an inspector appointed by the *préfet* to whom a report is submitted. Even if rejected by the inspector, the project can be declared *d'utilité publique* and authorised. The usual response that has developed to this totally unsatisfactory form of inquiry is the boycott. In the south-west, where a village referendum recorded 82 per cent against the Golfech power station, where the regional council and the *conseil général* were almost unanimous in opposition, and where the President of the Republic, in a speech at Mazamet on 17 November 1979 before the public inquiry had even been completed, announced that Golfech and two others would be built, the villages refused the use of town halls for the inquiry and picketed the portable 'town halls' brought in by the police. Both in the south-west and at Plogoff in Brittany the picketing of portable offices has turned to violence and the repeated use of tear-gas by the police. So far the government has pressed ahead regardless – the Flamanville power station was even started before the public inquiry was over and continued despite administrative tribunal rulings that the EDF was in breach of procedure, and at Belleville-sur-Loire the EDF was allowed by the Conseil d'Etat to go ahead with building while the demand for an annulment of building permission was being considered!

In 1979 and 1980 there began to appear the signs of a more rational anti-nuclear movement. What it criticised was not the development of nuclear power as such, but the technocratic style of decision-making in which an 'all-nuclear' choice was presented by the government without any public discussion or apparent consideration of alternatives, and by the blandness and secrecy with which all doubts about safety or the capacity to master such advanced technology were met. The campaign was led by the CFDT, the trade union movement closest to the Socialist Party. The accident in the Three Mile Island nuclear reactor at Harrisburg, Pennsylvania, in 1979 aroused a certain amount of anxiety, despite hasty French government assurances that the reactors in France, though of the same Westinghouse PWR type, were not of exactly the same design. In September 1979 the CFDT revealed that one of its members working on power station installations had discovered some cracks in the reactor vessels and supports and that no government or management body would take the responsibility for doing something about them. They could affect as many as twenty reactors already in service and the means of automatic checking and measuring of cracks in working reactors had not yet been perfected. The government announced that the cracks were superficial, the EDF that they were safe for five years – the unions, however, demanded repairs and checks before new reactors were charged and the minister, Giraud, agreed. About the same time a petition which by January 1980 had collected half a million signatures (*Le Monde*, 25 January 1980), was launched by the CFDT, the ecology movement, the

Socialist Party and the left-radicals demanding a more democratic debate on energy policy and the suspension of the nuclear programme. The ecologists, who planned to campaign in the 1981 presidential election, and whose votes could have been decisive at the second ballot, found that in 1979 their vote was highest in the constituencies where nuclear power stations or re-treatment plants had been sited – for example, round Flamanville and La Hague. The Socialist Party is somewhat divided, with some support for the nuclear programme. Communists are pro-nuclear.

There are some signs that the government has realised the need to spend more time convincing people about the nuclear programme and not just imposing it. The President has, as noted, intervened personally to persuade public opinion. Is the President not after all the man who declared on 26 January 1978 that 'anxieties must be answered in depth, not by a propaganda campaign. There could be no question of imposing on Frenchmen a nuclear programme to which they were profoundly opposed after being completely informed'? The Minister of Industry is going to great lengths – for instance, his statement to the Council of Ministers on 23 January 1980 – to stress that French policy is not simply 'all-nuclear' but includes the energy savings and developments of alternative sources outlined in the first paragraph of this section. Various bodies concerned with safety were set up. The Interministerial Commission for Nuclear Security was established by decree in August 1979. After the Creys-Malville demonstration, the President announced in his Vallouise speech on the environment (August 1977) the creation of a Conseil de l'Information Nucléaire on which the ecologists would be represented. This body was set up on 9 November under the chairmanship of the ever-popular Simone Veil, Minister of Health. Embarrassingly for the government, Mme Veil, by that time President of the European Parliament and no longer a minister, wrote to the Prime Minister in October 1979 demanding publicly that her committee be informed of any accidents or incidents, such as the episode of the cracks about which it had received no communication!

The policies for the protection of nature and for the development of nuclear power illustrate some of the contradictions of Giscard's presidential style: the ideal of the conservation of the natural environment conflicts, as in the mountain area policy, with the ideal of devolved local responsibility, and also of other national interests like independence in energy. It is presidential authority which imposes the final order of priorities: first nuclear power, second conservation of nature, third local responsibility.

CHAPTER 9

Social Reform

Giscard d'Estaing made it clear he wanted to be a reforming President. The removal of social injustice is an integral part, as we saw in Chapter 2, of his conception of a more cohesive national community. Where there is less injustice, there is less discontent; where there is less discontent, there is less upheaval; where there is less upheaval, there is more economic progress; where there is more economic progress, there is less discontent – and also more opportunity for the nation to 'reaffirm its rank in the world'. That reform was intended to be a major theme of the presidency was made clear from the start with votes for 18-year-olds, the liberalisation of abortion and the reform of the state monopoly in radio and television, all coming with a host of other measures in the first few months after the election. By 1980, however, there seemed to be universal agreement that social reform was the most disappointing aspect and unfulfilled promise of the presidency. 'Words not deeds', 'more reforms necessary', 'contrast between lucid analysis and insufficient action' – these were some of the judgements made by leading figures from the *majorité* (e.g. *Le Point*, 12 May 1980). Reform has indeed, as we shall argue in Chapter 11, been exceedingly disappointing in some fields – notably judicial reform and the liberalisation of information. A reason frequently given, however, by supporters and associates of the President for the drying-up of social reform after the initial flood is the difficulty of finding parliamentary support within the ranks of the *majorité*.

In the field of social policy, leaving aside for the moment civil liberties or institutions, the balance sheet of reforms is fairly creditable. On most of the criteria of the modern welfare state, France has made considerable progress in recent years: old people, handicapped people, those on the lowest wages, widows, those with housing needs, large families, working mothers, single-parent families have all benefited from actions and legislation undertaken. In this chapter some of the more conspicuous aspects of Giscardian social reform are considered – women's rights, education, *revalorisation* of manual work and capitals gains taxation, in particular. They reveal that the personal commitment of the President to combating social injustice is strong, that he has not always had the support of his own supporters, and also that the reforms belong in the tradition of the benevolently liberal conservative rather than the shockingly radical.

In one of those self-importantly laconic remarks which are his speciality, Giscard d'Estaing is reported to have said: 'I hope that of the ten or twelve lines that future history textbooks will allocate to my term of office, one or two will be devoted to my efforts to improve the situation of women.' After six years in office, he claimed his action on women's rights as the major success of his presidency: 'Je crois avoir été celui qui a inséré la femme française dans la vie de notre société' as he modestly and untranslatably put it (*L'Express*, 17 May 1980). the main instrument for the improvement of women's rights has been the Ministry for Women (*la condition féminine*). In 1979 this ministry also took over responsibility for family policy. A number of measures have been promoted: the 1975 law on equal pay, two-year parental leave from work, maternity leave progressively raised to six months and non-discrimination in education and training. There is a 1980 law to make lists at local council elections include a legal minimum of 20 per cent women. The minister is delegated by the Prime Minister to preside at the Comité Interministériel de l'Action pour les Femmes (CIAF) which considers the problems of women in relation to the entire range of state activities from women in universities to women in the armed forces. The minister also presides at the *comité interministériel* for the family. Some of this is liberal window-dressing or what feminists call 'tokenism' – as for example when Giscard d'Estaing boasted that there was a world-record number of women in his government. None the less, France had to catch up with its European neighbours in the matter of women's rights and of their capacity to take part in public and professional life, and a certain impetus has been given.

It was not as it happened, however, the Ministry for Women

that had the job of introducing the most important reform affecting women – abortion. Public opinion was in favour of the liberalisation of abortion and the reform, introduced at the very beginning of the Giscard presidency, was what launched the popularity of the Minister of Health, Simone Veil. The reform however had to be carried through Parliament with the help of the opposition. At its first reading in the National Assembly in November 1974 only 99 out of 314 *députés* from the pro-government majority supported it, but thanks to Socialists and Communists it was passed by 284 votes to 189. The law is not particularly liberal: operations have to be carried out by the tenth week of pregnancy whereas the limit in other European countries where abortion is legal ranges from the twelfth (Denmark, Luxembourg) to the twenty-eighth (Britain). A conscience clause allows doctors to refuse to carry out abortions and this has helped to ensure that a third of public hospitals do no operations of this kind at all. The number of legal abortions has settled down at about 150,000 a year – 35 per cent carried out in private clinics. The deaths and accidents associated with clandestine abortion have practically disappeared. The 1974 reform was provisional for five years and in November 1979 it was reintroduced – this time by the Minister for Women – and passed by 271 votes to 201, once again with opposition support. Not counting small numbers of abstentions and absentees, the main party groups divided as follows: Gaullists (RPR) 24 for, 116 against; *Giscardiens* (UDF) 45 for, 73 against; Socialists 114 for; Communists 86 for. The new divorce law making it possible for couples to divorce by mutual consent if their marriage had broken down – another early Giscardian reform – was also passed with massive opposition support and some hesitation by the *majorité* by 381 votes to 34 in June 1975. These early difficulties with government supporters in Parliament, accentuated later where reforms of capital gains taxation was attempted, are a factor in explaining why the pace of social reform slowed down so much as the 1981 presidential election drew nearer.

The 'Haby' reforms, named after the Finance Ministry official appointed by Giscard d'Estaing to be Minister of Education in 1974, were the main feature of educational change in the first years of the Giscard presidency. They fit into the context of the President's general ideas on social justice and into the general trend of postwar educational reform in France, both of which can be summed up in the phrase 'elitist egalitarianism', equal access for all but great advantages for the brightest and most motivated. In *Démocratie française*, discussing the need to eliminate privileges, Giscard d'Estaing argues that 'inequality of talent and determination are part of human nature; no justice comes from denying that. The establishment of a single system of secondary schools [*collèges uniques*] for all young French people will represent a powerful means for equalising their cultural intake' (1976, pp. 65–6). However, since individuals have different abilities, education 'must, by an effort of individualisation, adapt as closely as it can to the personality and gifts of each pupil or student. That is to say, that guidance [*orientation*] must be the general rule' (p. 82). The Haby reforms embody both of these principles, comprehensive access and a subsequent form of guidance that amounts to selection. Nursery education is open to all, there is no streaming by ability in primary schools, or holding back children who cannot read, and all pupils enter a *collège unique* at secondary level. However, *orientation* at the level of the *cinquième* directs about one pupil in five either towards the *certificat d'aptitude professionelle* or to classes in the technical *lycée* which prepare for apprenticeships. At the level of *troisième* (the end of compulsory schooling), of the pupils who are not already technically oriented and who stay at school (over half the original intake) two-thirds go to the *lycée* which prepares them for the *baccalauréat* and higher education, and the rest to the technical *lycée* to join the would-be apprentices or seekers of the *certificat d'aptitude professionelle*. The result in practice is that the children of working-class families end up on their own in the technical *lycée* being prepared for manual occupations. The idea of orienting pupils to studies that will prepare them better for life at work has been much criticised by teacher unions, which invariably criticise any reforms. Indeed in May 1968, an earlier period when educational reform was in the air, one of the criticisms made of education by unions at that time was that it was not oriented toward the jobs that were likely to be available. In higher education, the Minister for Universities appointed by Giscard d'Estaing, Alice Saunier-Seïté, has tried the same approach of attempting to fit university studies to the job market, and has been equally criticised. The other development in *lycées* which is viewed with concern is the increasing advantage which goes to the brighter pupils who take the maths *baccalauréat*. This is the road to all the high-status and secure jobs like medicine or public administration. In particular it is the road to Polytechnique and ENA.

Higher education in France is also 'elitist egalitarian'. Anyone with the *baccalauréat* can enrol at a university. Numbers, though, are so vast that there is no real guidance for first-year students, many of whom drop out. However, as Ezra Suleiman has eloquently described in his book *Elites in French Society* (1978), there are two completely separate systems of higher education: the one with open access, the other the highly selective *grandes écoles*. Would-be students have after graduation to compete for a place on the courses that prepare them for the entry exam to the *grandes écoles*. 'The creation of an elite was, of course, not an end in itself, for the *grandes écoles* all sought an elite that was trained for a specific task, an elite that was "useful" ... The practical nature of the training the *grandes écoles* dispense has always been their *raison d'être* and it has marked them off from the universities' (Suleiman, in V. Wright ed. 1979, p. 103). The political, administrative, commercial and industrial worlds have come in recent years to be dominated by former students of Polytechnique and the Ecole Nationale d'Administration, in particular by those who pass out high enough to get a place in one of the *grands corps*. Top ENA students go to the Inspection des Finances, the Conseil d'Etat, the Cour des Comptes, or the Prefectoral Corps from which they can go on detachment into ministerial *cabinets*, into industry, or into political life as parliamentarians and ministers. Furthermore the *grands corps* ENA graduates who go into political life advance farther and quicker than anyone else – for example, Giscard d'Estaing (inspector of finance) and Jacques Chirac (Cour des Comptes). Top *polytechniciens* go into the elite 'technical' *corps*: the Corps des Mines and the Corps des Ponts et Chaussées which are very well represented at the top levels of industry both public and private (see Suleiman, 1978, ch. 4). Access to these schools is open to all with the necessary ability and motivation. Unfortunately as reformers, including Giscard d'Estaing, have often bemoaned, 'one notices that the most gifted students from top civil service backgrounds, and by the same token Parisian, have, more than others the idea, the interest and the ability to accede to such schools. The result is that their entry is more and more numerous, and the recruitment tends to be circumscribed.

We must think of other routes for presentation and access and, therefore ... reconsider the operation' (1976, p. 67).

Another theme of social reform to which the President has made repeated references is *revalorisation du travail manuel* – the upgrading of manual work. The low status, low rewards, poor conditions of work and poor promotion prospects of manual workers and their poor position in terms of job protection and fringe benefits compared with management and clerical employees, are unjust in themselves and, by creating distaste for manual work and resentment among those obliged to perform it, threaten social cohesion and national economic development. Such is the view of Giscard d'Estaing himself (Council of Ministers, 21 February 1979; 1976, pp. 64–5), and of Lionel Stoleru, who included improvement in the status and rewards of manual workers as part of his formula for industrial survival in his influential book *L'Impératif industriel* discussed above. In 1980 Stoleru was the minister responsible for *revalorisation du travail manuel*. Measures introduced have included manual workers' savings books in which the state assists workers who want to save in order to set up on their own, state subsidies for the improvement of working conditions (FACT – Fonds pour l'Amélioration des Conditions de Travail) worth 46 million francs in 1976–7, exhibitions and a public campaign on posters and television designed to change attitudes to manual work, the development of team-work organisation in factories instead of the dehumanising assembly-line, the introduction in July 1976 of days off as compensation for overtime working, and the gradual introduction of retirement at 60 (law of 29 December 1975).

Such educational reforms, discussed above, as the teaching of manual work in secondary schools and the preparation for manual occupations are related to *revalorisation*. These reforms of course contribute to the maintenance of social divisions rather than to their effacement. The idea is to make manual workers more contented and more productive in their roles as manual workers. The *revalorisation* programme has all the Giscardian hallmarks: it is humane, it comes down from the top, it is not very revolutionary, and it is related to the twin national objectives of social cohesion and success in international economic competition.

The taxation system in France is not the enemy of privilege that it is in some countries. Taxes on goods and services bring in far more than income tax or profits tax. In the 1980 budget value-added tax was put at 253 billion francs, income tax at 116 and company tax at 51. The big difference between France and other European countries is that the huge cost of health and social security is not borne for the most part by the state but financed from employer and employee contributions (*cotisations sociales*). The employer pays the lion's share (60 per cent to the employee's 20 per cent, with the remaining 20 per cent from other public sources) and this vast *cotisation* plus fringe benefits adds 75 per cent on top of wages to the cost of employing a worker – variously described as a crippling burden to industry or as a valuable incentive to invest in high-productivity labour-saving machinery. The share of *cotisations sociales* in total public revenue receipts in 1974 was, according to OECD figures, 42 per cent. In consequence income tax in France is light – family allowances in fact exceed total income tax revenue. A married man with two children could expect in 1980 to pay about 10 per cent of his income in income tax if he earned 120,000 francs or about 7 per cent if he earned 80,000.

One attempt during the Giscard presidency to attack privilege through the tax system was the proposal to tax 'plus-values', or capital gains. It was a reform however that was blown badly off course. Giscard d'Etaing had been proposing measures to stop property speculation since 1962. No sooner was he elected President than he set up, in July 1974, the Monguilan Commission to report on the matter. The Council of Ministers decided in April 1976 to introduce a capital gains tax. The proposal, however, ran into a great deal of parliamentary opposition. Despite the fact that their leader Chirac was Prime Minister, the Gaullists rebelled. They and the left expressed their preference for a straightforward tax on capital. The National Assembly by pressure and by amendments gradually forced the government to retreat. Long-term capital gains, gains on second homes, gains on gold *napoléons*, half of the gains on property were exempted. The threshold for payment of the tax was raised. The project, almost totally disfigured, was finally adopted by Parliament in July 1976, but the following year the goverment, in a gesture designed to appease its supporters, decided to delay its application until July 1979.

Some reforms have not been directed towards the objective of greater social equality. The attempts to remedy the huge deficit in the health and social security systems, for instance, have led to the charge that a double health service – one for the rich, and one for the rest – was being introduced. Health and social security, as explained above, is largely financed by employer and employee contributions, not the state. Rising costs have forced contributions to rise some 20 per cent a year since 1973 but the deficit has continued to grow. In 1979 Jacques Barrot, the Minister of Health, put forward a plan based on various measures including a big cut in the annual growth rate of health service expenditure from 22 per cent down to the rate of growth of the economy (3–4 per cent) and an attempt to work out a new agreement with doctors. This would retain social security reimbursement to patients at an official rate of fees, not greatly increased, but leave certain categories of doctor free to charge above the official rate if they wanted to, with the patient paying the difference. This would cut the increase in costs but leave with the official fee the young doctors and the poorer patients. A battle was also engaged with the health insurance *mutuels* which reimburse to their members, often groups of public employees like teachers, the proportion of their medical expenses (called the *ticket modérateur*) that social security does not repay. This 100 per cent repayment is held to encourage excessive use of medical services. The attempt to outlaw it provoked the rare sight in May 1980 of a united 'day of action' with all unions taking part in strikes and marches.

Mention must finally be made of a policy areas where the French government has certainly not followed the enlightened and humane path that it has in others: immigration. Immigrants have played a considerable part in French postwar economic expansion, two-thirds of them are unskilled, and they perform, as in other countries, a lot of the unpleasant and menial jobs. Thirty-one per cent of workers in building and public works are immigrants, and 26 per cent of automobile assembly workers. Seven per cent of the population in France is foreign – the most numerous groups being Portuguese (0·9 million), Algerians (0·8 million), Italians (0·6 million) and Spanish (0·5 million). France has had a liberal regime for immigration and racial discrimination is relatively unpronounced. When economic recession and unemployment hit Europe in the mid-1970s, France, like other countries, began to restrict immigration. Immigration of workers (from non-EEC countries) and of families of immigrants already in France was banned in 1974 though the restrictions on families were subsequently eased and in fact, in deference to a Conseil d'Etat ruling and to protests from the Algerian government, whose citizens were the ones most affected, lifted in October 1977. Immigration dropped considerably. From 1964 to 1973 net immigration had been between 90,000 and 180,000, but in 1976 there was net emigration from France, the outflow of Algerians (– 60,000) being more than immigration from the rest of the world (+ 30,000). In June 1977 the minister responsible (Stoleru again) offered a repatriation bonus of 10,000 francs to any unemployed immigrant but there were very few takers.

The policy of not issuing work permits to foreigners was reaffirmed in 1977 and a big effort to control illegal immigration was undertaken. On 14 March 1979 measures were announced in the Council of Ministers to prevent the entry of foreigners into the country, or to expel them if they were already there, if they had no means of support, no proper documents, or if they were considered to be a threat to public order. Expulsion was to be an administrative, not a judicial decision and could be preceded by internment. The proposed law ran into parliamentary difficulties, however, and was thrown out twice by the Senate. It was subsequently reintroduced in a modified form which gave judicial guarantees to foreigners being expelled or interned beyond forty-eight hours.

The principal measure designed to reduce the number of foreigners in France was suspended because it clashed with foreign policy considerations. Thousands of expiring five- and ten-year residence permits issued to Algerians were not to be renewed, or renewed a year at a time. This was causing great anxiety and endless queues of permit-seekers. As a concession to improving Franco-Algerian relations this policy was suspended for review in 1980. On balance, apart from some action on housing and on certain aspects of discrimination against immigrants, one cannot regard the Giscard d'Estaing record on immigration as particularly liberal.

The next two chapters deal with other aspects of reform – institutions, including electoral reforms like the vote at 18 or the reform of local government, and civil liberties. Taken as a whole, these three chapters show that the liberal *élan*, which began with the law on abortion and the reduction of the voting age, has not been maintained. In particular, as we shall see in Chapter 11, the President evidently felt there was insufficient support from the pro-government parties in Parliament and outside, and from public opinion as a whole, to take the risk of judicial reforms like the abolition of the death penalty. Profound social reform has not really been the hallmark of the Giscard presidency.

CHAPTER 10

Institutions and Reforms

In 1967 Valéry Giscard d'Estaing called for 'a more liberal functioning of institutions'. In 1974 he became a President with a certain reforming zeal. Should we expect political institutions to have been greatly changed? During the election campaign he suggested that Parliament should be given back 'its independence on a certain number of subjects' (Europe 1, 11 April 1974). He declared himself 'favourable to an evolution of institutions in the direction of a regime that is more clearly presidential' (RTL 18 April 1974). In addition, 'the duration of the Presidential mandate must be reduced. Seven years is too long.' Looking wider than the Constitution, there was an expectation of a more devolutionist approach to the regions, an explicit pledge that Paris should have a mayor like all other towns and villages (*Enterprise*, 25 April 1974) and the view that young people should have the right to vote. As President, on the other hand, Giscard d'Estaing has stressed his duty to safeguard the Constitution, and to hand it over to his successors 'in the state in which I found it' (5 April 1979). 'The Fifth Republic is today the Republic that French people want,' he declared at a lunch to celebrate the twentieth anniversary of its Constitution on 28 September 1978, and promised that there would be 'no enfeeblement of institutions'. What we should expect therefore from the Giscard presidency, so far, is exactly what we have been given: minor but important changes in a liberal direction but nothing fundamental. This will be apparent if we look at four main areas: the Constitution and in particular the role of Parliament, electoral laws, regional and local government, and the French territories overseas.

The Constitution of the Fifth Republic, as was explained in Chapter 3, is not specifically presidential. Compared with its Fourth Republic predecessor, the big change is that Parliament has much less power to impede the executive – President and government. In practice it has been very presidential because that is the way General de Gaulle wanted it to be and that is the conception that has been shared by successive Presidents and their Prime Ministers and the parliamentary majorities on whom the Prime Ministers depended. So far no changes in the Constitution have been proposed which would either institutionalise presidential dominance or circumscribe it. The proposal to reduce the President's term of office, which had already gone through Parliament under President Pompidou but had been abandoned, was in 1980 finally rejected by Giscard d'Estaing. The idea of having a vice-president has been dismissed. Presidential supremacy over the whole range of policy has never been more pronounced.

Parliament

Parliament on the other hand has been, to a mild extent, the arena of 'a more liberal functioning of institutions'. There has been a constitutional change, some procedural changes and a change in the way government, the parliamentary majority and, to a lesser extent, the opposition behave. The power of Parliament in relation to the executive was a major issue in French politics in the 1950s. The return to power of General de Gaulle in 1958, the passage of the 1958 Constitution, the repeated electoral victories of the General's supporters all underlined one victorious theme: stability and progress depend on a strong executive free from the interference and harassment of the dividers and wreckers traditionally to be found in the French Parliament. In the Fourth Republic, firm government had been impossible: there had never been a parliamentary majority willing to give regular support to a government when unpopular decisions had to be faced. Any question to the government could end in a vote of no confidence and a new, short-lived coalition would have to be found. The Fifth Republic Constitution was a reaction to this state of affairs and there cannot, in consequence, be a constitution in history to compare with it for laying down in such meticulous detail all the ways and procedures by which the executive can avoid parliamentary harassment.

Government business has priority on the agenda (Article 48), the government can intervene when there is a deadlock between the National Assembly and the Senate (Article 45), the government may ask for delegated legislative powers (Article 38) which means making laws without the assent of Parliament, and the government's sphere of regulation covers everything that is not specifically a legislative matter. In addition the Constitution gives the government a procedure to end discussion of amendments and impose a single vote to decide a whole legislative text (Article 44), it lays down a time-limit for voting the budget (Article 47), it makes ministerial office incompatible with membership of Parliament but gives ministers the right to take part in parliamentary debates (Articles 25 and 31) and it lays down the precise dates of the two very short annual parliamentary sessions (five months in total – Article 28). The Fifth Republic remains a parliamentary regime because the National Assembly can by a motion of censure or a denial of confidence remove the government – but the procedure for bringing this about makes it as difficult as it decently could be. Article 49 prescribes that a motion of censure can only be put down if one-tenth of the Assembly's members have signed it, that the same tenth should not already have signed one that session, that no vote can take place for forty-eight hours (so that tempers and burning issues can cool), that to be carried the motion must command a majority of the entire membership (including absentees) and that only votes in favour of the motion are counted, so that absentees are in a sense counted in favour of the government. A lot of this, of course, is perfectly reasonable: a government must be able to govern, it is normal for governments today to be the main initiators of legislation, and political stability requires that governments are not constantly and frivolously overthrown. The problem in France is that the government, provided it has the support of a parliamentary majority, is just a little too safe from parliamentary scrutiny or criticism or control. Constitution, procedure and parliamentary practice are too restrictive of the opposition.

There have, however, been some moves towards 'a more liberal functioning of institutions'. First, Article 61 of the Constitution was amended, the first constitutional amendment of any significance since the change to the directly elected presidency in 1962. Before the change only the President, the Prime Minister, or the Presidents of the National Assembly or

Senate could ask the Constitutional Council to say whether a proposed law conformed with the Constitution or not. Now any sixty *députés* or sixty Senators can invoke the Constitutional Council. This amendment was voted, according to the terms of Article 89 of the Constitution by both houses meeting as a Congress as Versailles on 29 October 1979, with the parties of the left opposing it. Its object however was, in the words of the Prime Minister, 'to give the opposition the means to fulfil its function better', and the opposition has found it useful. By July 1978 parliamentarians had used Article 61 twenty-four times. On twenty occasions the initiative came from the opposition: fourteen times Socialist, twice Communist and four times joint Socialist–Communist. On six occasions (five Socialist, one joint) the Constitutional Council found the law not to be in conformity with the Constitution so it was not promulgated. Sometimes these were important: for example, on 12 January 1977 the Constitutional Council upheld a Socialist–Communist objection to a law authorising the police to stop and search any vehicle on the grounds that it infringed the Constitution's guarantee of individual liberty. So the amendment to Article 61 helps the opposition to play its part and is in line with the liberal inclination of President Giscard d'Estaing whose proposal it was.

Parliamentary procedure has been slightly modified too, to give the opposition more favourable opportunities to perform its role. Parliamentary questions to ministers have never had in the Fifth Republic the prestige as an instrument for controlling the executive that they have at Westminster. A minister in Great Britain can be put through quite a searching and punishing test by well-armed supplementary questions on issues of topical concern. Prime Minister's question time is particularly important as an arena of political combat. In an attempt to make parliamentary questions in France come nearer to having the immediacy and unscripted character they have at Westminster, a new procedure, *Questions au Gouvernement*, was introduced in 1974. Every Wednesday time is set aside for questions on any matter to be put to any minister, without prior notice. Half the time is allowed to the opposition and half to the majority. Unfortunately questions take the form of a speech by the questioner and a speech in reply by the minister. There are no supplementary questions so the minister may get away with an evasive or inaccurate answer. However, it is at least a chance for the opposition to demand a government statement on a matter of topical concern.

Another minor procedural change which again makes it slightly more difficult for the government to evade scrutiny concerns committees of inquiry and control (*commissions d'enquête ou de contrôle*) that Parliament can set up. Before 1977 these committees found life very difficult. They only had four months to produce their report, they had no power to compel witnesses to attend (so that the government and its officials could refuse to be investigated), and the Assembly could decide by majority vote that it did not want to publish the committee's report. In October 1977 the time-limit was extended to six months and publication of the report became automatic. However, the government can still refuse co-operation with the investigation, and of course the pro-government parliamentary majority can refuse opposition proposals to set them up, as for instance over the President's African policy.

There have also been some improvements in government behaviour. The government does not resort nearly so frequently to the steamroller of Article 44 – the 'blocked vote' which requires Parliament to swallow all or part of a Bill as a single package. There has been no resort since 1968 to the procedure for the granting of delegated legislative powers to the government. In December 1979 the government had some difficulty with getting the budget through because the Gaullist RPR, which normally supports the government, refused to vote for it until the government made a concession by cutting down expenditure. This the government refused to do, and resorted several times to the procedure outlined in Article 49. This enables the government to declare a text a matter of confidence. The text is automatically adopted unless a motion of censure is put down and carried in the constitutional manner. The Gaullists, unwilling to bring down the government by voting for a motion of censure, were thus rendered helpless, but the procedure was neither unconstitutional nor, under the circumstances, abusive. It also shows that governments in the Fifth Republic do occasionally have to fight for their life by asking for a vote of confidence.

The change that would have the most effect on parliamentary life would be having members of the opposition as presidents of some of the permanent committees. The six permanent committees in each house cover Laws, Finance, Defence, Foreign Affairs, Economic Affairs, and Cultural and Social Affairs (in the

Senate the last two are separate and Defence and Foreign Affairs
are combined). Each proposed law has to go to one or more
committee for scrutiny and a report which may propose
amendments. The committee chairmen occupy a very influential
role, have considerable resources at their disposal, and have much
more access to the administration than other *députés*. After the
1978 election it was reported that President Giscard d'Estaing
was particularly keen to see some of these chairmanships in the
National Assembly go to the opposition. However, the Gaullists
were strongly opposed on the grounds that such important
positions should go to those who had won the election, not to
those who had lost. The opposition were not willing to accept a
couple of token vice-chairmanships so all committees remain
firmly in the hands of government supporters.

France is still a country where executive power remains almost
immune from parliamentary scrutiny. The main reason is that the
President, who makes all the important policy decisions, is not
responsible to Parliament. Other factors are the wide extent of the
government's discretion in matters considered to be regulations
not laws, the low status of the opposition, and the procedural
restrictions which prevent the opposition from initiating debates
other than on motions of censure. Pierre Dabezier, writing on the
French role in Africa (*Le Monde diplomatique*, April 1980),
compared France with the United States where the President has
to seek parliamentary approval to engage military forces. In
France 'the President is in practical terms omnipotent . . .
Parliament has no rights other than that of general supervision,
more theoretical than real, over foreign policy. It is in particular
powerless from a budgetary angle . . . [since] the cost of
interventions is not itemised . . . Only 0·7 per cent of written
questions relate to French military actions . . . All demands for
commissions d'enquête having been rejected, one can say that the
executive – with the President of the Republic at the head – is free
of control in this domain'

Parliament in some ways, however, has become more assertive
in the last few years. The members of the *majorité*, while always
stopping short of bringing down the government, have been less
unconditional in their support of government legislation than in
previous Fifth Republic Parliaments. The Abortion Law was only
carried with opposition support, a proposed constitutional
amendment in 1974 which would have allowed ministers (who

have to give up their parliamentary seats on accession to government office) to return automatically to Parliament on leaving the government was thrown out; the government had to make big concessions over capital gains taxation in 1976; the Senate rejected the government's proposals on the expulsion of immigrants; and the Gaullists would not support the 1980 budget.

President Giscard d'Estaing for his part has, in one sense, remained faithful to his original conception of 'a more liberal functioning of institutions' and has been the author of some modest but concrete measures. We should not lose sight, however, of the fact that in another sense he has contributed to the weakening of Parliament. Under his presidency more and more decision-making has been centred at the Elysée and in the technocratic closed circuit of presidential and ministerial *cabinets*. As the ill-fated *programme commun* of the left put it: 'the head of state, in the conduct of internal and external policy, has exorbitant powers which he exercises without control'.

Electoral reform

Another reform initiated by the President, at the first Council of Ministers held within days of taking office, was the reduction of the voting age in France to 18. This was an effective reply to critics who had claimed he would not take such a step because young electors might be more likely to vote for the left. There have been various other and less radical changes to the electoral laws which can be conveniently recorded at this point. First, Frenchmen living overseas acquired the right not merely to vote (which they already had) but to register a proxy vote in any constituency of their choice, provided it was in a town of over 30,000 population, irrespective of whether they had any connection with it. This extraordinary measure went unnoticed through Parliament in the end-of-session rush in July 1977. However, a veritable scandal arose when it became clear that officials in French embassies were being given *carte blanche* and blank proxies by overseas residents to register these votes in marginal constituencies, vital for the government. This caused the defeat of at least one Socialist *député*, Georges Frèche in Montpellier. Secondly, a candidate now has to receive the support of 12½ per cent of all registered voters (usually around 18 per cent of those who actually vote) at the first ballot in an election in order to qualify for the second ballot. All elections in France (except for the European Parliament) are two-ballot. In the case of parliamentary and local elections, it is now customary in most constituencies for the four main parties to present a candidate at the first ballot and then, by agreement within each 'coalition', the second ballot usually consists of a dual between the best-placed candidate of the left and the best-placed candidate of the *majorité*. The 12½ per cent rule simplified the choice somewhat because it eliminated so many candidates. If it eliminated all candidates except one, then whoever came second was allowed to stand. In fact, what frequently happened in 1978 was that in some constituencies it eliminated all candidates of the left, so that the *majorité* had an unopposed run in the second ballot, or all candidates of the *majorité* so that the left was unopposed. In the constituency of the Communist leader Georges Marchais, all *majorité* candidates were eliminated by the 12½ per cent rule. The Socialist candidate was not eliminated but, respecting the pact between the two parties, withdrew. Marchais was thus the only candidate in the second ballot.

Finally, the Constitution was slightly amended on 18 June 1976 to tidy up the rules for presidential elections in the event of the death or serious illness of a candidate. The Constitutional Council can now postpone the election if a declared candidate dies, or is forced to withdraw in the week before the campaign starts, and must postpone it if such an event occurs during the campaign. The election is called off and recommenced if one of the two leading candidates at the first ballot (who alone go into the second ballot of a presidential election unless they choose for some reason to withdraw) dies before the second ballot or for some other reason has to give up. This amendment was obviously necessary: the possibility, however remote, of some accident leaving a single unopposed candidate (perhaps a Communist?) at the second ballot was a gaping loophole.

Local and regional government

In the field of local and regional government, the keynote of the presidency yet again has been 'a more liberal functioning of institutions', not radical change. Local government in France – or local administration as, not without significance, it is called – is commonly portrayed as exceedingly centralised. This is due partly to the fact that some public services like education, or the police, which in some countries are controlled by local authorities, are in France the responsibility of the central state. However, the picture of local administration as totally subject to control by the state stems from the French institution of the *préfet*. The *préfet*, installed like a colonial governor in a magnificent palace in the capitals of all the 101 *départements* of metropolitan and overseas France, is responsible for all state services in his *département*, exercises *tutelle* (somewhere between supervision and control) over the mayors and councils of every town and village, can suspend them, alter their budgets, act as their police chief, and presides in official uniform on ceremonial occasions. By the principle of hierarchy a mayor, as agent of the state, is subject to the authority of the *préfet*. In fact, this is not a complete picture of local administration. 'Local power' in the sense of power being wielded by locally elected political leaders, is a reality. This is mainly attributable to the fact that the office of mayor in a town or *conseiller général* in a *département* is often a base from which politicians go on to become *députés*, senators, or ministers. Indeed, those who, following the fashion in the Fifth Republic, start the *cursus honorum* at the top by going straight from the civil service to being a minister in the government, face the need to establish their political career on some local base so they seek election as councillors and *députés*. Eighty-three per cent of the *députés* elected at the 1978 elections were councillors, 46 per cent were members of both *conseil général* and municipal council (Frears and Parodi, 1979, p. 101). Though strictly speaking, therefore, political leaders like Jacques Chaban-Delmas, President of the National Assembly, former Prime Minister, and mayor of Bordeaux, are subject to prefectoral authority, the reality is clearly that they have much more influence than the *préfet*. To be the mayor of a big city is to be an important national political figure, to have the resources and the powers to exercise considerable initiative on behalf of one's city and to have the authority that comes with being elected for six years and not removable by party caucus or other means. In short, local government in France is presidential. The mayor of a French town is much better known to the public, much more influential and able to leave much more of a personal imprint on his city than the transient leader of the majority party on a city or county council in Great Britain.

There have been some modest reforms in the direction of 'transferring to local councils the powers that can be exercised at local level, as well as the necessary means to exercise them' (*projet de loi* – Senate, 20 December 1978). The first principle behind the new reform is that eventually the state should only keep 'the great attributions of sovereignty like foreign affairs, defence, justice and security, as well as responsibility for national economic and social policies' (including education?). Anything perceived as local should be decentralised 'now or in due course'. The second principle is that local councils must have financial responsibility for the powers they exercise. Under the law some of the supervision exercised by the *préfet* over council decisions is lifted, some of his powers over council budgets are modified, and mayors are given wider powers in such matters as town planning.

It was repeatedly emphasised by the President and ministers that basic units of local government would remain the 36,000 *communes* – the towns and villages of France, each with its mayor and municipal council – and the *départements* which, with their responsibilities for industrial development and public investment, constitute 'a level of administration quite indispensable to the country' (Secretary of State Bécam, *Le Monde* 28 October 1978). A further law in 1979 provided for a more satisfactory direct taxation system for local councils based on the value-added tax.

The most important reform in local government was the decision to restore to Paris the status of having a city council and a mayor. Paris had always had a council of sorts but no presidential figure called the mayor of Paris since the Commune in 1871. Indeed so many governments in French history have been overthrown in the streets of the capital that a mayor of Paris had always been considered too great a threat to the central government. Unfortunately for President Giscard d'Estaing the mayoralty of Paris, arising from this liberal reform, fell after the fierce election battle described in Chapter 4 to Jacques Chirac, the leader of the Gaullist RPR. Chirac is also a member of Parliament and president of the *conseil général* in the Corrèze, a rural *département* some 300 miles from Paris, but this did not deter him from assuming his role with gusto. Indeed, as mayor of Paris

Chirac tends to act as a rival head of state, making official overseas 'state visits', surrounding himself with municipally paid *chargés de mission*, presiding at vast official banquets and cultural manifestations around the city, and being as annoying as possible to the central government by such means as refusing to accept the cost of the Paris police as an item for the municipal budget.

One level of local government that has not been reformed and which remains with its original rather modest powers is the regional council. France has an extremely active policy for regional economic development but it is pursued mainly through central government agencies, often staffed by innovating technocrats, in which representatives of local councils participate to some extent in a consultative capacity. The twenty-two regional councils which are not directly elected but composed of the region's members of Parliament and delegates from the other councils in the region do, however, have some influence from the fact that their members and especially their presidents are often influential national politicians like Jean Lecanuet (former Minister of Justice) or Pierre Messmer (former Prime Minister). The region most recently to acquire its own council was the Ile de France (the Paris region) in July 1976. Regional councils are serviced by the *préfet de région* who is the *préfet* of the *département* where the regional capital is: for example the *préfet* of Haute-Garonne (Toulouse) is *préfet de région* for the Midi-Pyrenees region.

The regional councils may tax their citizens up to a limit of 55 francs per inhabitant (1979 figure). This taxation takes three forms: a tax on driving licences fixed by each region, a tax on vehicle registrations and a tax on registration or sales of property. The contribution by the motorist of so large a part of the region's budget is justified by the fact that most of the expenditure by regional councils is on roads. Other resources available to regional councils include, not surprisingly, government subsidies and loans. They have quite an important role in the co-ordination of the *départements* in matters of regional development – highways, national parks, tourism – and are consulted on economic planning.

The real regional development policies, however, come from central government bodies like DATAR (Délégation à l'Aménagement du Territoire et à l'Action Régionale). The *délégué* in charge of DATAR is responsible directly to the Prime Minister, takes the lead in proposing regional projects for economic development, arranges with other ministers and the National Plan for the necessary finance, and works with the *préfets de région* to ensure that plans are carried out. He is also a member of all the important financing agencies for regional development like the FDES (Fonds de Développement Economique et Social) and interministerial committees like CIANE (Nature and Environment), CIASI (Industrial Reorganisation), or CIAT (Aménagement du Territoire). Indeed, he is the main source of recommendations to CIAT and its executive instrument. It is DATAR that has been responsible for some of the most impressive regional projects like the development of the Languedoc–Roussillon coast-line for tourism. Another central government body which plays a part in regional economic development is the Conseil Central de Planification, created by Giscard d'Estaing and presided over by him.

There was a general expectation that Giscard d'Estaing was a 'regionalist', a believer in devolved powers, possibly because he was supported in the election by that ardent devolutionist Jean-Jacques Servan-Schreiber. Indeed JJSS was immediately appointed Minister for Reforms – but only lasted ten days in office because he criticised French tests of nuclear weapons in the South Pacific! Periodically there arise in France demands for regional autonomy – mainly from peripheral regions like Britanny which feel remote from Paris, are underprivileged economically and have a native cultural tradition of their own. In the Giscard presidency it is Corsica that has been the most active. There have been repeated strikes, marches, acts of violence, seizing of hostages and demands for autonomy. At the height of the troubles in August 1976 when two gendarmes were killed, a personal adviser from the President's *cabinet*, Jean Riolacci (a Corsican), was appointed *préfet* in Corsica. Various concessions were made: Corsica became two *départements* not one, a second university at Bastia was created, transportation improvements were promised but there was no concession to the idea of Corsican self-government. There is no evidence at elections that the demand for Corsican autonomy is very strong: Corsica, which with two *départements* is now entitled to four *députés* (the minimum for any *département* is two) sent back four supporters of the government and all RPR, the most Jacobin and centralist of all the non-Communist parties!

On regionalism Giscard d'Estaing has made his view quite clear. In a television interview on 16 June 1976 he said:

I am entirely hostile to the political fragmentation of France, because France ... would exhaust much of her strength and her external authority if she cut herself in little pieces on the political level. That is why I am, as you know, hostile to political regionalism. On the other hand, regional economic development has always seemed to me something very reasonable and very efficient. I am also, unlike some others, entirely favourable to France conserving all her cultures.

Reviewing this declaration, Jacques de Lanversin (1979, p. 75) remarks laconically that 'the position . . . of President Giscard d'Estaing seems to be a projection . . . of the line of moderate evolution pursued up to now'.

Overseas Territories

A final area of French public administration, usually left out of books on France, has also been the arena for modest but non-radical reform: the overseas *départements* and territories, known as DOM-TOM (*départements et territoires d'outre mer*). The DOM-TOM are considered to be integral parts of France, not colonies. They are widely scattered in the West Indies, in the Indian Ocean and in the Pacific. French Guiana is on the mainland of South America and the archipelago of St Pierre and Miquelon is in the mouth of the St Lawrence river between Canada and the United States (de Gaulle naturally visited it). There is a secretary of state responsible for the DOM-TOM. Some in the Pacific have territorial assemblies and high commissioners, but in other respects they have an administration similar to any other part of France. Their 600,000 electors send *députés* and senators to the French Parliament and vote in presidential elections and referenda — even European Parliament elections. France would not hesitate, declared the Secretary of State, Paul Dijoud (*Le Monde* 8 February 1980), to engage if necessary 'her atomic means' to defend her DOM-TOM.

Occasionally the desire for independence makes itself felt in one or other of the DOM-TOM. The French government is not favourable to independence but accepts it if there is strong evidence of a majority in favour. When the moderate majority in the territorial assembly in New Caledonia went *indépendantiste*, Dijoud dissolved it. The new election was won by loyalists but a majority of the Melanesian population which slightly outnumbers the whites, and feels underprivileged and discriminated against, is in favour of independence. Giscard visited the Pacific territories and spoke strongly to the whites, telling them they would even have to pay income tax, and adding: 'nothing great or lasting will be achieved in this territory if you do not allow the Melanesians the place that is theirs . . . France will do nothing which goes against the democratically expressed will of the inhabitants of this territory' (Nouméa, 17 July 1979).

Some territories have been granted independence in the last few years: Djibouti, Comores Archipelago and the joint Franco-British territory of New Hebrides, where the French insisted on guarantees for the French language and tried to delay independence, but where the English-speaking majority won a convincing victory at the polls. Djibouti in the Horn of Africa, the last French territory on the African mainland, was the scene of violence in 1976. There was conflict between the two main tribal groups the Afars (Ethiopian) and the Issas (Somali). The Somali Coast Liberation Front seized a bus-load of children from the French military school and two were killed in the subsequent rescue. French policy was reassessed and independence talks, attended only by some of the Issas, began. On 8 May 1977 there was a referendum in the territory and 98 per cent declared in favour of independence. The Republic of Djibouti was born, but 4,000 French troops remained there to guarantee its security in a very unstable part of Africa where Ethiopians and Somalis were at war.

The accession to independence that has been the most controversial concerns the Comores Archipelago, not far from Madagascar in the Indian Ocean. The problem was not the question of independence itself – there had been a practically unanimous referendum in the territory in December 1974 – but the French decision of June 1975 to seek ratification isle by isle. This was done so that the island of Mayotte, which ever since 1590 has been trying to resist rule by both Comores and Madagascar, could choose to remain part of France. The Comores were furious and a unilateral declaration of independence was made on 6 July 1975. The French, despite a great deal of criticism from African countries with whom they value good relations and who accused France of colonialism, pressed on with their policy. On 8 February 1976 a referendum among the 40,000 or so inhabitants of this tropical island, an impoverished but idyllic 'fruit-picking' economy, voted by 99 per cent to stay French. In May Mayotte was declared a 'territorial collectivity' – not quite up to being a *département* (unlike St Pierre and Miquelon with its 5,000 inhabitants who became one in 1976).

There are frequently accusations of French high-handedness and exploitation in respect of the DOM-TOM. The French test their nuclear weapons and extract nickel in Polynesia. They create settlements of refugees from South-East Asia in French Guiana. 'They asked us if we wanted Great Britain, Ireland and Denmark to join the Common Market [Pompidou's referendum, April 1972] but they didn't ask us if we wanted to!' complained Aimé Césaire, the Martinique Progressive Party *député* (*Le Monde* 15 December 1975), adding that the island could not develop its trade with America or Japan without going through France. He also repeated another criticism that is often made, that the DOM are never offered evolution to greater autonomy but the brutal choice of independence (without financial aid) or the status quo: 'the same old blackmail: empty stomachs or toeing the line'. Despite the efforts of the government to attract investment, economic development in the DOM-TOM and the level of wages – even of the SMIC (legal minimum wage) – are well behind metropolitan France. Paul Dijoud has declared that it is his 'ambitious policy' to bring the level of employment up to 'the equivalent of today's in metropolitan France' and to make the DOM in the Atlantic and the Indian Ocean (an unfortunate phrase) 'the aircraft-carriers of the French economy' (*Le Monde*, 9 February 1980). So no question of systematic preparation for independence: 'Vive le Québec libre' but not 'Vive la Guadeloupe libre'.

In no field of presidential action more than that of politcal and administrative institutions does the conservative liberalism of the President show more clearly. The changes in parliamentary powers and procedure are liberal but in no way threaten the concentration of powers in the presidency which Parliament has no power to control. The changes in local administration are liberal but in no way threaten the central government's monopoly of broad policy and planning decisions, and make no concession to regional autonomy. The approach to the DOM-TOM is liberal in its preparedness on occasions to recognise genuine demands for independence and to encourage economic development, but it in no way deviates from the central aim of perpetuating a direct French presence on which, to coin a phrase, the sun never sets.

CHAPTER 11

Civil Liberties

President Giscard d'Estaing aspires to leave behind him a more liberal society – a *société libérale avancée*, in fact. France is of course a country richly endowed with most of the civil liberties normal to a democracy – the right to vote secretly in free and regularly held elections, freedom to join political parties and interest groups, freedom to oppose the government and persuade others to do the same. These *acquis* should not be forgotten by readers of a chapter which concentrates, at the risk of seeming somewhat arbitrary, on just two aspects of civil liberties in which reform has not been as rapid as the President's liberal declarations might have led one to expect – the judicial process and freedom of information.

The judicial process

Of all the books on contemporary France in general and political institutions in particular – Jack Hayward's *The One and Indivisible French Republic* (1973) is an honourable exception – surprisingly few mention the question of justice. Yet the extent to which an individual is protected against the arbitrary use of executive power is as fundamental a political question as the means by which he participates in the choice of leaders. Judicial reform has been a frequent Giscardian theme and electoral programmes, such as the Programme de Blois introduced by the Prime Minister, Raymond Barre, before the 1978 elections, have made specific pledges. Indeed 'to perfect the guarantee of the rights of the individual' and 'to reinforce the rights of the citizen in dealings with the administration' were the first two headings of the Programme de Blois, and under the first there is a specific promise to introduce the *habeas corpus* principle which has given the right in England since 1679 to a person under arrest or on remand to be brought before a court. The reforms introduced by the Minister of Justice, Alain Peyrefitte, in 1980 did remarkably little to fulfil this promise. There continue to be serious problems surrounding the rights of accused persons; there have been a number of cases where the government appears to have interfered with the judicial process; the death penalty, abolished in almost all Western countries, including post-Franco Spain, is still carried out and the President has been very sparing in the use of his power of mercy; and illiberal laws continue to be proposed on matters like the expulsion of foreigners.

The argument is constantly advanced that the judicial system in France should be reformed to give more protection to the rights of the accused (e.g. Boucher, 1978; Cornec, 1977; Lombard, 1978; Hennion, 1976; Pradelle, 1979). That is not to say, however, as is frequently and wrongly supposed, that in France an accused person is presumed guilty until he proves himself innocent. There are two judicial systems, one for civil and criminal cases and the other for cases involving the administration. If a citizen is in dispute with an administrative body – for example, over whether planning permission should have been granted for the construction of a power station near his house – he can take the matter to the administrative courts and, on appeal, ultimately to the Conseil d'Etat with its prestige and, though part of the civil service, its reputation for independence from government. The judicial system for civil and criminal cases is summarised in simplified and diagrammatical form in Figure 11.1.

A number of objections can be formulated throughout the criminal procedure from the point of view of the accused's rights. First, there is the problem of *garde à vue*, the right of the police to hold someone in custody for interrogation (officially twenty-four hours plus twenty-four with the authorisation of the local state prosecutor – *procureur de la République* – with extensions in drugs or national security cases). *Garde à vue* may result either from a police arrest of a suspect or because the magistrate investigating an offence, the *juge d'instruction*, issues a warrant (*mandat d'arrêt* or *commission rogatoire*). Although the *procureur de la République* is a judge, he does not decide prolongation of *garde à vue* in open court nor does he have to give reasons. Indeed the idea that there is judicial supervision of

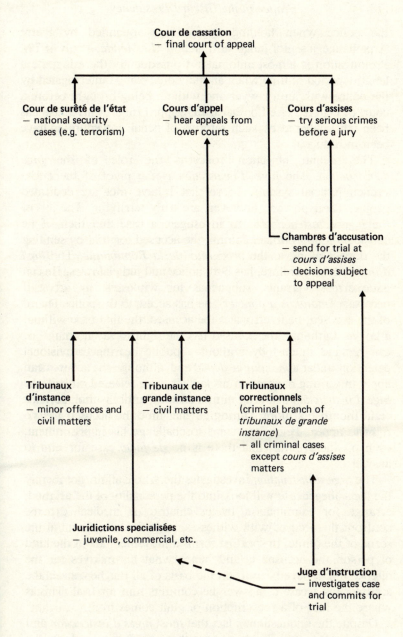

Cour de cassation
— final court of appeal

Cour de sûreté de l'état
— national security
cases (e.g. terrorism)

Cours d'appel
— hear appeals from
lower courts

Cours d'assises
— try serious crimes
before a jury

Chambres d'accusation
— send for trial at
cours d'assises
— decisions subject
to appeal

**Tribunaux
d'instance**
— minor offences and
civil matters

**Tribunaux de
grande instance**
— civil matters

**Tribunaux
correctionnels**
(criminal branch of
*tribunaux de grande
instance*)
— all criminal cases
except *cours d'assises*
matters

Juridictions specialisées
— juvenile, commercial, etc.

Juge d'instruction
— investigates case
and commits for
trial

Figure 11.1   French judicial system (civil and criminal).

the police when holding a suspect is qualified by Pierre Arpaillange, a senior judge, as a 'fiction' (*Le Monde*, 4 July 1979). Prolongation is almost automatic. Consequently there is quite a lengthy period of time when an individual can be interrogated by the police without a lawyer and without being brought before a court or charged (see Lombard, 1978, pp. 176–8). This abuse has been left unaltered by such reforms of penal procedure as have been introduced.

The second objection concerns the role of the *juge d'instruction*. The *juge d'instruction* is the pivot of the entire French judicial system. Those that I have met are dedicated people. Their powers, however, are truly terrifying. The job of the *juge d'instruction* is to investigate a case and then, if he considers it appropriate, commit the accused for trial by sending the dossier along to the *procureur de la République*. The *juge d'instruction*, therefore, has both police and judicial roles. He can issue arrest warrants, subpoenas for witnesses, by arrest if necessary (*mandats d'amener*), he has access to the police record of the accused, he interrogates the accused, the first time without a lawyer (although the accused has the right to say nothing), he can remand in custody without a public hearing (provisional detention under a *mandat de dépôt*) and, although the accused can apply in writing or through his lawyer to be released on bail, the *juge d'instruction* can keep him in custody until his trial, perhaps eight months or more. During all that time the accused has no right to appear before the court to challenge his imprisonment, even on the grounds that there is no *de facto* case for him to answer.

The *juge d'instruction* investigates the whole affair, not merely the facts alleged. He will look into the personality of the accused, arrange for examination by psychiatric or medical experts, confront the accused with witnesses, stage a re-enactment at the scene of the crime. In short he forms a judgement about the kind of person the accused is and hence what his motives for the offence might have been. If on the basis of all this he decides the accused has a case to answer he commits him for trial. This is where the idea of a presumption of guilt comes from.

Despite the unquestioned fact that most *juges d'instruction* and prosecutors try their hardest to see that no injustice is done, the third objection relates to the judicial procedure itself. British and American readers will be familiar with their own 'accusatorial' procedure in which the prosecution seeks to provide proof that the facts alleged against the defendant, that on such and such a day he committed such and such an offence, are true, and the defence seeks to show that the evidence is not adequate to establish those particular facts beyond reasonable doubt. The court does not have the criminal record of the accused before it. In France the procedure is 'inquisitorial'. The presiding judge interrogates the accused, referring to his background and previous criminal convictions. In doing this it is very difficult for the presiding judge not to sound like the prosecution. In any *tribunal correctionnel* in France you can hear the judge say sternly to the accused: 'Come on, Mohammed, you are obviously lying. You have committed this kind of offence before, haven't you? Short of money, were you? Why weren't you at work?' The prosecution (*procureur de la République* or *avocat général* – both members of the judicial, not the legal profession) and the defence may be invited to make comments or ask some questions during this process but the main questioning of accused and witnesses is done by the presiding judge. The *partie civile* (injured party) is also heard, and his lawyer makes a plea. Then the prosecution pronounces a *requisitoire* in which he specifies the sentence he considers necessary (by no means always the maximum, of course). Finally the defence plea (*plaidoirie*) is heard.

Unlike in England, there is no right to a trial by jury, except for certain very serious offences like murder or rape classified as *crimes* which must be tried by a *cour d'assises* consisting of three judges and nine jurors. The judges retire with the jurors and their votes are counted. A majority of eight to four (i.e. at least five jurors in favour) is required for a verdict of guilty. The penalty is also voted on and a simple majority suffices. The jurors swear to judge according to their 'conscience and *intime conviction*'. This old tradition in France is very different from that of the Anglo-Saxon countries. I sit as a magistrate in Great Britain and have often had the *intime conviction* that the accused was guilty but have supported a verdict of not-guilty because the evidence of guilt was not presented in a manner that was absolutely conclusive. Some may regard this as an argument in favour of the *intime conviction* principle. The memoirs of a distinguished French judge (Ullmann, 1978) refer to cases where criminals who were skilful at covering their tracks would have been undeservedly acquitted but for the *intime conviction* of the jury

(p. 155). For an accused person who is innocent, however, the *intime conviction* principle makes it more difficult to establish the truth.

It would be instructive at this point to digress further, but briefly, to compare two instances, one British and one French, of what many people believe to be errors of justice which led to the irrevocable penalty of death. The first case was the 'A6 murder' in Great Britain in 1961. James Hanratty based his defence upon an alibi – he claimed to have been in Rhyl, North Wales, at the moment the murder was committed. The most serious evidence against him was that the woman who survived the attack in which her lover was killed claimed to identify him. Apart from the woman's evidence, the other main factor that led to the conviction of Hanratty was that the prosecution was able to cast some doubts in court on the credibility of the witnesses for his alibi. The efforts of Hanratty's family and friends since the trial have produced much more solid support for the Rhyl alibi. It is conceivable that in France the powers of a *juge d'instruction* to investigate all aspects of the affair might have helped Hanratty to establish his innocence.

The French case is that of Christian Rannucci, guillotined in 1976 for the murder of an 8-year-old girl. The case is analysed by Gilles Perrault in his book *Le Pullover rouge* (1978). The most serious evidence against Rannucci was that he confessed to the crime. However, his confession came at the end of a very long period of interrogation under *garde à vue*, during which, so he claimed, he was maltreated. He also claimed that he confessed only because he had been too drunk to remember much about the day in question, that he certainly had been near where the body was found, and that the police told him that all witnesses had identified him. This was actually the contrary of the truth – most witnesses categorically said the man abducting the little girl was not him, had a different car, and wore a red pullover (subsequently found and much too large for Rannucci). Indeed, it was with the help of this famous red pullover that police dogs found the child's body. However, he repeated the confession (immediately after the police interrogation and with no lawyer present) to the *juge d'instruction* and all the psychiatric examinations ordered by the *juge d'instruction* started on the basis of the confession: 'the fact that he killed a child suggests that ...'. He subsequently never ceased to deny the charge but could not produce an alibi. Meanwhile the press had found him guilty and there was a strong public campaign for the death sentence, particularly because at about the same time an equally atrocious murder in Troyes had been punished by life imprisonment. If the French inquisitorial procedure might have prevented an injustice to Hanratty, the accusatorial procedure based solely on the proof of facts, not the *intime conviction* of jurors, would surely have produced a scintilla of reasonable doubt about the evidence against Rannucci.

Other aspects of judicial procedure which have been criticised as damaging to the rights of the accused include the excessive licence given to the press to publish stories about arrested persons which presume their guilt. There are no legal sanctions on this trial by press and it not only impairs a fair trial for the accused but, in serious cases, like the Rannucci affair, creates revengeful demonstrations outside the court and puts pressure on judges and jurors. Ullmann (1978, p. 139) rightly calls this 'an attack on the freedom of justice'. A final criticism of judicial procedure involves the Cour de Sûreté de l'Etat, which, at the request of the Minister of Justice, judges offences against the security of the state in peacetime – for instance, terrorism by Breton or Corsican autonomists. The court was established after the special military tribunals set up by de Gaulle to deal with OAS terrorism were declared illegal by the Conseil d'Etat in 1962. In 1975 the Cour de Sûreté tried the organisers of the *comités de soldats* – army trade unions in embryo – and in 1980 it was ordered to pursue the case of the synagogue bomb attack in the rue Copernic. Particularly criticised is the composition of the court in which two generals from the armed forces sit with the three judges. The elimination of these military figures was another specific and as yet unfulfilled promise from the government's election manifesto, the Programme de Blois.

The other big issue in French justice is the independence of the judiciary. When Pierre Arpaillange, at the time Director of Criminal Affairs and at the Ministry of Justice, wrote a report to his minister in 1972 (see Madelin and Michel, 1978, p. 337) saying that 'the crisis of justice is general', he was speaking not only of procedural defects but of the fact that the judiciary did 'not even appear in the eyes of the public to be an institution fully independent with respect to political power'. Still a judge himself, and therefore to some extent a testament to their independence, he continues to criticise the lack of a really independent judiciary (*Le Monde*, 5 July 1979). There are two problems: the status of judges as civil servants with a career involving promotion, and the capacity for the Minister of Justice to give instructions at least to the prosecution part of the judiciary. These two problems affect differently the two basic types of judge: the *parquet* judges – also called the *ministère publique* – who prosecute, and the *siège* judges who sit as judges in the court. The *parquet* judges are appointed and promoted by the President of the Republic on the proposal of the Minister of Justice, the *siège* judges by the same means but subject to an expression of opinion by the *conseil supérieur de la magistrature* composed of the President of the Republic, the Minister of Justice and nine others all named by the President. Six of the nine are judges, not elected but selected by the President from a list presented by the members of the Cour de Cassation. This procedure gives rise to the frequent complaint, just as frequently denied by Ministers of Justice, that only docile judges who issue the right sentences are promoted. There are elements of safeguard: for example a *siège* judge cannot be moved to another court, or even promoted without his consent. The *parquet* judges, in particular the *procureurs de la République* who are in charge of the administration of justice in their court area, are however directly subject to the authority of the minister. The *procureur-général* at the Cour de Sûreté de l'Etat, a transferred *siège* judge as it happened, resigned in January 1977 complaining that the Minister of Justice (Lecanuet) had tried to make him demand a stiffer penalty against a Corsican autonomist. A few months later the new minister (Guichard) decided that a *siège* judge could not be head of the *parquet* at the Cour de Sûreté de l'Etat because 'his statutory independence would not be compatible with the instructions that the government might be required to give him' (*Le Monde*, 18 January 1977).

In recent years there has developed, especially among the younger judges, a Syndicat de la Magistrature (see Marc Robert, 1976), which takes a militant line on various judicial matters: the independence of judges, the rights of the accused, *garde à vue*, or the Cour de Sûreté de l'Etat. Some actions by SM members have been much criticised. A *juge d'instruction* in September 1975, for instance, remanded an employer in custody because an accident at his factory had killed a workman. This caused a furore amongst employers' associations and among parliamentarians of the pro-government majority. Indeed, a former Gaullist Minister of Justice, Jean Foyer, argued (*Le Monde*, 2 December 1975) that *habeas corpus* was needed as a protection against 'red judges'! Another SM *juge d'instruction* was disciplined in 1974 for allowing a journalist to observe and write an article on his work. The SM even organised a judges' strike in November 1979 against a proposal by the Justice Minister to tighten control over recruitment of judges.

The allegation of government interference with justice has been made frequently during the Giscard presidency. The two most serious cases, the Abu Daoud and Klaus Croissant affairs in 1977, when political considerations seem to have intervened, both concern the difficult problem of international terrorism. Daoud was a leading member of the PLO (Palestine Liberation Organisation) and alleged to have been involved in the attack on the Israeli athletes at the Munich Olympic Games in 1972. He was arrested in Paris on 7 January 1977. Demands for his extradition were presented by both West Germany and Israel. Four days later the demands had been rejected and Daoud, to the gratification of Arab states, was taken to the airport and sent off to an Arab destination. Normally extradition is a lengthy procedure because many documents have to be assembled. This time the *chambre d'accusation* was convened in special session, and rather than remand Daoud in custody and adjourn the case, it decided on the spot and in an unprecedented manner to reject the extradition demands. This decision caused Pierre Arpaillange to write a stinging series of articles (*Le Monde*, 21 June 1977 *et seq.*) on the lack of judicial independence, and Raymond de la Pradelle (1979, p. 235) to write 'justice . . . has appeared in perfect submission to the solicitations of those in power'.

European collaboration in the control of international terrorism has been an important Giscard theme. Klaus Croissant was a German lawyer associated with the Baader–Meinhof terrorists. He was arrested in France in October 1977 and West Germany demanded extradition, on the grounds that he faced criminal charges in his own country. The extradition decree was signed by the Prime Minister at the instant of the court decision, and on 16 November Croissant was bundled out of the country the same day by helicopter, before any appeal could be lodged. A Syndicat de la Magistrature judge who protested publicly about this procedure was disciplined by the Ministry of Justice. There are numerous other recent examples of alleged political interference in judicial matters: the dismissal of the complaint by *Le Canard enchaîné* that the police had installed listening devices at its offices, for instance, or the police raid on party headquarters and the arrests of Socialist leaders that followed their symbolic protest pirate radio broadcast in June 1979. The nature of the inquiry into the curious murder of Jean de Broglie, a *Giscardien député*, in December 1976 caused opposition *députés*, after new aspects came to light in 1980, to demand the arraignment of Michel Poniatowski, Minister of the Interior at the time, before the Haute Cour de Justice. The National Assembly went so far as to set up a committee to consider this request – but made a political associate of Poniatowski its *rapporteur*!

Another important judicial and social issue where liberal reform has been conspicuous by its absence is the death penalty. It still continues in France and is carried out by the singularly revolting, if historic, method of the guillotine. From 1958 to 1977, thirty-eight murderers were condemned to death. In fifteen cases the judgement was over-ruled by the Cour de Cassation, in sixteen cases the convicted person was pardoned by the President of the Republic, and in seven cases he was executed. President Pompidou pardoned all but Buffet and Bontemps, the two killers of a prison nurse. At the time of writing, Giscard d'Estaing has pardoned four and withheld Presidential mercy from three murderers of children. One of these was Rannucci, whose case gave rise to serious doubts about a judicial error, an argument that was put to the President by Maître Lombard in the audience that is always accorded to the defence lawyer.

The President and his Minister of Justice, Alain Peyrefitte, are both proclaimed opponents of the death penalty but have been surprisingly timid in proposing its abolition. In the presidential election campaign (11 April 1974) Giscard d'Estaing said that he 'felt a profound aversion to the death penalty', Peyrefitte on 25 August 1977 said that he found the principle 'horrifying'. There have been in addition, a number of cases in recent years (see Ullmann, 1978) where juries have refused to pass the death sentence as requested by the prosecution, and the majority in public opinion opposed to abolition is far from overwhelming (55 per cent against, 37 per cent for, according to a poll in June 1979). Both President and Minister of Justice expressed the view, however, that the time was not ripe for a change. In his press conference of 21 November 1978 Giscard d'Estaing argued that 'it is necessary to establish in French society a state of security and justice such that it is apparent one can suppress the death penalty'. It is true that there are some worrying cases of violent public reactions against crime. The 'legitimate defence' association (under the chairmanship of a former president of the Cour de Sûrêté de l'Etat − Romério) has been founded to support those who take the law into their own hands against intruders or burglars, their actions resulting in a reported twenty-one deaths. Peyrefitte, despite the fact that there is clear evidence of a parliamentary majority for abolition (though not a majority of government supporters), refused to allow the Assembly to vote on the subject in 1979 and refused to bring forward a Bill on this matter in 1980. When a *député* tried to raise it by proposing to delete the cost of an executioner from the 1980 budget, the government employed Article 44 which, perhaps appropriately, guillotines amendments, in order to prevent a separate vote.

The reform of the penal code, that Napoleonic monument that still ensures that a boyhood 'theft of a fish from a pond' will be recorded in an individual's *casier judiciaire* for the rest of his life, was promised by Giscard d'Estaing who set up a revision committee by decree in November 1974. The code, in order to reduce the arbitrary power of courts, specifies maximum and minimum penalties for every offence. The committee wanted, in the name of the principle that courts judge 'the offender not the offence', to abolish minimum penalties, leaving wider discretion for leniency to the judges. However, it became clear from a *conseil restreint* at the Elysée on 22 February 1980, that the reform proposals had been effectively buried and that the President and government were more interested in raising the level of penalties for acts of violence.

A *projet de loi* entitled 'Security and Liberty' was introduced at a Council of Ministers on 30 April 1980 and was met by a barrage of hostile criticism. Its main proposals concerned the raising of minimum sentences and the elimination of suspended sentences for certain types of serious crime and also of pre-release parole except for first-time offenders. It also removed the requirement for 'double instruction' for serious crimes. The *procureur de la République* could decide to commit a case direct to the *chambre d'accusation* for investigation and committal to the *cour d'assises* without the preliminary investigation of the *juge d'instruction*. As a fulfilment of the promise on *habeas corpus*, it was singularly feeble. An accused caught in the act can be tried on the basis of police evidence and without an investigation by a *juge d'instruction* by a rather summary and much-criticised system called *flagrants délits*. Under the new law this becomes *saisine directe* (virtually the same thing) but such an accused could only be remanded in custody pending the hearing by a judge and not, as before, by the *procureur de la République*. The only other concessions to *habeas corpus* were that judges would henceforth be responsible for the detention of foreigners under sentence of expulsion and of prisoners in psychiatric establishments. In all other respects the rights of those held in *détention provisoire* or *garde à vue* remain unchanged.

The final point that needs to be made in reviewing a poor record in liberal judicial reform relates to some of the anti-libertarian laws that have been proposed. They were referred to in the last chapter on institutions because Parliament and the Constitutional Council have been, to their credit, particularly vigilant, and the laws have not been adopted – at least, not in their original form. On 12 January 1977 the Constitutional Council questioned a law that would have authorised police to search any vehicle on a public road, provided its driver or owner was present. In 1979 a law permitting the refusal of entry to foreigners or their expulsion if they were without means, without the necessary work permits, or a threat to public order, and for them to be held in 'administrative internment' pending their departure was proposed but, as described in the last chapter, was considerably amended.

At the beginning of the President's term of office there were, as we have seen, a number of reforms in matters like the laws on abortion and divorce. There were proposals in the air for others: the suppression of the *casier judiciaire* (an individual's police record which has to be presented when applying for a job) or of short prison sentences, or the introduction of *habeas corpus*. So far nothing much has come of any of these. The liberal reforms of judicial procedure have been very minor: improved access to legal aid, abolition of court costs in civil cases (though not lawyers' fees, of course), and a limit of six months placed on provisional detention for first offenders if their offence carries a maximum penalty of less than five years. The liberal elements of the 'Security and Liberty' proposals were of minor importance and outweighed by the tougher sentence objectives.

Two points on the positive side of the balance sheet merit a mention. The *médiateur*, introduced during the Pompidou presidency to act as an ombudsman for complaints by the public about maladministration, has had his powers widened so that he can propose administrative reforms. He deals with 5,000 cases a year and about half the reforms he proposes are adopted. Finally, in the judicial field, President Giscard d'Estaing has been active in proposing an *espace judiciaire européen* – a European system of justice extending outside national frontiers which would help in the control of crimes like international terrorism. If this was achieved, control, detection and extradition might become more effective and less arbitrary.

The areas of policy such as foreign affairs or military affairs where President Giscard d'Estaing has appeared able to act as he liked, in an almost omnipotent manner, subject to no checks or balances whatever, have been areas where there has been no resistance from public or parliamentary opinion and a high level of consensus from powerful groups like the armed forces or the administration. The meagre balance sheet of judicial reform indicates how in some areas, where sensitive electoral issues are involved, where there is opposition from the President's parliamentary supporters and from within the administrative hierarchy itself, the President is not all-powerful to decree reform *tous azimuts*. Some doubts, however, must remain over the President's will to bring about radical judicial reform.

News and information

The freedom of information is another important aspect of civil liberties. France is a country with a free press and with freedom of expression. Most of the past excesses of government censorship of television and radio have disappeared. However, three sizeable clouds remain in this relatively clear sky. The first is the main-tenance of government or presidential control by means of appointments to key media posts rather than by censorship. The second is the concentration of the written press into fewer and fewer hands. The third is the deferential behaviour towards those in power of so many journalists and producers – particularly on television which has over three times the coverage of all the written press combined. The last point is the most serious. If it were otherwise, the other factors – pro-government appointees in top jobs, and the concentration of ownership – would have much less importance. The result is that though there is freedom of expression in France, there is a surprising absence of informed public debate. The most striking instance has been referred to once or twice already: the presidency of the Republic takes on more and more of executive and policy leadership in France, yet presidential actions are never given serious investigation or outspoken criticism, except by a handful of up-market newspapers like *Le Monde* or *Le Canard enchaîné* which retain an unrivalled reputation for independence.

One of the first acts of President Giscard d'Estaing, in the first flush of reforms that included abortion, divorce and the lowering of the voting age, was to dismantle the ORTF, the radio and television monolith and the Ministry of Information that controlled it. Government control of radio and television news began in the Fourth Republic under Guy Mollet. Alain Peyrefitte, Information Minister under de Gaulle in 1962, described in his book *Le Mal français* (1977, p. 69), how he discovered on his appointment as minister that there were buttons on his desk with which he could summon the directors of television and radio news programmes and that at 5 o'clock every day they expected to be told what the main outline of the evening news bulletins should be. He instituted some reforms of the ORTF but also, in the severe words of Ignacio Ramonet (*Le Monde diplomatique*, November 1979), 'implanted a veritable totalitarian system for information by instituting the SLII (Service de Liaison Interministérielle de l'Information) which assembled at the ministry every morning top civil servants, chiefs of ministerial *cabinets* and directors of television news to determine jointly the summary of the evening television news: subjects to emphasise and themes to be proscribed were explicitly defined. This gross form of censorship lasted seven years.' Georges Pompidou in his election campaign in 1969 promised liberalisation and under the premiership of Jacques Chaban-Delmas from 1969 to 1972 this promise was kept. News and current affairs units in ORTF were free of government control. Various factors brought this period to an end – a scandal about bribes to producers to allow unofficial commercial advertising, the political flop of Pompidou's 1972 referendum on EEC enlargement in which nearly half of the electorate abstained, the growing threat of a Socialist–Communist victory at the 1973 parliamentary elections, complaints about left-wing television bias from Gaullist parliamentarians, and the fall from favour of Chaban-Delmas. The Ministry of Information rose phoenix-like from the ashes.

President Pompidou said at a press conference in September 1972: 'whether one likes it or not ... the television journalist is not like other journalists ... Television is regarded as the voice of France.' President Giscard d'Estaing on 8 January 1975, by contrast, pointedly declared: 'radio and television organisations are not the voice of France. Television journalists are the same as other journalists.' Setting up the new structures to replace the ORTF, he wrote to the presidents of the new programme companies: 'the public authorities do not intend to manage [your company] through you. They delegate that role entirely to you, until the expiration of your term of office . . . without ever intervening in your responsibilities for management or information' (see National Assembly report on *Information publique*, 15 September 1979, p. 27). Instead of one massive ORTF, the law of 7 August 1974 created seven separate organisations: a transmission company (TDF), a production company to make and sell television films and other programmes (SFP) an audio-visual research institute, a national radio network (Radio France), and three separate television channels, TF1, Antenne 2, and FR3 – the last being responsible for regional programmes.

Under the 1974 legislation the state retains its overall control of radio and television. The state monopoly in broadcasting was retained in the sense that there is no independent commercial television channel, nor local commercial radio stations. In radio, the monopoly is more theoretical than real because commercial radio networks transmitted from just outside French territory have very large national audiences in France: Radio Luxembourg (RTL), Radio Monte Carlo (RMC) and, the station with the largest audience for news in France, Europe 1. The French state has a predominant financial interest in these commercial networks through the nationalised firms of Sofirad and Havas. RTL and Europe 1 make all their programmes in Paris from where they are relayed by cable (by courtesy of TDF and the Ministry of Posts and Telecommunications) to transmitters just over the French border.

Loopholes which permitted challenges to the monopoly by pirate local radio stations, notably Radio Fil Bleu set up by the

Giscardien parliamentary candidate in Montpellier, have been plugged by a new law in 1978. It was under the same law that the Socialist Party's symbolic protest radio station – Radio Riposte – was raided by the police in 1979. A blind eye, however, has been watching other ventures like the CGT's pirate station in the depressed steel towns of Lorraine, Radio Acier – Coeur de Lorraine. The 1974 law also set up a watchdog parliamentary delegation for radio and television, supervisory arrangements for finance and the power to appoint the governing boards of the companies and their chairmen.

The basis of financial control is the television licence fee, fixed by the government, the licence allocation committee, a civil service body that distributes resources between the companies, government adjustments in the form of direct grants (see Kuhn, 1980), and regulations covering expenditure. The dependence of TF1 and A2 on licence fee allocations is reduced by their growing revenue from advertising (60 per cent of the revenue of TF1 in 1978, 52 per cent of A2's).

The third and most important source of control has been through government appointments to key positions in radio and television. There has been ministerial intervention in appointments to news departments, for instance of the TV news presenter J.-P. Elkabbach to A2 in 1977, which has gone beyond the government's legal right to appoint the boards and the chairmen. A case much commented upon was the dismissal of Maurice Siegel as director-general of Europe 1 in October 1974 through the pressure of Denis Baudouin, former press attaché of Pompidou, chairman of Sofirad and Délégué à l'Information (government information service). The first chairman of A2, a rather independent-minded man, Marcel Jullian, was replaced at the end of his first three-year term of office by a senior civil servant, M. Ullrich. It is however on the wide range of appointments to top posts in the media of people close to President Giscard d'Estaing that the allegations of 'l'Etat UDF' and the surreptitious control of information are based. The new chairman of Sofirad, for instance, in replacement of Baudouin, is Xavier Gouyou-Beauchamps, formerly in charge of Giscard's press service at the Ministry of Finance and the Elysée. Head of Radio Monte Carlo is Michel Bassi, a journalist and biographer of the President, former Elysée press service chief, and president of the *Giscardien* Association for Democracy. Yves Cannac, formerly deputy secretary general of the President's *cabinet*, has become head of Agence Havas. Henri Pigeat, Baudouin's successor as Délégué à l'Information is now managing director of the worldwide French news agency Agence France Presse. The Délégation Générale de l'Information became in 1976 the Service d'Information et de Diffusion and was attached to the Prime Minister's office. When the television production company (SFP) was in deep financial trouble, Henri de Clermont Tonnerre, another associate of the President, was appointed to direct it. It should be said, however, that the directors of the three TV channels themselves have connections that are Gaullist rather than *Giscardien*, and that the Ministry of Information has not been revived, although Jean-Philippe Lecat, who was Minister of Information under Pompidou, is now Minister of Culture and Communication. Most observers agree that actual censorship is at an end. Thomas Ferenczi, in a critical article (*Le Monde*, 5 December 1975), concluded that the reality was 'the exercise of a multi-form control on the most powerful media of information' but that the Elysée did not intervene directly as it used to. 'Controlled liberalism' was the expression used by Patrick Jarreau (*Le Monde*, 4 November 1977).

The President's own regular television appearances, until 1980 normally in the form of relaxed-looking interviews with three or four respectful journalists, are very carefully prepared. An official from the President's *cabinet* has the job of arranging with the selected journalists the questions to be asked, the collation from ministries of the relevant information to be included in the replies, the drafting of questions and replies, and communicating to the journalists the presidential decision on the order in which the questions are to be taken.

The National Assembly, on the initiative of the Gaullists, set up a *commission d'enquête* to look into the question of information in 1979. It had the effect, however, in the words of *La Croix* (25 July 1979) of 'a sword stroke in the water', largely because each party group decided to prepare its own blatantly partisan report. Let it suffice to say that the conclusion of the UDF group – 'Never, since the origin of the Fifth Republic, has there been a period when information has been more free ... than since 1974' – did not receive unanimous endorsement.

As far as the written press is concerned the picture is depressing, not because of government control or interference, but because of the catastrophic decline in the readership of Paris dailies and the concentration of ownership this is bringing about as titles close or are sold. The largest provincial newspaper group, controlled by Robert Hersant, now owns three Paris dailies – *France-Soir*, *Le Figaro* and the dying right-wing *L'Aurore* – and is interested in a fourth, *Le Parisien libéré*, which lost half its circulation during a prolonged strike.

Hersant is a rather right-wing, indeed allegedly pro-Vichy, former Radical – extremely anti-communist, and now a supporter of the *majorité*. In fact both the UDF and the RPR endorsed his (unsuccessful) candidature in the 1978 parliamentary elections. It is said, however, that the Elysée views with unease this concentration of ownership. Hersant is running into considerable difficulty with some of his plans – especially the dream of all French newspaper proprietors to have a big Sunday paper of the kind that flourishes in Great Britain or America. There are insuperable distribution problems through normal channels on a Sunday in France when almost all news kiosks are closed. In addition Hersant's employees would not accept what is already done on a larger scale for *Le Figaro* and *L'Aurore*, the use of common sports and entertainment pages in both *Figaro-Dimanche* and *France-Soir-Dimanche*. Both titles have closed. The other big publishing group, Hachette, is the leading press distribution company. It sold *France-Soir* to Hersant and no longer publishes a Paris daily. It is strong in weekly magazines and moving into the provincial press. Various attempts have been made to start new dailies – *J'informe* (pro-government – quickly closed down) or *Le Quotidien de Paris* – without success. *Le Matin*, founded by Claude Perdriel, the owner of the pro-Socialist weekly *Le Nouvel Observateur*, is a promising exception to this rule. Perdriel is reportedly considering starting a pro-Socialist daily in the Lille area to replace *Nord-Matin* bought up by Hersant. The really flourishing sections of the press are *Le Monde*, whose circulation is built on its extraordinary reputation for independence and record, and the provincial press. Most of the provincial press is political by being virtually non-political, and concentrates on local news items. The Paris dailies of the Hersant group can be relied upon for virulently anti-communist news stories, especially at election times. The important political weeklies, *Paris-Match*, *L'Express*, and *Le Point*, are *Giscardien* in orientation. Circulation figures for the main dailies and weeklies in France are given in Table 11.1. In 1980 observers were agog to see if Jacques Chirac could find some support in the press for a presidential campaign against Giscard d'Estaing. The vigilance of the parties is tremendous: the UDF group saw fit to include in their part of the parliamentary report on *information publique* that 'since Charles Lignet has taken control of *Le Progrès de Lyon*, the Lyon activities of the Prime Minister, who is an elected member for that city, are no longer mentioned'.

Table 11.1   Newspapers in France: Principal Dailies and Political Weeklies (circulation in thousands, 1977–8)

Paris dailies	France-Soir	530
	Le Monde	429
	Le Parisien libéré	359
	Le Figaro	327
	L'Aurore	289
	L'Humanité (Communist Party)	151
	La Croix (Catholic)	122
	Le Matin (pro-Socialist)	105
	Libération (Trotskyist)	30
Provincial dailies	Ouest-France (Rennes)	663
	Le Progrés (Lyon)	390
	La Voix du Nord (Lille)	375
	Sud-Ouest (Bordeaux)	368
	Le Dauphiné Libéré (Grenoble)	325
	La Nouvelle République du Centre-Ouest (Limoges)	274
	La Dépêche du Midi (Toulouse)	255
	La Montagne (Clermont-Ferrand)	251
	Nice-Matin	239
	Le Républicain Lorrain (Metz)	211
	Les Dernières Nouvelles d'Alsace (Strasbourg)	207
	Midi-libre (Montpellier)	186
	Le Provençal (Marseille – owned by Gaston Defferre, the Socialist mayor)	182
Political weeklies	Paris-Match	564
	L'Express	538
	Le Canard Enchaîné	500
	L'Humanité Dimanche	400
	Le Nouvel Observateur	342
	Le Point	250

It is the absence of any real political debate in those media like television or provincial newspapers which have an audience from all social classes that is the most striking defect of French news and information. In Chapter 3 on the powers of the presidency I suggested one of the reasons: ambivalent feelings about the office of President. Although the presidency exercises more and more political power in France so that no policy initiative of any importance in any field, be it foreign or economic or social or environmental, comes from any other source, there remains a feeling that one must be careful not to be insulting to the dignity of the head of state. I can think of no other political leader in a democracy who benefits from such respectful indulgence. Another factor is the importance of the Communist Party in France. The electoral success of the left in 1978 would have brought the Communists into government as coalition partners. A lot of those responsible for news are very reluctant to do anything that might help to bring this about. A third factor is the tradition of government and Elysée appointments, dismissals and interference in radio and television. A fourth factor, connected probably to the preceeding three, is that there are far fewer serious current affairs programmes on television and radio. The air-time that in other countries is devoted to the analysis and investigation of public issues hardly exists in France. Even political scandals leave scarcely a ripple behind them. Where but in France would the main news story about the Bokassa diamonds affair (concerning an alleged gift to Giscard d'Estaing when he was Minister of Finance) be the fact that it was mentioned on the main television evening news?

Analysis of a week's broadcasting in Great Britain and France revealed some staggering differences. Television programmes, other than news and regional news, that could broadly be classified as analysis, comment, or debate, on contemporary public issues constituted 800 minutes across the three British TV channels and 440 for the three in France. Other 'public themes' such as documentaries with some contemporary political or social relevance represented 305 minutes on British TV, 175 on French. The differences in radio were even more marked. Radio 4 in Great Britain broadcast 2,000 minutes of analysis, comment and debate, including extended news programmes. In France, considering the three networks with a national audience, France Inter (Radio France) had 565 minutes, Europe No. 1 715, RTL (Luxembourg) 505. It is true that Radio 4 has a more middle-class audience than the three French programmes. A listener to Radio 1, highly popular amongst young people, would be exposed to much less news analysis than the French radio audience. On the other hand the analysis for Great Britain has excluded local radio, both BBC and commercial, which has a high output of local news and controversy including phone-in programmes on local issues, and national light music programmes like Radio 2 which carry a surprising amount of comment in the form of interviews with political and interest group leaders. The analysis has also excluded minority programmes like France-Culture and BBC Radio 3, which in any case approximately balance one another in terms of relevant output.

In assessing the likely impact of analysis and comment programmes one has to consider, of course, not merely the quantity of such programmes, or the size and character of the audience, but the actual tone and content. We have already referred to the respectful tone towards authority displayed by French radio and television commentators. As far as the content of programmes is concerned there are some uncomfortably wide gaps. First, the figures quoted above completely conceal the fact that in France there are virtually no programmes at all to make critical assessments of important aspects of government policy – notably defence and foreign policy initiatives. As far as I am aware there have been no in-depth programmes on French television or radio analysing developments like the President's African policy which has included French military intervention, or his defence policy with a strengthened role for nuclear weapons in a framework of *sanctuarisation élargie*, or French policy on the sale of arms or nuclear technology. I am writing this paragraph on a day in which a BBC peak-hour television programme, *Panorama*, examines whether it is sound policy or not for Great Britain to develop its chemical and bacteriological warfare capability. The second observation relates to a point repeatedly made in this book: the lesser role of interest groups in French political life. Interest groups in Great Britain and America are much more successful in performing an 'agenda-setting' function in political life: in determining what are to be the issues which predominate in public debate and decision-making. The vastly greater allocation of television and radio air-time to comment, debate and analysis gives interest group leaders much greater opportunities to campaign publicly, to prepare their membership and public opinion for action, and almost to conduct negotiations on the air. In France it is only the occasional violent or spectacular manifestation, such as a national 'day of action' or a big rally, which, by being a big news story, gains some reporting by television and radio.

To conclude this review of those two important aspects of civil liberties – justice and information – it must be said that it would be absurd to expect President Giscard d'Estaing, however powerful the presidency has become, to have reformed absolutely everything in one term of office. A political leader in a democracy would soon cease to be a political leader if he tried to change too much too fast. The judicial system in France, with everything clearly laid down in a written code, has a great deal to recommend it. It is also a part of French history and culture. Furthermore the judiciary and the police exist as a very large body of people whose attitudes and style are not subject to instant change by decree. As far as information is concerned, it is unreasonable to blame a political leader for trying to maintain the support of influential news media. Giscard d'Estaing has at least gone some way in a liberal direction by cutting out direct government control of television news, for instance, or by renouncing his presidential right to prosecute the press for outrages to presidential dignity.

One must remember, too, another obstacle to radical reform in the field of civil liberties: the tradition of loyal opposition does not exist in France and in the minds of the administration and the authorities is the fear of anarchy and upheaval which might result if control was loosed. Indeed one of the central themes of the Giscard presidency has been the search for the kind of consensus between political opponents on which a *société libérale avancée* could be based.

In fact, in civil liberties, as a number of writers have remarked, it is a change of attitudes that is really needed more than a reform of structures. Raymond Kuhn (1975, p. 35) compares French television and radio with the BBC and concludes:

the BBC's charter does not provide any more independence from government control than the various statutes of the French radio and television services have done. The BBC's Board of Governors is chosen by the government and approved by the Queen. The relative freedom from government interference which the BBC enjoys in practice is dependent not on legal texts but on the willingness of British politicians to abstain from meddling in the running of the corporation.

He might have added that those responsible for news at the BBC would not be expected to defer to the intervention of politicians and would be defended if they did not. Pierre Arpaillange, a monument himself to judicial independence from government, makes a similar point about judicial reform (*Le Monde*, 4 July 1979) and *habeas corpus*:

it is astonishing that all the legal experts who, at the Elysée, at the Prime Minister's office, or at the Ministry of Justice, have the job of advising the head of state have not suggested that first of all the existing regulations concerning the police and *garde à vue* should be applied. It could be a waste of time to improve texts and codes if those which exist already are utilised either little or badly, or if their spirit is not respected.

CHAPTER 12

Democracy in France

Interest groups and democracy

'Our project', writes Valéry Giscard d'Estaing, 'is a modern democratic society, liberal by the pluralist structure of all its powers, advanced by the high degree of its economic performance, social unification and cultural development.' Neither collectivism, which crushes the individual, nor classic liberalism which leaves the individual too unprotected: such is the *société libérale avancée* to which the President aspires to lead his country. In guise of conclusion, therefore, some reflections on France as a model of liberal democracy are appropriate.

France in the Fifth Republic has all the normal attributes of political democracy. The citizen can choose his leaders at free and regularly held elections. He is allowed to oppose the government and to join organised groups to promote his interests. Subject to the reservations expressed in Chapter 11 about *garde à vue*, the power of a *juge d'instruction* to remand in custody for prolonged periods, and government interference in radio and television, the citizen is protected by the rule of law and has access to a variety of information and opinions. There are the watchdog institutions, not always entirely effective perhaps, of a constitutional council and a Parliament. However, French democracy has something more, something which other Western democracies in the 1980s do not have: executive power that can impose its will.

Is this a democratic or an undemocratic characteristic? Liberal democracy is a system of government where executive power is limited. If the people, even by the democratic process, will absolute power to a leader, the system of government ceases to be democratic. The first modern referendum – 'Napoleon Bonaparte, shall he be consul for life?' – would, even under universal suffrage, have negated democracy. Should democracy, however, confer the power to govern effectively or does its essence continue to lie in the series of restraints and checks and balances with which institutions and society prevent the government from abusing its powers?

British and American democracy have evolved towards the latter conception. In America it is quite explicit. From the framers of the Constitution on, the Americans have been animated by the idea that political power must be held in check. Presidential power finds itself constrained at every turn by Congress, with the power to withhold laws and money, by public opinion, because elections for Congress or presidency are so frequent and, with all their primaries and nominating conventions, so arduous, by interest groups who are immensely well organised to put pressure on Congress or on public opinion, by press and television whose right to free speech is guaranteed by the First Amendment. The Constitution enshrines the separation of powers between executive, legislature and judiciary, as well as between federal and state governments. The economic system is based on an ideology which resists government intervention. The mythology of the American way of life is based upon notions of self-reliance and the capacity of groups of citizens to act collectively in their own interest or in the interests of their local community. This healthy tradition has however led to a state of affairs, where, it has been claimed, the office of President of the United States has become impossible. The measures that circumstances require can never be carried into effect. When President Carter proposed a plan of action to reduce America's dependence on imported oil, for instance, interest groups were easily able to mobilise sufficient opposition to block it.

In Great Britain the myths are different, but the reality is the same. Governments are supposed to govern. The party that wins a general election has a 'mandate' to carry out what it said it would carry out. In fact the reality is that if the government cannot carry with it the principal interest groups affected by any policy, the chances of implementing that policy successfully are very slight. The various attempts to establish a prices and incomes policy, to restructure major industries, or even to build a third London airport provide examples. Relatively autonomous centres of power like local councils can frustrate policies, as in the case of the abolition of selection in secondary schools, promised to the electorate by a national government. In this pluralist model of decision-making where power is not concentrated but diffused, 'the government is essentially a broker, obliged to modify its policies and to bring about concessions in the light of evolving circumstances. Decision-making is rarely "heroic", and only rarely results from the imposition of rationally calculated policies, but is rather the negotiation of marginal adjustments to the status quo. It necessarily precludes major shifts in policy which would be offensive to certain groups who could jeopardise the harmony of social institutions' (Wright, 1978, p. 184).

From the standpoint of democratic theory, there are many arguments in favour of a pluralist version of democracy. First, pluralism is a natural expression of democracy. Where there is no freedom for groups to organise and to attempt to influence government there is no democracy. Secondly, the idea that the citizen is a better judge of his own interests than the government, that it is desirable that he should be able to influence decisions, and that his consent can be awarded or withheld, is a strong element of democratic thought in Locke, John Stuart Mill and others including French radicals like Alain. Indeed, the last argued for 'perpetual resistance' to authority.

Pluralist theories however assume that where all groups are free to exert pressure, no group will predominate. Much of the immobilism, though, to which the most pluralist democracies have come stems from the power of veto which some interest groups have acquired over public policy. The power of American medical interest groups to impede the introduction of a free health service, of groups in farming or transportation that effectively control the government agencies supposed to regulate them, or of British trade unions to veto the anti-inflation or industrial restructuring policies of successive governments provide examples. Grant McConnell, writing about America in terms equally applicable to Great Britain, claimed that 'a large number of groups have achieved substantial autonomy for themselves and the conquest of important segments of government and public policy . . . It is not "rule" as normally conceived; it is the fragmentation of rule and the conquest of pieces of governmental authority by different groups' (1966, p. 7). Some writers like Peter Jay (1976) or Samuel Brittan (1975) go even further and argue that the coercive power of some interest groups, particularly large unions with a monopoly position in the supply of labour, act as such a barrier to any government policy to control inflation that it poses a threat to the stability and even the preservation of a democratic system of government.

Appearing from time to time as a theme in this book, notably in the chapters on foreign affairs and the economy, has been the assertion that the executive in France does not have the 'problem' with interest groups that political leaders have in other Western democracies like Great Britain or the United States. France, as far as this aspect of democracy goes, presents a paradox. While the government has been able to pursue its main economic policy choices without being blown off course by interest groups, there are many areas of government policy where group influences are manifest. One such area is foreign affairs and defence where the 'Gaullist' view of France as a world-ranking nuclear power with a rather majestic foreign policy independent of America sets limits to the range of presidential options. Within those limits, as we have seen, the President is much freer to act than other Western leaders. Other policy areas in which interest groups are quite effective at preventing change are education (Wright, 1978, pp. 184 and 196), judicial and penal reform, local government reorganisation, or agriculture. This list, it will be noticed, covers much of what one might call the French way of life, traditional social institutions as well as the consensus image of France's place in the world.

If groups can prevent change in aspects of policy that would affect these traditional institutions, why cannot they have more influence on decisions affecting industry and the economy? A number of explanations have been offered involving the role of the state in French society, the role of the new technocratic elite, and the distinction made between legitimate and 'dynamic' groups on the one hand and selfish and negative ('Malthusian') groups on the other. Other elements of explanation include the low membership and solidarity of potential veto groups like unions, or the fact that the industrial economy has been sufficiently dynamic to leave little room for genuine discontent. Finally, a considerable part of the debate about the allocation of resources to important sectors in difficulty – small farms are a good example – has been exported out of France to international arenas like the EEC where the French government can fight shoulder to shoulder with the most negative of groups to extract resources from an international budget.

The idea, derived from Rousseau, of the general interest which is distorted and threatened by pressure groups but preserved and expressed by the state is a strong theme in French public life. In France, says Suleiman (1974, p. 350) 'the concept of the general interest has been marked by an aura of sanctity and the administration has been seen, and has seen itself, as the guardian of the general interest'. He does however go on to argue that this is to some extent mere rationalisation and that civil servants invoke the general interest to justify their own definition of what is a legitimate and representative private interest and what is not. Hayward (1975a, p. 5) notes that groups have been 'unwilling or unable effectively to resist initiatives from senior officials that have sought, with substantial success, to monopolise a legitimacy that derives from acting in the public interest'. Whereas in Great Britain, he continues, 'the government is conceived as operating on the same plane as other political actors and is not outside or above them', in France 'the government's claim to represent the public interest is given greater credence and weight'. This is an important distinction between France and the Anglo-Saxon democracies because the essence of the pluralist theory of democracy is that there is no such thing as an objective 'general interest' defined by those in power. 'In the United States the concept of the general interest has never achieved intellectual respectability, and countless have been those ready to deny the existence of an interest transcending that of groups' (Suleiman, 1974, p. 349). The dilemma is that 'recent attacks in the United States on the pluralist system of democracy have based their case on the fact that a decentralised federal structure has afforded groups undue influence on policy-making, has excluded a large segment of the population from having any influence on the decisions that affect their lives, has diluted national values, has denied the existence of a national interest and, finally, has wiped out the distinction between public and private'.

Many observers, French and foreign, accord to the technocratic elite in France a high place in the capacity of the French political system to resist pressure from groups. Hayward contrasts the 'self-confident assertiveness of an administrative elite accustomed to operate in a country ... where weak parties had seldom been the main agency for channelling innovations in public policy' with the British civil service 'wedded to the task of preserving political cohesion' (1975a, pp. 12–13). The greater success of economic planning in France he attributes to the planners' ability 'to bypass the incrementalist obstacles, represented in particular by the traditional ministries' (p. 5) – a view that, as we saw in Chapter 7, might be challenged by Diana Green. This success, says Hayward, is 'thanks largely to assertive techno-bureaucratic change agents with access to the levers of public power'. He quotes Stanley Hoffmann (1974, p. 450) who accords the same priority to 'new men and new attitudes as well as the tradition of dependence on the state. Consequently, in the period of rapid industrial development when the watchdog became a greyhound, those who had been holding the leash had to learn to run.'

Suleiman's main argument is that the administrative elite is able to define what constitutes an *interlocuteur valable*, dynamic and representative 'professional organisations' whose demands concord with government policy, and what are mere 'lobbies' (in franglais a very pejorative word) which seek 'limited and selfish ends' for their members and are of 'highly questionable legitimacy' (1974, p. 337). The administration is greatly helped in its capacity to do this by some of the attributes of the groups themselves. Labour unions, for instance, can be ignored most of the time for three reasons. The first is that, other than in a few occupations like teaching, unions only represent a minority of employees. Less than one in four manual workers belongs to a union, and institutions like the closed shop are unknown, indeed illegal as being contrary to the freedom of the individual. The second is that unions are deeply divided. Instead of having a series of unions affiliated to one peak organisation as in Great Britain (TUC) or America (AF of L-CIO), there are three separate peak organisations, each with its own branches in each sector of activity. The largest is the CGT (Confédération Générale du Travail) which is closely aligned with the Communist Party and whose general secretary Georges Séguy is a member of the party's Bureau Politique. The other two principal ones are pro-Socialist – the CFDT (Confédération Française et Démocratique du Travail) and the more moderate Force Ouvrière, which derives from a postwar split between Communists and non-Communists in the CGT. The three organisations very rarely manage to work together for anything more than the occasional symbolic protest march. Thirdly, they tend (even some branches of the moderate FO) to have revolutionary or messianic aims. French labour unions grew out of a syndicalist tradition which stressed the insurrectional general strike rather than collaboration in existing institutions as the way to achieve the aims of the working class. This has meant much less in the way of such mundane things as organisation or the accumulation of funds for strike pay, and much less discipline or solidarity in pursuing limited group aims. It has also meant much less respectability as an economic 'partner' of government. The pro-communist CGT in particular is simply not regarded as a body with a constructive point of view to contribute, nor does it behave like one. Cohen graphically described in his book on economic planning in France (1969) how the planning process was mainly a dialogue between the civil servants and the representatives of industry, who shared the same background and had the same crisp volumes of statistics and projections. The unions on the other hand were not even sure whether they should be there at all as if their presence would underwrite and sanction an economic system to the overthrow of which they were supposed to be dedicated. Their attitude to participation in this kind of economic decision-making is rather like that of the late critic F. R. Leavis to a writer he disliked: 'to read him would be to condone him'. 'We have the good fortune in France', the former Prime Minister Edgar Faure remarked in an interview with the present author, 'to have revolutionary trade unions.' Thirdly, in addition to the ineffectiveness of unions to organise resistance to government economic policy and their lack of legitimacy as a partner in the eyes of government, there has been a dynamic economic climate for most of the Fifth Republic's twenty-three years. With industrial output, productivity, living standards and spending on public services rising rapidly with, until the recession of the mid-1970s, very little unemployment, and all this happening in a new industrial society, not an old one set in its ways, there is not much real discontent for 'negative' groups to mobilise.

The legitimate groups that are accorded access tend to become, in Jack Hayward's phrase, 'more like pressured groups than pressure groups' (1973, p. 58). Consultative bodies, involving trade associations or farm organisations, help the government with technical information and can be used as channels through which government policies and government support can be transmitted.

Contacts are also important because they enable the administration to explain its point of view and to convince the groups of the importance of decisions already taken. If the groups do affect decisions taken by administrators, this is likely to be the result, not of a compromise worked out between the administration and the groups, but of the government's awareness of the intensity of opposition to a particular programme . . . Contacts with interest groups are important more for the communication of policies than for anything to do with the actual substance of these policies. (Suleiman, 1974, p. 327)

If 'negative' groups, like unions or the small shopkeepers that periodically stage a riot or burn down a tax office, have little influence on government policy and little capacity to frustrate it, what about the influence of the 'legitimate' or 'dynamic' groups? One of their characteristics, as we noted in our summary of Suleiman's thesis which was derived from interviews with top-level officials in the administration, is that their demands or views concord with government policy. The problem, of course, methodologically unsolvable, is to know to what extent the former moulds the latter or whether there is a natural identity of views so that the 'dynamic' interest group finds itself pushing at an open door or whether, in important areas of policy, groups and government are so interlocked as to form one entity. One interesting example of this is PEON, the consultative commission on the production of electricity from nuclear power which we encountered in Chapter 8. It is an officially constituted body which groups together government officials and leaders of public and private industry. Some of them, for instance the directors of the Creusot-Loire company who form part of the Framatome consortium or of CGE and its subsidiary Alsthom, the sole French manufacturer now of turbo-generators for Framatome, have a financial stake in the development of nuclear power in France. Massive public investment in nuclear power and its rapid development has been French government policy since the Middle East oil crisis in 1973. It does not follow from this, however, that private interests have colonised public policy. Public sector interests – CEA (atomic energy) and EDF (electricity) – are leading participants in PEON and in the arguments in favour of developing nuclear power. Finally, the government itself did not require pressure from private or public sector interests to be convinced of the need to reduce French dependence on imported oil. In addition, as we saw in Chapter 8, the government played an activist role in knocking heads together in the restructuring of the nuclear power industry, in the choice of the Westinghouse process, and in the choice of CEA and Creusot-Loire (Framatome) and not CGE as the sole constructors of nuclear power stations – a battle that was fought out inside PEON. Simonnot records (1978, pp. 273–8) that PEON itself had something of a battle in 1974 with the Ministry of Finance which had reservations about PEON's projections for electricity consumption, about the cost of the vast programme it advocated, and about its observations on 'insufficient' prices and indexation in nuclear power contracts.

The story of nuclear power in France is not the story of a powerful interest group taking over government policy (as in the case of the roads lobby in Great Britain and the Ministry of Transport) but of fusion between private interests, public sector industry and government. Even the individuals involved cannot really be separated into categories of private and public. Most of the membership of PEON (public or private) was trained for the public service at Polytechnique and worked in the public service as members of the Corps des Mines or the Corps des Ponts et Chaussées. They move from sector to sector: for instance, André Giraud was head of the CEA before becoming Minister for Industry, Roger Gaspard was a member of PEON as director general of EDF and later as chairman of the steel company Schneider which, associated with Creusot-Loire in the Empain group of companies, is part of Framatome. PEON is undoubtedly a 'dynamic' and 'legitimate' interest group but it is also part of government. The same story of close identity between industry (public or private) and government rather than of pressure by the former on the latter holds true for other policy areas we have examined. The government, in the shape of the DGA (Délégation Générale à l'Armement), is the promoter and marketing director of the aviation and armaments industries. Marcel Dassault, the great French innovator in the aircraft industry, may be a Gaullist *député* but it would be wrong to see sinister pressure and covert influence in the enormous amount of government finance for Dassault aviation, in the form of contracts and subsidies, and the immense pressure applied by the French government to persuade NATO air forces to re-equip for the 1980s with French Mirages, made by Dassault, rather than American aircraft. The same point could be made about the restructuring of industry discussed in

Chapter 7. The capacity of big French firms like Renault, Peugeot–Citroën, or Matra to obtain favourable treatment from the government is only partly to be regarded as successful advocacy by interests. In the government's industrial policy of ensuring a French national 'champion' to be competitive internationally in each vital industrial sector, government and privileged interlocutors from dynamic firms are partners in one common struggle. This is in marked contrast with the corporatist style of economic management in Britain through what Hayward (1975a, p. 12) calls the 'toothless tripartism' of government, CBI (employers) and TUC (unions), a 'semi-permanent three-party coalition'. The presumption that group consent is an indispensable prelude to action has generally resulted in timid and irresolute decision-making.

The action of private interests and the government engaged on behalf of France in a common international struggle extends to other policy sectors. The willingness of the French government in EEC negotiations over matters like common axle weights or fork-lift trucks to act, as other governments do for their domestic industries, as spokesmen for French firms indicates of course that there is consultation between administration and interest groups but not necessarily that the former is acting under pressure. French agriculture, at first sight the epitome of 'negative' interest groups with its small farmers, and its frequent violent demonstrations over low prices, is under the leadership of the FNSEA increasingly recognised as being effective and influential. The voice of French farming, due, it is assumed, to the electoral weight of agriculture, is heard loud and clear in Brussels. H. Mendras (1980), in an optimistic book on France, stresses that farmers 'have rejoined the ranks' of those with proper living standards (p. 35), that the 'rural world . . . is in good health' (p. 27). One explanation for the greater success of agriculture as an interest group is that, in the battle for the allocation of resources, French farmers are no longer in competition with other parts of the domestic budget but with farming interests in other EEC countries who want access to French markets or restrictions on French exports, or EEC governments who are opposed to higher prices for commodities in surplus. In these battles government and farmers are partners against the foreign foe, and the leading farming groups are welcomed to the ranks of the dynamic and the legitimate.

To summarise this attempt to resolve the paradox of French interest groups, those groups considered legitimate have been absorbed as a part of the machinery of government while those considered negative do not, with the possible exception of unions in education, have the capacity or the cohesion to frustrate government policy or to resist change. Some of these 'negative' groups, like unions or environmentalist pressure groups, have acquired considerable influence on policy in other democracies, but for cultural and historical reasons, and perhaps because in a burgeoning new industrial economy there has not been much mobilisable discontent, they have acquired remarkably little in France.

I have dwelt on the place of interest groups in relation to the state and the administrative elite because I believe this to be the 'efficient secret' of French government in the Fifth Republic. As the balance shifted from Parliament to the executive, from unstable coalitions to a permanent parliamentary majority, from a fragmented electorate to one that gave sustained support to the government of the day at successive parliamentary and presidential elections, the balance between private power and public power has tilted in favour of the latter. The efficient secret, however, which has allowed French governments to pursue reasonably coherent policies in foreign and domestic affairs for two decades and to implement what they have decided has an anti-democratic side to it. France is, as we saw in the chapters on defence or the environment or civil liberties, a country where there is no proper debate on major policy choices: tactical nuclear weapons, military interventions in Africa, the nuclear energy programme, the siting of nuclear power stations. The last is a good example of a case in which local interest groups, inspired possibly by selfish motives rather than the public interest, are simply not given adequate constitutional opportunity to express objections.

Democracy and the Giscard presidency

French democracy in the 1980s presents a number of curiosities encountered from time to time throughout this book. It is a pluralist democracy and yet, for the reasons discussed above, interest groups play a subdued role. It is a political democracy, not a bureaucratic dictatorship, and yet political and economic leadership is virtually monopolised by an administrative elite trained for the public service. It is a parliamentary democracy in the sense that the government is responsible to the National Assembly and can be removed by it, yet France has the most remarkable and uncontrolled concentration of executive power to be found in any Western democracy. Constraints on executive power exist, in Parliament or in the mass media, for instance, but they do not constrain. Finally, and the greatest paradox of all, France is a legitimate democracy, with accepted political institutions, with over twenty years of stable and effective government continuously supported by an electoral majority, with a high degree of national cohesion over matters like presidential leadership or French independence in foreign affairs and defence, and yet everywhere is the fear that the whole edifice would collapse – economy, security, order, freedom, legitimacy, everything – if the voters ever voted for the opposition. The Communists would take over; the army would take over; the 'intermediaries' like political parties or interest groups would take over. In other words, France is a stable and democratic republic so long as the same people continue to govern it.

Valéry Giscard d'Estaing as a political leader expresses these contradictions of French democracy. In economic life, for instance, he is an advocate, as we saw in the chapter on his ideas, of liberalism, but it is an 'organised liberalism'. Economic policy has seen some liberal innovations such as the scrapping of price controls but the firm direction by the state of energy policy or the restructuring of industry continues. *Démocratie française* is filled with hymns of praise to pluralism and dire warnings about the danger of interest groups 'privatising power for their own profit and imposing their objectives or views to the detriment of the general interest' (1976, p. 150). Groups who make excessive demands and will not seek compromise 'commit an act of social violence' (p. 141). Consequently (p. 150 again), though it must be neither all-pervasive nor arbitrary, 'the pluralist state must be strong'.

The risk of France evolving 'towards a technocratic regime' was evoked by Giscard d'Estaing in a speech to mark the twentieth anniversary of the Constitution in September 1978. 'The political stability of France gives the administrative services the means to act in a framework of continuity. Modern problems require highly developed technical expertise. But political power which springs from the citizens' vote must not be made occult and subordinate to technocracy . . . This risk is redoubtable.' Under the presidency of Giscard d'Estaing this danger has increased. More and more prominent political leaders, like Giscard himself, Chirac, or Rocard, come from ENA and the *grands corps* of the administration. More and more ministers appointed by Giscard are technicians like Barre or François-Poncet, not politicians with a background in Parliament or party. Indeed, in June 1980, of forty-two ministers and secretaries of state in the government, twenty-three were of civil service origin and seventeen of these had served in ministerial *cabinets* at some time. The 'occult' and unaccountable power of the *cabinets*, particularly those at the Elysée and the Hotel Matignon, has never been more pronounced. Economic life too, with public sector and private, as has been repeatedly stressed, is dominated by the innovating technocrats, mostly educated at Polytechnique, many from the *grands corps* of public administration. Suleiman (1978, pp. 232–6) and others have remarked that the most striking characteristic of the French economy is that the leadership roles in the public service and private industry are occupied by the same type of men, that in a remarkable number of cases the president-directeur-général of a big private firm comes from the civil service, that public service and dynamic private industry are so 'interpenetrated' that the distinction between them has effectively disappeared. It is difficult to apply with a sure hand any litmus test of democratic theory to this phenomenon. On the one hand an uncontrolled administrative elite dominates the state. On the other, however, those members of the administrative elite who have crossed the boundary and become political leaders responsible to an electorate are much better equipped by training and occupation than politicians in most other democracies to impose their priorities on the technical experts in the administration and not be dominated by them.

The third contradiction expressed by the Giscard presidency is that which exists between the President's desire for a 'more liberal functioning of institutions' and the 'solitary exercise of power' by himself. Parliament has been given a somewhat better opportunity to exercise its function of control on the executive. We noted in Chapter 10 that its members can invoke the Constitutional Council and that the government does not abuse its procedural advantages as it used to. Parliament has acted as a constraint on presidential power in so far as the parliamentary supporters of the President and his governments, Gaullists especially but *Giscardiens* as well, have been prepared to express their objections to presidential reforms or initiatives in everything from capital gains taxation or the death penalty to nuclear strategy. The difficulty of gaining parliamentary acquiescence has frequently been stated as the reason for a slowing of the pace of reform. Local government has been given words of encouragement and some measures of reform, like the change in the status of Paris City Council, to favour its independence.

Accompanying the 'more liberal functioning of institutions', however, has been the continuation of presidential power in as concentrated a form as ever. In Africa, in the Middle East, in East–West relations, the actions of President Giscard d'Estaing are, within the limits of the Gaullian consensus on French independence and prestige, accountable to no one. With a wave of his sovereign hand, he sells a nuclear power station to South Africa or withholds it, moves paratroops into the Central African Republic or Mauritania, or Chad, or Zaïre, or withdraws them. He conserves the urban and rural environment from despoliation by high-density building or vast skiing resorts and he imposes the biggest nuclear power programme for electricity generation in any Western country. In neither case is any notice taken of the views of local councils or local citizens. He breaks up the old ORTF radio and television monolith in order to 'let a hundred flowers bloom'. Censorship and the Ministry of Information are, as we saw in Chapter 11, at an end. Yet radio and television still abstain from critical scrutiny of presidential initiatives and everywhere in radio and television one finds associates of the President in top jobs.

Finally there is Giscard d'Estaing and the paradox of a regime with stable, effective and accepted political institutions which is considered too vulnerable to withstand a change of government. This is one of the contradictions that he has, short of actually helping the opposition to win, tried his best to resolve. This is where the theme of *décrispation* has been important in the Giscard presidency, if not exactly crowned with success. The aim has been to institute more normal relations between the elites of majority and opposition, to end the 'civil war' of French political life, in order to bring them into line with the reality of a national consensus about the political institutions and even some of the policies, particularly in defence and foreign affairs, of the Fifth Republic. 'Beyond the quarrels and discords', writes Thierry Pfister (*Pouvoirs*, no. 9, 1979, p. 153), '. . . political debate in France has, for twenty years, evolved in the direction of a strengthening of the national consensus. The opponents of the Gaullist regime, whether centrist, Socialist, or Communist, have been obliged to take account of the achievements and many of the themes of the Fifth Republic that they categorically rejected before. Even if they propose to alter these policies, they begin by taking them in charge. The stability of governments in the Fifth Republic has enabled actions to be engaged which cannot simply be switched off from one day to the next. Public opinion has become used to certain themes, and certain ideas which have presided over the life of the country for twenty years.'

Giscard d'Estaing has done what he could to prepare the country for the peaceful alternation of power from government to opposition which is 'fundamental to advanced democratic societies' (1976, p. 154). He has tried, as we saw in Chapter 4, talking to opposition leaders or using his influence to persuade the parliamentary majority to elect opposition committee chairmen in the National Assembly. He was unsuccessful. His Prime Minister, Chirac, tried to persuade him not to wait for 1978, but to dissolve Parliament and hold early elections, with the obvious corollary that a victory for the left would be followed by a resignation of the President. Instead he made it clear that he would stay in office whoever won the election, and appoint a government that corresponded to the choice made by the country. This was a very courageous position to adopt because it counteracted to some extent one of the favourite themes of the majority, that upheaval and collapse for the regime would follow a win by the opposition. It was undoubtedly in the period around the 1978 parliamentary election that President Giscard d'Estaing showed his qualities as a democratic political leader at their best.

What will the enduring monuments of the period 1974–81 be? It is hard to point to any significant new departure and declare it specifically Giscardian. Despite innumerable presidential declarations, they were not seven years of vigorous social reform. There were no great innovations in the Constitution or in civil liberties. The style of the presidency returned to the Gaullian model. So did foreign and defence policy, both in manner and in content, with, as its most notable features, the Franco-German entente in Europe, the military adventures in Africa and the policy of *sanctuarisation élargie* applied to nuclear defence strategy.

They were seven difficult years for the economy but France pursued a more coherent, rational and effective response to the problems of inflation, unemployment and international competitiveness than did most countries. A determined attack was kept up against the worst sources of potential discontent from bad housing to retirement pensions. Despite an unemployment level of 1½ million, national cohesion was preserved – something that would have been considered impossible in the 1960s. All in all, France continued to be what it had become under Presidents de Gaulle and Pompidou – an efficiently governed state, one of the world's leading industrial economies, a difficult partner in the European Community and the Atlantic alliance, and a democracy in which there are far too few constraints on executive power. Continuity of all this, not change, has been the hallmark of the Giscard presidency.

What of Giscard d'Estaing as a man and as a President after seven years of 'doing that for which one was destined', as he put it in a 1976 radio interview? The reforming language, the generosity of ideas, the liberal outlook which found such strong expression in the opening years of the presidency, culminating perhaps in *Démocratie française* and his speeches to 'mes chères françaises et mes chers français' before the 1978 election, grew fainter as the 1981 presidential election drew nearer. No doubt the difficult world economic climate throughout all the seven years dimmed his hopes of being a President for good times of expansion and change. No doubt the rather opportunistic rivalry of Jacques Chirac and the Gaullists, with a strategic position as the largest parliamentary group in the pro-government coalition, prevented some presidential reforms, and it certainly exercised its influence over foreign policy. Giscard d'Estaing was at his most adventurous when the feeling that he had the confidence of the country was greatest: the initial burst of reforms from abortion to the break-up of the ORTF television and radio monolith in 1974, the tougher handling of the economy after the 1978 election. In late 1979 and 1980, however, as the one real moment of accountability for a French President drew nearer, the tone changed. Vainglorious postures were struck in defence and foreign affairs: the melodramatic and purposeless summit meeting with Brezhnev in May 1980 provides the best example. At home the big liberalisation of the judicial process, which had been the subject of preparation and a report, and which had been promised in the Barre government's 1978 election manifesto, the Programme de Blois, dwindled into the feeble, indeed repressive, measures of the Alain Peyrefitte 'Securité et Liberté' legislation in 1980. Executive power, as exercised in the Elysée Palace or in ministerial *cabinets*, is still as immune from scrutiny or accountability as it was before. Presidential patronage has created an *état*-UDF, especially in the realm of information and the media, just as it once created an *état*-UDR. The brief references in this book to the 'scandals' of the Bokassa diamonds, the de Broglie murder, the Boulin suicide, or the incident of votes for Frenchmen living abroad, have been intended to show how in France executive power can still suppress scrutiny, or political influence be used to obtain favours, or that the administrative apparatus of the state is still not politically neutral.

Jean Lecanuet, a leading supporter of Giscard d'Estaing, promised (*Le Point*, 16 June 1980) that 'after 1981 the spirit of reform will reappear'. In the meantime the achievements of the presidency are the achievements of a rational centralised administration, such as the reorganisation of industry and energy supplies to make the French economy more secure or the prevention of discontent by action to alleviate hardship. But it has not been a period when the French state has become more liberal. Giscard d'Estaing has lived up to his 1974 election slogan, *un vrai Président*, but he has not yet won the affection accorded to his predecessors.

I want to finish on a personal note. I have written this book the way it is because I am English. If I were American or French I would have felt differently about the Giscardian experience. Great Britain is going through a frustrating period of its history in which it has seemed unable to face and to resolve certain fundamental problems – mainly concerned with economic and industrial adaptation to a world in which it has no empire. Many British people, therefore, admire and rather envy the vigorous and effective way that France has set about its political and economic renewal in the last twenty-five years. The French are very fortunate to have had leaders of the intelligence, clarity and authority of de Gaulle, Pompidou and Giscard d'Estaing. In the case of the latter, I admire greatly his capacity to rise above day-to-day concerns and to try to prepare his country for the future. However, I think that few English people would care to live under a regime in which such unrestricted power was conferred even on such a sage. The problems of Great Britain, and of America too, are the problems of democracy – that is to say, they stem from a political system in which the authorities cannot compel people to accept even what is considered good for them. It is very irritating to live with Anglo-Saxon pluralist democracy at the present time, where pressure groups have acquired the power to frustrate all policies including those which seem manifestly to be in the public interest. If you ask me if I admire the lucidity and authority revealed by the French political system under Giscard d'Estaing and his predecessors, I have to say yes. If you ask me, however, do I want the same style of authority here, I have to reply: not on your life.

Bibliography

Anderson, Malcolm (1973), *Conservative Politics in France* (London: Allen & Unwin).

Audouard, Yvon (1976), *Diner avec Giscard* (Paris: Plon).

Avril, Pierre (1967), *Le Régime politique de la Ve république* (Paris: Librairie Générale de Droit et de Jurisprudence).

Bassi, Michel (1968), *Valéry Giscard d'Estaing* (Paris: Grasset).

Bienaymé, Alain (1979), 'La politique des revenus en France', *Revue économique*, January, pp. 162–78.

Boucher, Philippe (1978), *Le Ghetto judiciaire* (Paris: Grasset).

Brittan, Samuel (1975), 'The economic contradictions of democracy', *British Journal of Political Science*, pp. 129 ff.

Cerny, P. (1980), *The Politics of Grandeur* (Cambridge: CUP).

Chaban-Delmas, Jacques (1975), *L'Ardeur* (Paris: Stock).

Christensen, S. A. (1979), 'Nuclear power plant siting: a comparative analysis of public intervention in the siting process in France and the United States', *Denver Journal of International Law and Policy*, Winter, pp. 343–66.

Cohen, S. S. (1969), *Modern Capitalist Planning* (London: Weidenfeld & Nicolson).

Colliard, Jean-Claude (1971), *Les Républicains indépendants, Valéry Giscard d'Estaing* (Paris: Presses Universitaires de France).

Cornec, Jean (1977), *A quoi çu tient: 40 histoires sur la justice* (Paris: Robert Laffont).

Crisol, P., and Lhomeau, J. Y. (1977), *La Machine RPR* (Paris: Fayolle).

Deligny, Henri (1977), *Chirac ou la fringale du pouvoir* (Paris: Moreau).

Duclaud-Williams, Roger H. (1978), *The Politics of Housing in Britain and France* (London: Heinemann).

Elleinstein, Jean (1979), *Une certaine idée du communisme* (Paris: Julliard).

Fabre-Luce, Alfred (1974), *Les Cent Premiers Jours de Giscard* (Paris: Robert Laffont).

Frears, J. R. (1978), *Political Parties and Elections in the French Fifth Republic* (London: Hurst).

Frears, J. R., and Parodi, Jean-Luc (1979), *War Will Not Take Place: The French Parliamentary Elections of March 1978* (London: Hurst).

Fry, Earl Howard (1976), 'Executive policy-making in Gaullist France: the case of Franco-Soviet Relations 1958–74', UCLA PhD dissertation.

Giroud, Françoise (1977), *La Comédie du pouvoir* (Paris: Fayard).

Giscard d'Estaing, Valéry (1976), *Démocratie française* (Paris: Fayard).

Goodman, Elliott R. (1975), *The Fate of the Atlantic Community* (New York: Praeger).

Green, Diana (1980), 'The budget and the Plan', in *French Politics and Public Policy*, ed. Philip G. Cerny and Martin A. Schain (London: Francis Pinter).

Grendel, Frédéric (1978), *Raymond Barre* (Paris: Desforges).

Grosser, Alfred (1967), *French Foreign Policy under de Gaulle* (Boston, Mass.: Little, Brown).

Hamon, Léo (1977), *Une république présidentielle?*, 2 vols (Paris: Bordas).

Hanley, D. C., Kerr, A. P., and Waites N. H. (1979), *Contemporary France, Politics and Society since 1945* (London: Routledge & Kegan Paul).

Hayward, Jack (1973), *The One and Indivisible French Republic* (London: Weidenfeld & Nicolson).

Hayward, Jack (1975a), 'Institutional inertia and political impetus in France and Britain', Political Studies Association conference, unpublished paper.

Hayward, Jack (1975b), 'Employer associations and the state in France and Britain', in *Industrial Policies in Western Europe*, ed. Steven J. Warnecke and Ezra N. Suleiman (New York: Praeger).

Hennion, Christian (1976), *Chronique des flagrants délits* (Paris: Stock).

Hill, Christopher, and Wallace, William (1979), 'Diplomatic trends in the European Community', *International Affairs*, January, pp. 47–66.

Hoffmann, Stanley (1974), *Decline or Renewal? France since the 1930s* (New York: Viking).

Irving, R. E. M. (1973), *Christian Democracy in France* (London: Allen & Unwin).

Jay, Peter (1976), *Employment, Inflation and Politics* (London: Institute of Economic Affairs, Occasional Paper 46).

Jonas, Joseph-Jacques, and Nourry, Anne (1978), *Giscard de tous les jours* (Paris: Fayolle).

Kohl, Wilfrid L. (1971), *French Nuclear Diplomacy* (Princeton, NJ: Princeton University Press).

Kolodziej, Edward, A. (1974), *French International Policy under de Gaulle and Pompidou* (Ithaca, NY: Cornell University Press).

Kolodziej, Edward A. (1980), 'France and the arms trade', *International Affairs*, January, pp. 54–72.

Kosciusko-Morizet, Jacques-A. (1973), *La Mafia polytechnicienne* (Paris: Editions du Seuil).

Kuhn, Raymond (1975), 'Government and broadcasting in France 1969–1975', University of Warwick, Working Paper No. 8.

Kuhn, Raymond (1980), 'Government and broadcasting in France: the resumption of normal service?', *West European Politics*, May, pp. 203–18.

Kulski, W. W. (1966), *De Gaulle and the World* (Syracuse, NY: Syracuse University Press).

Lafont, Hubert, and Meyer, Philippe (1979), *La Justice en miettes* (Paris: Presses Universitaires de France).

Lagroye, Jacques, Lord, Guy, Mounier-Chazel, Lise, and Palard, Jacques (1976), *Les Militants politiques dans trois partis français* (Paris: Pedonne).

Lancel, François (1974), *Valéry Giscard d'Estaing de Chamalières à l'Elysée* (Paris: Belfond).

Lanversin, Jacques de (1979), *La Région et l'aménagement du territoire*, 3rd edn (Paris: Litec-Droit).

Lecomte, Bernard, and Sauvage, Christian (1978), *Les Giscardiens* (Paris: Albin Michel).

Lellouche, Pierre, and Moisi, Dominique (1979), 'French policy in Africa', *International Security*, Spring, pp. 108–33.

Le Pors, Anicet (1977), *Les Béquilles du capital* (Paris: Editions de Seuil).

Lombard, Paul (1978), *Mon intime conviction* (Paris: Robert Laffont).

McConnell, Grant (1966), *Private Power and American Democracy* (New York: Knopf).

Madelin, Philippe, and Michel, Jean-Pierre (1978), *Dossier J, comme justice* (Paris: Alain Moreau).

Mendras, H. (ed.) (1980), *La Sagesse et le désordre, France 1980* (Paris: Gallimard).

Pellissier, Pierre (1977), *Un certain Raymond Barre* (Paris: Hachette).

Pellissier, Pierre (1979), *La Vie quotidienne à l'Elysée au temps de Valéry Giscard d'Estaing* (Paris: Hachette).

Penniman, Howard R. (ed.) (1975), *France at the Polls: The Presidential Election of 1974* (Washington, DC: American Enterprise Institute for Policy Research).

Percheron, Annick, *et al.* (1978), *Les 10–16 Ans et la politique* (Paris: Presses de la Fondation Nationale des Sciences Politiques).

Perrault, Gilles (1978), *Le Pullover rouge* (Paris: Editions Ramsay).

Peyrefitte, Alain (1977), *Le Mal français* (Paris: Plon).

Poisson, Georges (1979), *L'Elysée: histoire d'un palais* (Paris: Librairie Académique Perrin).

Pouvoirs (1979), no. 9, 'Le Giscardisme'.

Pradelle, Raymond de la (1979), *Aux frontières de l'injustice* (Paris: Albin Michel).

Robert, Marc (1976), *On les appelle les juges rouges* (Paris: Téma).

Sanguinetti, Alexandre (1977), *L'Armée pour quoi faire?* (Paris: Seghers).

Sauvy, Alfred (1978), *La Tragédie du pouvoir* (Paris: Calmann-Lévy).

Seguin, Daniel (1979), *Les Nouveaux Giscardiens* (Paris: Calmann-Lévy).

Simonnot, Philippe (1978), *Les Nucléocrates* (Grenoble: Presses Universitaires de Grenoble).

Stoffaes, Christian (1978), *La Grande Menace industrielle* (Paris: Calmann-Lévy).

Stoleru, Lionel (1969), *L'Impératif industriel* (Paris: Editions du Seuil).

Suleiman, Ezra (1974), *Politics, Power, and Bureaucracy in France* (Princeton, NJ: Princeton University Press.

Suleiman, Ezra (1978), *Elites in French Society* (Princeton, NJ: Princeton University Press).

Tint, H. (1972), *French Foreign Policy since the Second World War* (London: Weidenfeld & Nicolson).

Todd, Olivier (1977), *La Marelle de Giscard* (Paris: Robert Laffont).

Touraine, Alain (1979), *Mort d'une gauche* (Paris: Galilée).

Ullmann, Jean (1978), *Mémoires d'un président de cour d'assises* (Paris: Fayolle).

Verrier, Patrice (1971), *Les Services de la présidence de la république* (Paris: Presses Universitaires de France).

Victorri, Jacques (1979), 'Le role du secteur publique dans la politique économique', *Revue économique*, January, pp. 72–87.

Wallace, William, and Paterson, W. E. (eds) (1978), *Foreign policy-making in Western Europe* (Farnborough: Saxon House).

Warnecke, Steven J., and Suleiman, Ezra N. (eds) (1975), *Industrial Policies in Western Europe* (New York: Praeger).

Wilson, Frank L. (1971), *The French Democratic Left 1963–1969: Toward a Modern Party System* (Stanford, Calif.: Stanford University Press).

Wright, Vincent (1978), *The Government and Politics of France* (London: Hutchinson).

Wright, Vincent (ed) (1979), *Conflict and Consensus in France* (London: Frank Cass).

Zysman, John (1975), 'French electronics policy: the costs of technological independence', in *Industrial Policies in Western Europe*, ed. Steven J. Warnecke and Ezra N. Suleiman (New York: Praeger).

Zysman, John (1977), *Political Strategies for Industrial Order* (Berkeley, Calif.: University of California Press).

Index